Consuming Nature

Consuming Nature

ENVIRONMENTALISM IN

THE FOX RIVER VALLEY,

1850–1950

Gregory Summers

 University Press of Kansas

Published by the University Press of Kansas (Lawrence, Kansas 66045), which was
organized by the Kansas Board of Regents and is operated and funded by Emporia State
University, Fort Hays State University, Kansas State University, Pittsburg State University,
the University of Kansas, and Wichita State University

Library of Congress Cataloging-in-Publication Data

Summers, Gregory.
  Consuming nature : environmentalism in the Fox River Valley, 1850–1950 /
Gregory Summers.
    p. cm.
  Includes bibliographical references and index.
  ISBN 0-7006-1486-9 (alk. paper)
    1. Environmentalism—Fox River Valley (Wis. and Ill.)   2. Fox River Valley (Wis. and
Ill.)—Environmental conditions.   I. Title.
  GE198.F69S86 2006
  333.7209775'6—dc22

2006011174

British Library Cataloguing-in-Publication Data is available.

Printed in the United States of America
10 9 8 7 6 5 4 3 2 1

For Shari, Shane, and Cassandra

CONTENTS

ILLUSTRATIONS

ACKNOWLEDGMENTS

When I began this book many years ago, I had no idea how long I would live with it, how difficult it would be to complete, or how much help I would need along the way. Already, the hours of research and writing are fading from memory. But I will never forget those who lent a hand.

Without question, the most important debts I owe are to my family: my wife, Shari, and our children, Shane and Cassandra. Like me, they lived with the project for years, and their love and encouragement helped immeasurably. My parents, Neel and Elsie Summers, and my in-laws, Arlie and Marcia Steinwand, were equally supportive, offering kind words and occasional child care when both were most in need.

Professionally, I was aided by many wonderful colleagues. At the University of Wisconsin–Madison, William Cronon was a model graduate advisor. His patient counsel did much to shape the early stages of the work. The same holds for Eric Schatzberg and Colleen Dunlavy. Just as important were my fellow students, who offered friendship as well as thoughtful advice. Marsha Weisiger, William Philpott, Lynne Heasley, Louise Pubols, and Amy Butler Greenfield were especially generous. At the University of Wisconsin–Stevens Point, where I now teach, I am equally fortunate in co-workers. In particular, I am grateful to Rixey Ruffin for reading numerous chapters and for always being willing to talk; and to Brian Hale who interrupted many a long day's writing to share a laugh. In the Fox River Valley, Paul Wozniak served as a guide to the region's industrial and environmental history. Finally, I owe special thanks to Ari Kelman, Jared Orsi, and Paul Sutter, all of whom read various drafts of the manuscript and improved it in countless ways.

There are several institutions without which I could not have written the book. While a graduate student, I received financial assistance from the U.S. Environmental Protection Agency. Later, a fellowship at the Institute for Research in the Humanities in Madison allowed me to complete the work. For help in my research, I relied on staff members at a number of libraries, among them the State

Historical Society of Wisconsin in Madison, the Outagamie County Histori-
cal Society in Appleton, and the Area Research Center in Stevens Point. Last,
I am indebted to Nancy Scott Jackson and the staff at the University Press of
Kansas for their support of the project.

Consuming Nature

Introduction

A River of Paper?

On the wintry morning of December 17, 1948, some three hundred residents of Wisconsin's Fox River Valley packed the circuit courtroom in the Brown County Courthouse in Green Bay. They had braved temperatures in the teens to attend a public hearing being conducted by the state Committee on Water Pollution (CWP) to investigate the contamination of the lower Fox River. On one side near the front of the room sat the underdogs: Virgil Muench, Arthur Kaftan, and Donald Soquet. The three were local attorneys for the county chapter of the Izaak Walton League, a national organization of sportsmen and the plaintiff in the hearing. On the other side was the lone but powerful figure of Adolph Kanneberg. Kanneberg was a longtime veteran of such proceedings. In 1927, he had helped to create the CWP, and for most of its history he served as its chairman. But on this day, Kanneberg had switched roles. He now stood before the committee on behalf of the defendants in the hearing: the valley's mighty paper industry, the largest employer in the area and the biggest contributor of pollutants to the Fox River.[1]

For nearly a century, the valley had been a place defined by its river, and especially the paper the river helped to produce. Manufacturers were first drawn to the Fox in the 1870s, lured there by the fall of its waters and the tremendous power it generated. Although the river traveled barely 35 miles between Lake Winnebago and Green Bay, it dropped 170 feet along the way, releasing enough energy to fuel decades of industrial growth.[2] By 1948, twenty-one pulp and paper mills operated in the valley. They relied on the river for everything from the transportation of raw materials and the generation of electricity to the use of water for manufacturing. The mills, in turn, sustained the local economy, providing jobs, revenue, and the promise of future development. More than a hundred thousand people lived along the banks of the lower Fox, in modest towns such as Neenah, Menasha, Appleton, Kaukauna, De Pere, and Green Bay (Figure 1). For them, the Fox was a river of paper, and paper was a way of life. Unfortunately, this way of life now threatened the river that made it possible. Decades of pollution from the paper industry had poisoned the Fox, rendering its waters a danger to wildlife and public health. The hearing by the CWP was meant to determine both the cause of the problem and its potential remedies.[3]

During four days of testimony spanning two and a half weeks, state investigators heard from scientists, politicians, manufacturers, commercial fishermen, sportsmen, and local residents. The case against the paper industry appeared strong. Muench and his fellow attorneys first called researchers from the state Board of Health, who testified that portions of the Fox had become almost lifeless, the result of chemical pollutants that stripped the water of oxygen. More than 90 percent of this pollution came from the paper mills, they said, and little could be done to restore the river until the contamination stopped. To illustrate pollution's effect on wildlife, the league's attorneys introduced two small buckets, one filled with fresh water and a dozen minnows and the other with water drawn from the Fox. When the minnows were transferred from the first bucket into the second, all of them died within minutes. Finally, the league questioned area residents who added their own impressions of life along the polluted waterway. Farmers complained of having to fence off livestock to prevent their drinking from the river, parents worried about children going swimming, and sportsmen described the loss of fish and wildlife. Nearly everyone grumbled about the stench. "It's almost impossible to sit out on the porch," one resident pleaded.[4]

In the face of these complaints, the valley's paper industry urged citizens to remain patient. Adolph Kanneberg led the charge, reviewing his twenty years of leadership as chair of the CWP. "Much has been done in the matter of cleaning up our streams," he argued. Since 1927, the CWP had reduced many types of waste, from canneries, dairy farming, and municipal sewer systems. Yet when it came to pollution from the paper industry, he confessed, "we were stymied." According to Kanneberg, local mills had already spent

Figure 1. Map of the Fox River Valley, Wisconsin.

nearly a million dollars seeking an answer. But solutions to the problem were too expensive, he claimed, and would place an unfair burden on the industry. "It seems to me there should be a little more tolerance in feeling of the paper mills and better public understanding of this problem," he concluded. "That's why I am here." Although Kanneberg struck a cooperative tone, occasionally the manufacturers he represented made explicit the threat he implied. During the questioning of J. M. Conway, president of the Hoberg Paper Mills in Green Bay, Arthur Kaftan suggested that the industry cared more about earning a profit than saving the river. Conway responded bluntly. "I will say this," he declared, "if you . . . would say to Hoberg right at this moment . . . put in a system to eliminate this pollution or else, we will take the 'or else' right now. That is we will close the mill definitely."[5]

In the end, the CWP decided in favor of the Izaak Walton League. State authorities ordered thirteen companies to reduce the waste they discharged into the Fox. The decision was the first of its kind in the valley, and it began a decades-long political battle over the cleanup of the river. Taking place as it did in the late 1940s, the contest occurred before environmentalism became a national movement in the United States. Yet like many better-known events of the period—from the 1950s battle against Echo Park Dam to the first Earth Day in 1970—the antipollution campaign in the Fox River Valley was part of the new environmental politics then taking shape. In particular, it was marked by a conflict between industry's right to use natural resources in the production of goods and services and the public's right to enjoy a clean and healthy environment in full possession of its aesthetic, recreational, and ecological value. In Wisconsin, the issue happened to be water quality. Elsewhere, it was suburban sprawl, the destruction of wilderness, or the loss of habitat and wildlife. In every case, Americans struggled to balance their use of nature against the growing need to protect the environment from harm. "Shall the mills or the streams be sacrificed?" asked the Green Bay *Press-Gazette* in 1948. The choice was unappealing then, and it remains so today.[6]

The story that follows is about the origins of this dilemma. Like many histories of environmentalism, it involves more than pollution. In the case of the Fox River, what made the issue so difficult were the dramatically different ways in which manufacturers and pollution opponents defined the river's value to the community. According to Adolph Kanneberg and his paper industry clients, the Fox was a means of production, an economic resource that sustained the local economy (Figure 2). Consequently, during the hearing, they appealed to the long-standing tradition of conservation in Wisconsin, an approach to the management of resources that emphasized cooperation between state authorities and manufacturers and values such as efficiency and scientific study. On the other side of the debate were the attorneys for the Izaak Walton League. Throughout the hearing, they characterized the Fox in more personal terms, describing its aesthetic, recreational, and ecological value to area residents. "In what way does the polluted condition of the Fox River affect you?" they asked repeatedly of the witnesses they called. People answered by describing their frustration with the terrible stench, their fear of swimming and fishing, and

Figure 2. Kimberly-Clark paper mill in Appleton, ca. 1948. Courtesy of the Wisconsin Historical Society, Image No. WHi-28350.

their concern for fish and wildlife. "I demand as a citizen and property owner of this state," one resident pleaded, "that my rights be upheld to give me the proper use and enjoyment of my home." These kinds of demands — focused as they were on the interests of individual residents — were central to the emerging politics of environmentalism in 1948. Unfortunately for manufacturers, they had little apparent connection to the importance of nature to industry (Figure 3).[7]

Historians often explain this widening conflict between economic production and environmental protection by pointing to the growth of consumption in the United States. According to this argument, rising prosperity in the twentieth century gave Americans new opportunities to enjoy the comforts of nature, including outdoor recreation, scenic beauty, and wildlife. The more people valued these so-called natural amenities, the more they objected to their loss as a personal threat. This was certainly the case in the Fox

Figure 3. Kids frolicking in the waters of Green Bay at Bay Beach City Park, ca. 1930s. Courtesy of the Henry Lefebvre Collection of the Neville Public Museum of Brown County, Image No. 18.1988.5603.

River Valley. Pollution had been a problem in the Fox River for decades, yet the issue remained a narrow concern, drawing attention only from manufacturers, health officials, and a handful of sportsmen. Most people tolerated the blighted waters and foul odors of the stream as an unfortunate but necessary evil, part of the cost of making paper. But beginning in the 1920s, a broadening segment of valley residents came to value the Fox River in ways that moved beyond its utility to manufacturers. By 1948, it was not just sportsmen who treasured the river. In the budding prosperity of the postwar era, people from all walks of life found the means to enjoy the Fox as a place to go fishing, swimming, or boating; an inviting location along which to buy a home; and a pleasant backdrop for weekend picnics and Sunday drives with the family. Together with rising pollution, these new consumer-oriented demands on the Fox caused many citizens to question its traditional use by the paper industry.

This much is well understood. Unfortunately, the idea that prosperity alone defines consumption's influence on environmentalism does little to explain why valley residents turned against the use of their river for production. This book offers a closer explanation of consumption's role in the pollution debate by stepping back from the conflict itself to explore the changing material context in which it took shape. Specifically, it describes the creation of what might be called a consumer society in the Fox River Valley between 1850 and 1950. Consumer society can be defined in many ways. But in strictly material terms, it is perhaps best used to describe a world in which the role of nature as a means of production had all but disappeared from the ordinary experience of daily life. Few people in 1948, no matter what their occupation, acquired even a fraction of the goods and services they used directly from the natural landscape. Energy came from utilities, food from grocery stores, and transportation from automobiles. The list of commodities available to consumers was nearly endless. In almost every case, the relationship between a commodity's consumption and the raw natural materials from which it was produced was so obscured by complex systems of production and distribution as to be invisible.[8]

The evolution of consumer society resulted, above all, from the growing human ability to control nature. Yet this ability was experienced differently by Americans depending on their relative involvement with production and consumption. In the case of production, the control of nature was apparent in nearly everything that manufacturers and other producers did: the vast amounts of resources and energy they used, the mounting volume of goods and services they produced, and consequently, the profound transformations they caused in the natural landscape. But in the case of consumption, people's dependence on the manipulation of nature became increasingly hidden from view. By the mid-twentieth century, consumers relied on industrial production for nearly everything they used, from food, clothing, and shelter to the growing array of conveniences that symbolized the good life in America. In effect, they exercised the same control of nature as producers: they used vast amounts of resources and energy, they consumed a mounting volume of goods and services, and consequently, they caused profound transformations in the natural landscape. But always they did so at a distance, far removed from the great manipulations of nature that made their consumption possible.

Exploring this aspect of consumer society suggests that its influence on environmentalism involved more than prosperity. In effect, consumption served as a filter in people's interactions with the material world, screening out nature's unpleasant realities while at the same time creating new attachments to its recreational and aesthetic charms. Qualities such as scenic beauty, wilderness, and clean air and water are natural parts of the landscape. But what transformed these qualities into amenities during the twentieth century — or, in other words, what caused Americans to value certain aspects of nature enough to seek their protection — was the way in which industrial development tamed the landscape and made it available for use by consumers for outdoor recreation, tourism, suburban home-buying, and the general improvement of their quality of life. In other words, the enjoyment of natural amenities relied as much on the control of nature as it did on nature itself, on things such as affordable energy, paved roads and automobiles, and the mass production and distribution of goods and services. These things, too, were comforts derived from nature. Yet because so few consumers took any direct role in creating them, it was all too easy to assume that using natural resources for production and enjoying the great outdoors were entirely separate and competing demands.

Again, this was the case in Wisconsin's Fox River Valley. "The people of this otherwise clean and happy valley have two important interests involved in the hearings," explained the Green Bay *Press-Gazette* in 1948. "There is a serious conflict between the recreational and health interests on one hand and economic advantages on the other." If state authorities forced the mills to close down, argued the paper, "the economic loss to the community would be tragic." At the same time, the public's right to enjoy a clean, healthy river was indisputable. "If [the mills] have done their utmost and no solution appears on the horizon, what then?" wondered the *Press-Gazette*. "That is the hardest question to answer." Since the mid-twentieth century, this tension between using nature for production and protecting the landscape from harm has complicated environmental politics throughout the United States. But ironically, it is a debate whose opposing sides have more in common than anyone realized, either at the time or largely still today. Admittedly, to recognize this irony offers no easy solutions for the environmental problems we continue to confront. Nonetheless, it may well suggest a more useful starting point from which to carry on the discussion.[9]

Readers should be aware of two caveats before proceeding. First, unlike many histories of environmentalism, this story looks more at consensus than conflict. Between 1850 and 1950, Wisconsin's Fox River Valley experienced relatively stable patterns of social, political, and economic development. Throughout the period, the economy remained tightly bound to agricultural and industrial production, its politicians were conservative and resistant to change, and its racial and ethnic makeup was nearly homogenous. The valley was not immune from unrest. There were occasional labor strikes, agricultural protests, and countless local disputes, many of which suggested alternate paths of development. But for the most part, the region's civic and professional leaders either ignored or defeated these possibilities. Included in their ranks was a varied list of modern professionals: state and local politicians, regional planners, road builders, public utility managers, university professors, retail merchants, conservationists, farmers, and manufacturers. They shared a powerful vision of progress, a set of goals defined almost exclusively in material terms: higher incomes, shorter workdays, larger profits, better roads, burgeoning cities, rising productivity, falling prices, improved technology, greater prosperity, growing convenience, and more development of every kind. Together, they built a consumer society in the region, gradually creating the technological and economic systems that separated production and consumption. Perhaps most important, their efforts were generally embraced by local residents.

In many ways, the history of environmentalism can be written as an effort to oppose exactly this vision of material progress. Yet this book is primarily about those who embraced it. Because of the unanimity that characterized people's attitudes toward such consumer-oriented development, the valley makes an ideal place to examine its influence on environmental politics. To be sure, few citizens who confronted the paper industry in 1948 were environmentalists in the usual sense of the word. They cared deeply about the fate of the river, but their interest in nature remained largely self-serving. What's more, they offered no fundamental critiques of modern society, and they embraced the growing freedom they enjoyed as consumers in a thriving economy. Still, in challenging the industrial use of the river, valley residents advanced the notion that progress had limits, that there were unwelcome consequences to industrial and commercial development that deserved reconsidering. In this sense, their uncritical acceptance of consumption makes the Fox River Valley a useful case study: if an environmental critique of progress emerged here, then understanding its origins may offer lessons relevant to American environmentalism more broadly.

In drawing these lessons, readers should keep in mind a second cautionary note: environmentalism cannot be explained by consumption alone. The history that follows describes one aspect of environmentalism in Wisconsin—the way it was shaped by consumer society. It is not intended to explain environmentalism in its entirety. In the Fox River Valley, many factors contributed to people's growing concern for the river. Although some forms of pollution were gradually reduced during the twentieth century, the concentrations of other contaminants increased, leading to the overall deterioration of the Fox. At the same time, new scientific discoveries empowered valley residents to demand the treatment of industrial waste in ways that once might have seemed impossible. Finally, the gradual strengthening of Wisconsin's law and regulatory framework gave citizens new, more powerful tools to effect political change. By 1948, all these factors would contribute as much as consumption to the debate over the Fox River.[10]

Yet so profound was consumption's influence on people's interactions with nature that its impact on environmentalism continues to be felt today. Consequently, it is worth asking exactly how this relationship evolved. In chapter 1, I offer a brief history of the production-minded politics that governed water pollution in the Fox River Valley until 1948. The majority of the book then describes the gradual creation of an infrastructure of consumption in the region and its corresponding impact on people's use of nature. Chapter 2 begins with the nineteenth century, and argues that nature played a more noticeable role than would later be the case as a means of production for valley residents. Chapter 3 explores the years between the 1890s and 1920s, a period whose environmental history is often narrated through the politics of conservation. By contrast, I describe the more significant expansion of industrialization generally, especially how the increasingly intensive use of nature paradoxically obscured its productive role in the lives of valley residents. I examine the impact of this industrialization on consumers in chapter 4, which looks at how modern technology allowed people to benefit from the use and control of nature without participating directly in the work involved in the effort. Given the fading visibility of natural resources, chapter 5 describes how state and local developers—including conservationists—en-

couraged valley residents to utilize nature as a playground for outdoor recreation. Finally, chapter 6 returns to the 1948 pollution hearing to discuss the
influence of consumer society on opposition to the paper industry.

The book concludes with a brief consideration of the relationship between consumption and the meaning of nature in American environmental
politics. Throughout the text, I strive to use the words *nature* and *consumption* cautiously. By *nature* I mean the nonhuman, material world, a collection of things that sustain human comfort, whether this comfort involves
productive resources, enjoyable amenities, or both. By *consumption,* I mean
the use of various commodities produced from the material world. Rarely
did anyone in the Fox River Valley speak of nature, in particular, this way.
Yet by looking carefully at how people's interactions with this "nonhuman,
material world" changed over time, I hope to make clear the ways in which
their ideas of nature shifted as well. Inevitably, the more people relied on
consumption during the twentieth century, the less they viewed nature as a
means of production — a source of work, hardship, and resources. Instead, it
became synonymous with the great outdoors, a place of escape, recreation,
and beauty in an urban-industrial world. Yet fundamental to both these understandings of nature is the growing human ability to control the material
world, an ability that was gradually masked by the very technological and
economic systems that made it possible. Nothing is more important to the
future of environmental politics in the United States than negotiating the
paradoxical influence of these competing understandings of nature. On the
one hand, the remarkable ease with which Americans now enjoy the great
outdoors inspires new demands to protect the environment from harm. On
the other hand, the increasing detachment between consumers and natural
resources makes it easy to forget that material comfort is a product of using
nature. Politically, the end result is an environmental debate that grows more
polarized and difficult to resolve each year. "Shall the mills or the streams be
sacrificed?" The answer, of course, is that neither can be easily abandoned
without jeopardizing both human survival and the nonhuman world upon
which we depend.[11]

1

The Voice of Industry

It would be easy to assume that Adolph Kanneberg's appearance at the 1948 pollution hearing in Green Bay was a disingenuous ploy on the part of the paper industry. Who better to depict the industry's cooperation with state authorities than the man legally authorized to demand its assistance? Who better to reassure valley residents that manufacturers sincerely wanted to end pollution than the man charged with safeguarding the public interest? And most pointedly, who better to secure a lenient ruling from the Committee on Water Pollution (CWP) than the man who created the organization and served as its chairman for twenty years? If manufacturers wanted to hide an ugly record of water pollution behind savvy public relations, they could have chosen no better spokesman than Adolph Kanneberg.

Yet this reading of events would be too cynical. Kanneberg's approach to pollution control was no different in 1948 than it had been in 1927 when he wrote the legislation creating the CWP. Under Kanneberg's leadership, the CWP had pursued the best practices of conservation, encouraging scientific study, technical innovation, and efficient management to improve Wisconsin's lakes and streams. In the Fox River Valley, manufacturers had cooperated with Kanneberg's system for twenty years, albeit sometimes grudgingly. During that time, there had been little public awareness of the issue, to say nothing of opposition. If growing numbers of valley residents were now angry at the paper industry, then according to Kanneberg, this was only because people failed to understand the scientific, technical, and economic difficulties involved in reducing pollution. Thus, when the retired chair of the CWP agreed to represent the valley's paper industry, he was anything but disingenuous. Kanneberg sought to defend his own record of pollution control as much as the actions of manufacturers. Any reasonable examination of the evidence, he believed, would vindicate both their efforts.[1]

To better understand the paper industry's case in 1948, it is helpful to view it as Adolph Kanneberg did, through his twenty years of experience as Wisconsin's chief regulator of water pollution. In many ways, Kanneberg's approach to pollution control was shaped by his personal and political history. Kanneberg was born in 1870 in Germany, and his family moved to Wisconsin when he was just three years old. A graduate of the University of Wisconsin in 1894, he entered law school and became a practicing attorney three years later. Kanneberg thus entered professional life during one of the most tumultuous moments in Wisconsin's history. Dubbed the Progressive Era by later historians, the years between 1890 and 1920 witnessed unprecedented increases in the pace of industrialization, urbanization, immigration, and the use of natural resources. Confronted with these perplexing changes, the people of Wisconsin sought to preserve American democracy and free enterprise within the increasingly technological world of big business and big cities. For guidance, they turned to leaders in science, industry, and politics who mounted a campaign to restructure Wisconsin's society. Their collective efforts were driven by what one historian called "the most pervasive notion of the day: *that technological innovation, combined with the systematic application of expertise, must ultimately produce 'progress.'*" Adolph Kanneberg was caught up in this maelstrom of political reform, and he adopted many of the values of his fellow progressives, including the desire to enter politics himself. In 1920, Kanneberg ran for state attorney general as a progressive Republican. He was defeated, but his effort won the notice of party officials who appointed him in 1923 to the state Railroad Commission, a three-person regulatory agency whose oversight responsibilities had recently broadened beyond the rails to include several other activities deemed public necessities: gas, electric, and telephone service as well as transportation along navigable waterways.[2]

It was from this unlikely position that Kanneberg began his career in water pollution control. During a three-day period in the summer of 1925, thousands upon thousands of fish died in the Flambeau River near the central

Wisconsin city of Park Falls. Fish kills were not uncommon at the time. But the awful magnitude of this incident called attention to the problem in a way that others had not. "Fish Die Like Poisoned Rats," screamed the headline in the local newspaper. Most of the deaths took place just downstream from one of the city's paper mills. "There, strewn along the shore from the power dam as far as the eye could reach, were the white bellies of dead and dying fish." Volunteers worked hastily to remove and dispose of the bodies. Within days, they had pulled ten tons of fish from the river, but estimates put the total loss at closer to thirty. So many fish had died by the time the crisis passed that some people assumed there were no more left in the river to be killed.[3]

More clearly than anything, the Park Falls incident revealed the lack of public authority in Wisconsin to regulate water pollution. At the time of the fish kill, control of the state's waterways was divided among three agencies. The state Conservation Commission had clearest jurisdiction to prevent pollution. A 1917 statute declared unlawful the contamination of streams by any "substance deleterious to fish life," and even authorized the commission to punish violators with fines and imprisonment. A second agency was the state Board of Health. Wisconsin statutes authorized the board to regulate water pollution when it affected people's health or comfort. Finally, the state Railroad Commission was charged with regulating the level and flow of all public waterways in an effort to preserve the rights of citizens to open navigation.[4]

On paper, Wisconsin seemed to possess an adequate legal framework for pollution control. But in practice, manufacturers throughout the state remained free to dump their waste in local streams without fear of penalty. The situation in Park Falls typified the difficulties of regulation. As one newspaper reported shortly after the fish kill, "nothing of an unusual nature so far as is known is going into the river, that hasn't been going in for years." It was clear that waste from the city's paper mill lay at the heart of the disaster. Yet none of the three state agencies with a potential claim to jurisdiction seemed likely to intercede. Weakest of the three was the Railroad Commission. Unless pollution actually obstructed the Flambeau River enough to impede navigation, the commission had virtually no power to involve itself in the matter. Likewise, the state Board of Health was similarly handicapped. Because pollution at Park Falls had harmed fish and not people, the board was rendered helpless. The same could not be said for the Conservation Commission. The massive destruction of fish in the Flambeau seemed tailor-made for the commission to exercise its authority to protect the state's wildlife. Yet, as several observers pointed out, the commission was unlikely to act. State law allowed the commission to impose fines and prison sentences on polluters, but it created no less confrontational remedies, such as the ability to require the treatment of waste. Although it was relatively easy for the commission to punish sportsmen in this way, it was another matter entirely to penalize important manufacturers, even when their careless behavior killed thousands of fish. "How stern would have been the justice meted out to the angler who had been bold enough to have taken more than his share of these beauties," asked one journalist in Park Falls, noting the double standard. Taken together, the numerous shortcomings in Wisconsin's statutes meant that industrial pollution went unregulated.[5]

It was Adolph Kanneberg who took it upon himself to address the problem. Kanneberg likely grew familiar with Wisconsin's rivers from his service on the Railroad Commission, which dealt in numerous cases with the use of streams as navigable waterways. His experience led him to believe that controlling water pollution was "the most important problem . . . confronting the people of the state." Despite the Railroad Commission's dubious jurisdiction in Park Falls, Kanneberg used the incident as a platform on which to construct a new program of pollution control for Wisconsin. On October 1, 1925, Kanneberg together with representatives of the state Conservation Commission and the Board of Health held a public hearing in Park Falls. His stated aims, to "make a fair presentation to the public," to "seek the cooperation of the paper mills," and to "show the value of conservation from an economic standpoint," clearly illustrate the outlines of the program he had in mind.[6]

Testimony at the Park Falls hearing closely mirrored that heard in Green Bay twenty-three years later. Kanneberg listened to local residents who described the extent of the fish kill, state scientists who explained the characteristics of various wastes and their impact on aquatic life, and manufacturers who pledged their willingness to cooperate to improve the streams. The most important witness, perhaps, was John D. Rue. Rue was a scientist and an expert on the paper industry from the Forest Products Laboratory, a research arm of the U.S. Forest Service located in Madison. As Rue explained, most paper in Wisconsin was manufactured by using wood pulp, a typically white, fibrous material that could be dyed and bound into sheets in various ways, depending on the product desired. Some companies manufactured their own pulp from trees, which they debarked, ground into chips, and chemically treated to extract the needed fibers. Others simply purchased whatever pulp they required. In either case, water was vital to manufacturers, serving as a means of carrying, screening, and treating pulp as it traveled through the complex machinery that produced paper.[7]

Not surprisingly, when manufacturers returned the water they took from Wisconsin's rivers, it contained a variety of contaminants. In general, there were two types of waste from paper mills that contributed to stream pollution. The first and least serious was fiber waste. Because manufacturers used water to move pulp through their mills, they inevitably lost a certain percentage that remained suspended in the water they discharged back to the streams. According to Rue, this so-called white water carried away between 7 and 20 percent of the fiber used by the industry, depending on the efficiency of individual mills. This insoluble pulp tended to gather on streambeds, where it formed thick layers of sludge that inhibited the growth of plant and animal life. In addition to its biological effects, fiber waste also represented a substantial loss to manufacturers in raw material, the value of which some estimates placed in the range of millions of dollars per year nationwide.[8]

Even more threatening to fish and wildlife was a second category of waste, the many chemical pollutants that paper mills routinely discharged into the rivers. Depending on their products, manufacturers added a variety of substances to the pulp they used, some serving as fillers to change the paper's texture, others as dyes to alter its color. But in general, a given mill used only small amounts of these substances, and their concentrations in rivers remained diluted enough to be harmless. The same could not be said, however, for the chemicals used to manufacture the pulp itself. Here, the so-called sulphite process was especially damaging.[9] The technique, first invented in 1874, utilized digesters, large steel containers in which wooden chips were mixed with calcium bisulphite and then heated with pressurized steam. This cooking process decomposed nearly all of the wood except for its cellulose fiber, or pulp, which manufacturers screened out, washed, drained, and used in the production of paper. Unfortunately, the process also created a substance known as sulphite waste liquor, a mixture of sugars, acids, alcohol, wood fibers, and sulphur dioxide left over once the useful pulp was removed. Unlike other chemical pollutants, vast quantities of sulphite liquor were produced each year—roughly a ton of waste for each ton of pulp manufactured. According to Rue, "in almost all cases [this liquor] is dumped into the streams." Once placed in a river, the sulphur dioxide in the liquor tended to bond with free oxygen, essentially stripping the water of air for use by aquatic life. In other words, if the sulphite liquor became concentrated enough, fish in the river would suffocate.[10]

As the hearing in Park Falls revealed, it was exactly this dynamic that led to the fish kill along the Flambeau. Testimony showed that the local paper company discharged roughly 73,000 gallons of sulphite liquor into the river per day. By comparison, the 3,000 residents of the city of Park Falls typically generated 100,000 gallons of sewage. But the oxygen demand of the sulphite liquor was twenty-six times greater than that of the sewage. During the hottest months of the year, oxygen levels in the river were already naturally low because the water's ability to absorb oxygen was reduced as temperatures rose. Shortly before the fish kill, the company had discharged an unusually large volume of liquor into the stream. When combined with the hot weather, the effects of this pollution stripped the river of its remaining oxygen and suffocated the fish.[11]

So it was that Wisconsin's first-ever public hearing on water pollution revealed an obvious violation of state law. Yet Adolph Kanneberg and his colleagues from the Conservation Commission and the Board of Health decided against prosecuting the manufacturer in question. Their rationale, which Kanneberg discussed at length in the months that followed, is a near-perfect example of the production-minded conservation ethic so prevalent in America at the time. It also neatly summarizes the views that Kanneberg still held in 1948, when he came to the defense of the paper industry in the Fox River Valley.

First, like many conservationists, Kanneberg began from the premise that to protect natural resources was, in essence, to safeguard democracy. The widespread destruction evident in Park Falls had resulted, Kanneberg believed, from careless and inefficient production practices. "We have been so absorbed in our wasteful methods of making quick money out of some of our natural resources," he explained, "that we have scarcely noticed the passing of our forests and the pollution of our waters." In this way, Americans were being denied the full benefit of the country's natural wealth. In the case of Wisconsin's rivers, these benefits included more than fish. "Our demand for purification of waters [is] on higher ground," Kanneberg declared. "It is in the interest of the health, comfort and happiness of all the people—to recover our common law rights in our public waters, the rights of navigation and all the incidents thereof, including hunting, fishing, bathing, boating, the drawing of water and recreation generally."[12]

Despite this sweeping and idealistic philosophy, Kanneberg had a keen appreciation for the pragmatic as well, a second trait he shared with conservationists of the era. In the case of Wisconsin's paper industry, substantial scientific, technical, and economic factors tempered Kanneberg's repugnance for the needless waste of resources. In particular, although manufacturers might conceivably have used a variety of methods to reduce or treat their waste, in Kanneberg's view, these techniques remained too costly to offer a practical alternative to pollution. "No economical process of treating sulphite waste liquor has been discovered," he explained. "To prevent the discharge of the same into the streams would put every paper mill in the state out of business." The pulp and paper industry was among the most important in Wisconsin, ranking third in overall employment and generating a payroll of $20 million a year. Its impact on related industries was incalculable. "For every ton of paper produced more than ten tons of raw material are required," said Kanneberg—materials such as wood, coal, lime, and various chemicals. "The right of the public to have the public waters remain in a reasonably pure state is undisputed," he affirmed. But authorities could only push so hard. "Agricultural and industrial development must not be unduly hampered."[13]

Resolving this conflict between the public's right to clean waters and its need for continued development was, according to Kanneberg, a simple matter of finding better methods of treating industrial waste. Here, Kanneberg displayed a third trait common to conservationists of the period: faith in science and rational management. Wisconsin's laws were as much to blame for harming the rivers as manufacturers, Kanneberg believed, because they failed to encourage the required scientific and technical innovations to mitigate pollution. "Before any action can be taken against an industry, it is necessary to know what can and what cannot be done by that industry," he argued. Kanneberg had no use for the fines and jail sentences provided under the current statutes: "You cannot go about purifying your waters in that way," he noted. Instead, Kanneberg insisted that the problem required a new centralized agency, one authorized to encourage scientific investigation of pollution, develop new methods of treatment, and enforce restrictions where possible. "If we are going to find a way to purify our streams," he concluded, "it must be through an agency that understands the problems."[14]

In the aftermath of the Park Falls hearing, Kanneberg set out to build exactly this kind of agency. Kanneberg himself authored the legislation used by lawmakers in 1927 to create the state Committee on Water Pollution. Membership of the CWP was composed entirely of existing government officials: the state sanitary engineer, the state chief engineer, plus one person each from the Board of Health, the Conservation Commission, and the Railroad Commission. In this way, Kanneberg sought to provide the committee with the kind of disinterested expertise necessary to balance the interests of navigation, public health, and protection of wildlife. Despite limited funding, the new committee received impressive authority to control pollution in Wisconsin. Lawmakers directed the organization to investigate all problems relating to the contamination of surface waters, establish regulations concerning the installation of treatment facilities, and, perhaps most significant, compel violators to reduce the waste they discharged into the environment.[15]

In 1927, few people doubted the wisdom of the approach to conservation represented by the new Committee on Water Pollution. As Kanneberg traveled throughout Wisconsin promoting his legislation, in fact, he found it difficult enough merely to garner popular interest in the pollution issue: "The public seems not yet to realize sufficiently that the present movement to conserve our natural resources cannot be successful without the active support of the public." Most citizens apparently remained content to entrust the issue to industry and state officials. A few voices among Wisconsin's conservation leaders did question the logic of scientific study. "The way to purify the streams and keep them pure is to stop dumping refuse into them," one critic asserted. To spend years merely investigating water pollution was "as nonsensical as it would be to put scientists to observing a highway that was being littered with refuse instead of [chasing] the offenders away." Yet most commentators applauded the CWP, including the state division of the Izaak Walton League and many newspapers that endorsed the new agency. "Whether or not we are admirers of industry and industrial institutions," cautioned the editors of the Milwaukee *Sentinel,* "the fact must not be lost sight of that upon them we depend largely for general prosperity. Co-operation on sound, scientific lines is the answer to the problem, and scientific study must precede intelligent action."[16]

With this mandate, the CWP began its oversight of Wisconsin's surface waters. Not surprisingly, Kanneberg himself became a member of the CWP and served as its chairman, a position he would hold until his retirement from public life in 1948. Under Kanneberg's leadership, the agency did much to further the cause of pollution control in Wisconsin, sponsoring the scientific study of rivers and lakes; establishing standard methods for the treatment of waste; and educating local officials, manufacturers, and the general public about the pollution problem. Its many achievements brought steady improvement to the condition of Wisconsin's surface waters. Though critics would eventually grow frustrated with the slow pace of change, especially concerning the paper industry, Kanneberg and his colleagues on the CWP had every right to believe they were making progress in reducing pollution.

One of the earliest and most important actions of the CWP was simply to assess the condition of rivers and lakes. Although much was known by the 1920s about the makeup of various municipal and industrial wastes, no comprehensive effort had yet been made to track their presence in Wisconsin's environment. Learning more about pollution from the paper industry was among the CWP's principal aims. In February 1926, even before the committee had been created, state health officials met in Milwaukee with paper manufacturers from throughout Wisconsin, including the Fox River Valley. The two groups agreed to begin joint studies of mill waste in order to determine how best to bring it under control. Employees of the mills would gather regular water samples from the rivers and then send them to state scientists for analysis. In part, this cooperative approach was necessitated by a lack of funding. The Board of Health, and later the CWP, had no money to hire their own personnel to collect samples. But the approach spoke as well to the conservationist belief that cooperating with polluters, not confronting them, was the first step to more enlightened industrial practices. There was no discussion in Milwaukee of forcing an immediate halt to pollution. Rather, "the object was to arrive at some definite basis for cooperation between the state and the pulp and paper industry." The joint surveys of water quality would continue under the CWP, and the data they provided gave the committee invaluable information in its effort to control pollution.[17]

Results from the initial round of surveys were compiled by the state Board of Health, which issued Wisconsin's first major analysis of water pollution in 1927. The report found a chemical soup of contaminants throughout the state. In the lower Fox River, waste from the valley's paper mills posed the most serious threat, particularly sulphite liquor. As the river flowed north from Lake Winnebago, conditions were favorable to fish life. But the gradual depletion of oxygen from the water began almost immediately and grew worse with each passing mile. Between Appleton and Kaukauna, officials noticed that the water became turbid. Fibrous material and deposits of sewage were readily apparent, as was the characteristic odor of paper mill wastes. By the time the river reached De Pere, enough oxygen had been removed from the stream that conditions were found to be intolerable for some species of fish. At Green Bay, "thick sludge deposits were found," and the "highly colored, turbid" water emitted gas that smelled unhealthy and foul.[18]

According to the report, improving the river would pose serious technical and economic problems. Experiments showed that storing sulphite liquor for several days in man-made ponds helped to reduce the amount of oxygen it would later consume in the Fox. But storage was prohibitively expensive given the large quantities of material involved. "The ultimate solution of the sulphite waste liquor problem," concluded the board, "lies in [its] utilization as a fuel or in the manufacture of valuable by-products rather than in treatment." The idea of somehow recovering and using the waste liquor was hardly new in the 1920s. Such a large amount of material was being discarded, in fact, that manufacturers had searched for years for a means of transforming it into marketable commodities. Unfortunately, they met with little success. Although chemists found methods of producing a number of useful by-products, including alcohol, glue, tanning extracts, and a road binder to reduce dust along highways, none offered an economical solution—at least in the opinion of the paper industry. Demand for such products was low and could be supplied by a small number of plants. What's more, because the sulphite liquor was so corrosive, it was extremely expensive to handle. Simply dumping it in the river remained the most cost-effective means of treating the waste.[19]

Armed with information from this first statewide investigation, Adolph Kanneberg and the CWP began an aggressive program of cleanup efforts in the Fox River Valley. Among the easiest issues to address was the problem of fiber waste from the paper industry. Unlike the situation with sulphite liquor, eliminating wood pulp from the effluent of the paper mills was both technically possible and economically feasible. The solution came in the form of "save-all" equipment, devices designed to recover and reuse much of the pulp residue that mills otherwise wasted. Save-alls were of two basic types: screens that filtered out solid material from the wastewater, and sedimentation tanks in which fiber was allowed to settle and collect before the remaining water was discarded. Most paper companies were eager to install such equipment once the CWP encouraged them to do so. Not only did the save-alls reduce pollution and improve stream conditions, but they offered mills dramatic savings in raw material. With the new equipment in place, companies were able to recover as much as 90 percent of the wood fiber they once discharged into the rivers, pulp they could utilize in the production of certain kinds of paper. Within just a few years, the reduction of these "white-water wastes" became a pronounced success in Wisconsin's conservation campaign.[20]

A second problem in the Fox River Valley to be tackled successfully by Kanneberg and the CWP was sewage disposal. By the 1920s, these municipal wastes threatened water quality as much as pollution from manufacturers. Although sewage appeared to have little effect on fish and wildlife along the river, according to most observers, the bacteria it introduced in the stream posed a critical danger to public health. Here, as happened with fiber waste from the paper industry, Kanneberg found that a solution depended less on overcoming scientific uncertainties than on simply encouraging people to implement known methods of treatment. In the case of sewage, the major obstacle was the cost of installing treatment facilities, which far exceeded the meager budgets of many towns and cities. Beginning in the late nineteenth century, communities throughout Wisconsin had constructed sewer systems as a means of safeguarding the public health. Yet by 1920, less than half of these provided even partial treatment for municipal sewage. Most communities, including those of the Fox River Valley, simply dumped their waste raw into nearby rivers, relying on the water's natural capacity to absorb, dilute, and carry away the sewage. This practice worked well in the 1880s and 1890s, when pollution levels remained low. By the 1920s, in contrast, the rapid increase in population had begun to tax many streams to their limit. Even so, despite the growing problem, few local officials were eager to spend the millions of dollars that new treatment facilities required.[21]

Help came, ironically, from the economic depression of the 1930s. As unemployment climbed and commerce stagnated, the federal government searched for ways to put Americans back to work. The mounting need for sewage treatment plants was a natural fit. By the mid-1930s, federal money generated by the Public Works Administration and other New Deal agencies began flowing into Wisconsin's cities, earmarked specifically for the construction of public sewage systems. In the Fox River Valley alone, municipalities spent $5.6 million on a series of treatment plants, nearly half of which came from the national government. According to the Milwaukee *Journal*, "communities were sold the idea that industries prefer to settle in cities that are equipped to handle industrial wastes; that a city saves in doctor bills and funeral expenses where health is protected; that streams that reflect the blue of the sky attract tourists and fish for the tourists and the home folks." Lofty rhetoric aside, it was federal money that most convinced local officials to treat sewage. Between 1936 and 1939, Neenah, Menasha, Appleton, Kaukauna, De Pere, and Green Bay each took advantage of the opportunity for help.[22]

Consequently, by the late 1930s residents in the Fox River Valley had good reason to believe that the CWP's cooperative, pragmatic approach to conservation was gradually eliminating pollution from their river. "With stream clean-up activities along the Lower Fox River, the pollution load is steadily decreasing which should result in material improvement from the fisheries point of view," reported L. F. Warrick, state sanitary engineer and member of the CWP, in a 1938 letter to a Green Bay assemblyman. "Much of the domestic sewage and a substantial amount of industrial waste are now receiving treatment." Editors at the Green Bay *Press-Gazette* agreed, noting that the Fox River, "decent, comfortable and law-abiding, [had] responded to the new sewer system good-naturedly and with alacrity," resulting in "a constant and highly satisfactory improvement." If problems remained, most people believed, they required only continued patience and further study to remedy.[23]

Unfortunately, several problems did remain. Throughout the late 1930s, there were troubling indications that rising population and production levels in the valley were outpacing whatever improvements were being achieved through save-alls and sewage treatment facilities. First, during the fall of 1936, 5,000 to 6,000 ducks died mysteriously in Green Bay. Officials who examined the bodies blamed a bacterial infection, potentially caused by effluents released from the new sewage treatment plant. But many citizens pointed to industrial pollution in the Fox as the real culprit. "They've got to find a 'goat,' and we're it," complained the manager of the treatment facility. The situation seemed only to worsen during the following autumn, in 1937. Once again in Green Bay, a massive duck kill occurred, adding to suspicion that industrial pollution in the lower Fox was to blame. Meanwhile, upstream from the bay, thousands of fish died suddenly along the Fox River between Appleton and Kaukauna. "Their bodies are littering the shores and jamming the river locks," reported the Appleton *Post-Crescent.* "You could pick up a wagon load of pike almost anywhere along the river," said a deputy game warden. Immediately, nearly everyone suspected low oxygen levels in the stream, caused at least in part by wastes from the valley's paper industry.[24]

These incidents, reminiscent as they were of the fish kills of the 1920s, drew the attention of Adolph Kanneberg and the CWP. Much as he had done in Park Falls a dozen years earlier, Kanneberg traveled to Appleton to hold a public hearing on the issue. For two days in November 1937, the committee heard testimony from the usual collection of witnesses: citizens who had observed the fish kill, representatives of the paper industry, game wardens, and city officials. The evidence was inconclusive. Tests conducted along the Fox showed that oxygen levels both before and after the incident were low, but still within acceptable levels for sustaining fish. "Something out of the ordinary must have happened," concluded the superintendent of the city water plant. Attention focused on the Interlake Pulp and Paper mill, located just upstream from where the dead fish appeared. Company officials admitted that on the morning in question, employees had flushed a large settling tank containing two years' worth of sludge left over from the production of sulphite pulp, washing the contents into the Fox. They maintained, however, that nothing in the acidic mixture of chemicals was harmful to fish. The company even supported its claim with data from a lab experiment conducted by an Interlake chemist in which several groups of minnows were able to survive for sixty-five hours in tanks filled with varying concentrations of sulphite waste. Although members of the CWP questioned the methodology of the mill's experiment, all agreed that further investigation was necessary.[25]

When the CWP issued its ruling two months later, it made essentially the same decision that Adolph Kanneberg had rendered in Park Falls in 1925: to defer restrictions on pollution by the paper industry until more feasible methods of dealing with its wastes were discovered. The committee did order the Interlake Company to avoid further dumping of sludge into the Fox. But on the larger question of sulphite liquor, the agency remained cautious, ordering the company to "do its part in installing . . . utilization or treatment facilities as soon as a practical and effective system was made available." No such system was available, of course. But much as Kanneberg had argued in Park Falls, balancing the value of the paper industry against the harmful impacts of pollution still required looking to science more than regulation as a means of protecting Wisconsin's rivers.[26]

This patient, cooperative, and largely technical approach to conservation was again highlighted two years later, in 1939, when the CWP published the results of yet one more investigation of the Fox River. This particular survey, which began in the fall of 1938 and lasted for nine months, addressed continued complaints from citizens in Green Bay concerning foul odors and the decline of commercial fishing in the region. Its results, which were announced by Adolph Kanneberg and several colleagues from the CWP at a public meeting in Green Bay, proved once and for all the responsibility of the valley's paper industry. "Pollution in Fox River Is Caused by Mills," read one local headline. According to the report, 90 percent of the pollution in local waters came from the valley's sulphite mills. Sewage and fiber residue still contributed to the overall degradation of the river. But even if such waste could be completely removed from the Fox, the report explained, sulphite liquor would continue to render the water dangerous to fish and people alike. Investigators found the stream nearly devoid of oxygen by the time it reached De Pere. "No relief can be expected from the conditions observed in Green Bay until equipment which will remove at least the major portion of the oxygen-consuming material in waste sulphite liquor is installed," the report concluded. Despite this damning evidence against the paper industry, the CWP once again declined to order reductions in pollution. As Kanneberg made clear, the economical treatment of sulphite liquor was not yet possible. Consequently, the CWP could offer only further scientific study and the continued cooperation of the paper industry.[27]

Just one month later, in a public display of this cooperative approach, Kanneberg called together representatives from Wisconsin's leading producers of sulphite pulp. The group, consisting of ten mills located along the Fox and Wisconsin rivers, met in Appleton to design a research program intended to solve the sulphite problem once and for all. "There has been some progress made," said Kanneberg, in explaining the rationale behind the meeting, "but we felt it wasn't enough." By the end of the day, the mills organized the Sulphite Pulp Manufacturer's Research League, to be funded entirely by the voluntary assessment of fees to individual corporate members. The league would use this money to conduct research on various methods of utilizing sulphite liquor. According to Dr. C. A. Harper of the state Board of Health, who also attended the meeting, scientific investigation was likely to benefit the industry as much as the rivers. "Protection of water is the first thought," he explained. But the new league's investigations might be profitable, too. "Much of the material which has been wasted in the past can be utilized as a result of the studies made," he pointed out. Clearly, although many people in Wisconsin, including perhaps Kanneberg himself, had grown frustrated with the slow pace of the industry's progress, the CWP remained committed to scientific investigation and the search for "feasible" treatment methods as the best means of ending pollution.[28]

In the years immediately following the creation of the Sulphite Research League, the question of pollution receded from public consciousness in the Fox River Valley. The onset of World War II made the region's manufacturers more important than ever, because many products of the paper industry proved vital to the war. Under these circumstances, few resources remained for the treatment of industrial waste. Progress did not halt entirely, though. In August 1946, the CWP announced a major breakthrough in combating pollution along the beleaguered Fox River. According to L. F. Warrick, the chief sanitary engineer, Wisconsin was "within sight of success in the fight to eliminate paper mill waste pollution of our principal rivers." Researchers with the Sulphite League had apparently discovered a means of extracting yeast and other marketable by-products from the spent sulphite liquor, thus allowing manufacturers to reduce their waste while preserving the bottom line. Market surveys suggested that the paper companies might even make a profit from the process, regardless of the need to use it as a means of pollution control. Newspapers portrayed the announcement as vindication for the "decades of patient and willing collaboration" between government and industry. "It is a story of tolerance on the part of the state officers who had the statutory power to compel compliance with the anti-pollution laws, but who were willing to wait for the paper industry to develop feasible solutions." Manufacturers planned to construct a pilot plant along the Wisconsin River to try the process. If it worked, then an end to pollution would finally be at hand.[29]

Here, it seemed, was the long-promised fulfillment of Adolph Kanneberg's scientific, economically sound approach to pollution control. But by 1946, the public response to the news was less favorable than state officials might have hoped. Many did welcome the apparent cure for pollution as a credit to citizens for their thoughtful restraint. "It wasn't always easy to tolerate these wastes," admitted the *Press-Gazette*. "But generally the population knew that it was not the fault of the paper mills. . . . Candid discussion [and] sympathetic treatment were more a spur to the paper industry than a flood of kicks and blame." Yet lurking within the apparently placid citizenry was a growing resentment of the paper mills and the damage they had caused. As the *Press-Gazette* itself reported just three weeks later, an increasing percentage of area residents believed that pollution had robbed them of a valuable public resource. In this particular instance, local parks commissioners had asked the city council for money to build outdoor swimming pools. According to the newspaper, the action "was unquestionably dictated by public opinion. The people of Green Bay with two large rivers flowing through the heart of their city, and with miles of bay shore bordering their homes on the north are painfully aware of the fact that they and their children have been cheated out of the great privilege of a clean place for swimming." Though residents still valued the paper industry, their frustration with its pollution of the river was nearing a boiling point.[30]

That point would come finally in 1948, when several public displays of anger would lead the CWP to convene yet another hearing on the pollution of the Fox River, this time in Green Bay. For Adolph Kanneberg, the new attacks on the paper industry seemed a misguided effort to derail Wisconsin's pollution control program at precisely the moment when it was bearing fruit. Kanneberg had retired from public life in February 1948, but he nonetheless agreed to appear in Green Bay on behalf of the Sulphite Manufacturers Research League. His argument was simple. "If I didn't have the utmost confidence that the mills will continue to attempt to clean their waste," he assured his former committee, "I would not be here. My position is the same today as it was [in 1927] and that is why I am here." The paper industry needed time. Scientific investigation should not be rushed, nor should penalties be imposed without careful thought to the economic costs. "Now we will go along with you, your Izaak-Walton League, we will go along with any citizen," Kanneberg pleaded. "If you have any leads to offer we will follow them up. We will do anything in our power to solve this problem," he urged, "but we cannot . . . plug up the sewers because these paper mills are too vital for this community."[31]

Despite all that Kanneberg did to defend the paper industry and his own twenty-year history of pollution control, his former colleagues on the CWP eventually ruled against him. As later chapters will argue, their decision marked a fundamental shift in Wisconsin from a political system of resource management dominated by production to one influenced by the mounting demands of consumption. At the core of this transformation were the changing standards by which area residents valued the Fox River, especially the growing belief that natural amenities, not production, comprised the stream's most important contribution to the community. "The right of the majority of the people for a clean river ... must be restored, regardless of the expense involved to those that are guilty of polluting," said one reader in a letter to the *Press-Gazette* during the hearing. Increasingly, his fellow citizens agreed.[32]

For Adolph Kanneberg and the paper industry, natural resources were most important for their use in production. Thus, in the absence of feasible alternatives, Kanneberg believed that conservation required allowing mills in the Fox River Valley to continue polluting the stream. Kanneberg made this decision repeatedly as chair of the CWP, despite the damage caused by sulphite liquor and despite the existence of several promising but costly methods of treatment. "The committee always attempted to enforce the law when there was a method of doing it," Kanneberg testified. But enforcing the law, he insisted, was always economically impossible. "By that you mean not profitably possible?" asked Virgil Muench of the Izaak Walton League. "It is possible," replied Kanneberg, "but it will put the mills out of business and obviously you would rather have this waste going into the river than not have the mills." Throughout the proceedings, various witnesses from the paper industry echoed this logic, arguing that companies were trying hard to solve the problem. "The thing that we need in this program ... is not money, so help me," pleaded one engineer with the Sulphite Research League, "it's ideas." According to another industry scientist, Wisconsin was "twenty-five or thirty years ahead of all other states" in its program of waste reduction in the streams. If citizens now blamed the mills for failing to end pollution, he argued, they might just as easily "castegate [*sic*] doctors for not solving cancer. We are working on it."[33]

In contrast to Kanneberg's production-minded approach, opponents of the paper industry argued for a broader view of resource management. The

Fox, they insisted, contributed many things to valley communities beyond its service to manufacturers. "This thing is more important than just the paper mills making money," urged one participant. "Let us assume for a moment that the sulphite problem could never be licked," added Virgil Muench in questioning one industry executive. "Do you think your mill would have the right to continue to pollute this water to the health hazard of the people here? Isn't there a moral problem involved?" According to witness after witness, the answer was yes. Their testimony provides a list of the many demands beyond production that citizens made on the stream. "It is very discouraging to have a home on the Bay, where it is impossible to fish and swim and enjoy the beauties of nature," one resident testified. "I am being robbed from the standpoint of depreciating the valuation of my property," stormed another. "We couldn't use the porches on our house a great part of the summer [because of the smell]." Many people spoke out on behalf of their children. "They don't have any enjoyment out of our home at all as far as the water is concerned," said one resident about his riverside farm. "The Bay is the front part of my property, the front part of my yard," said another. "The neighborhood children who have gone in [to swim], have come out with their eyes swollen and their lips swollen." Others noted pollution's impact on their enjoyment of wildlife. "Fish and wildlife are not found along our shores that should be," complained the curator of a local museum. Still others condemned the cost to taxpayers. "I seriously object to spending Six Hundred thousand dollars for swimming pools when we are surrounded by what should be such beautiful waters for recreation and swimming," the same curator protested.[34]

In previous years, members of Wisconsin's CWP had often dismissed the enjoyment of natural amenities as an issue of secondary importance in the management of streams. Fishing, swimming, boating, and scenic beauty were individual pursuits, not as significant to the public good as a river's contribution to industrial production. Yet by 1948, as testimony in the hearing made clear, a growing number of valley residents considered natural amenities an obvious matter of public concern. How, then, could the CWP justify a regulatory policy that consented to the destruction of these same amenities? This was the question at the heart of the case presented by the Izaak Walton League. "We believe the people of Wisconsin are entitled as a matter of law and public right to clean water," declared A. D. Sutherland, president of the league's State Division. Again and again, league attorneys hammered at the CWP's traditional approach to conservation, especially its reliance on scientific study, technical innovation, and cooperation with industry. What good was it that mills had reduced the percentage of fiber wasted in manufacturing if rising production levels led to an increase in the absolute volume of pulp dumped in the stream? How reliable was the CWP's scientific research if nearly all of it was funded and conducted by the very industry being regulated? Perhaps most important, if there were several known methods of treating or utilizing sulphite waste, why couldn't the mills be required to use them, albeit at some cost to overall profits? "It seems to me as a listener that everybody here is on one side of this idea, and you mills are on the other side," one critic of the paper industry charged. "You have had a great many years to study this question. The only thing [the mills] are waiting for is an order, an order to make them clean up." Other citizens were even more direct. "I just want to make this one plea," begged a resident of De Pere. "For God's sake, do something right now. Something should have been done long ago. Don't wait!"[35]

In the end, the decision by the CWP was a tacit admission of the shifting political priorities in Wisconsin. The concerns of production still carried obvious importance in resource management. But increasingly, so too did the mounting demands of consumption. Not surprisingly, the CWP's ruling failed to bring an immediate improvement in the condition of the Fox. Nevertheless, it demonstrated that valley residents would never again so easily accept the control of their river by manufacturers. "Citizens in the Fox River Valley are thoroughly aroused," proclaimed one member of the Izaak Walton League in the midst of the controversy. "It is no longer a question of 'if' municipalities and industry will clean up, but 'when' they will clean up." Understanding the origins and significance of this demand requires looking back to the emergence of consumer society in the valley and the ways in which it gradually altered the use of nature in local life.[36]

2

Working with Nature

Citizens in the Fox River Valley had once been much less troubled by the pollution of the local river. In the summer of 1895, the waters of the lower Fox dropped to less than half their normal flow, the result of a yearlong shortage of rainfall. At the time, the region's cities depended on the stream to carry away a variety of wastes, including sewage, garbage, and various by-products of manufacturing, all of which entered the river untreated. But in the midst of the drought, the amount of water available to dilute this refuse dropped steadily, and the contamination of the Fox grew more noticeable throughout the summer. In Appleton, residents obtained their household water from the Fox, taking in roughly a million gallons a day. According to local newspapers, it was nearly unusable. "Three inch blood-suckers have been drawn from the taps of private houses," railed the *Crescent*. "Is there nothing before us but to look forward to having the sole water supply coming from the sewer-pipes of neighboring cities," the paper asked. "It would perhaps save expense to connect our water mains to their sewer mains and the effect would be practically the same."[1]

Much as happened in 1948, the declining condition of the lower Fox River led to a hearing in Green Bay. But this time, the meeting was not prompted by outraged citizens, nor did pollution stand at the center of debate. Instead, local manufacturers invited Wisconsin's governor and all the state's federal representatives to Green Bay to discuss the failing waterpower. The meeting took place on September 3, with the governor and several politicians arriving in the city to hear the complaints of businessmen and manufacturers from throughout the region. Because federal law required that the Fox remain navigable, the valley's paper companies were restricted from using what little water still flowed down the stream. Thus, as early as May, factories had begun laying off workers and reducing production as the river slowly dried up. By July, the situation reached crisis proportions: mills shut down completely, leaving thousands of people unemployed; local electric companies cut off power for lighting; and residents grew impatient for the water level to rise. At the Green Bay conference, businessmen and politicians discussed the issue for two hours before adjourning for a tour of the river. By the end of the day, they decided to petition the United States Congress to approve a diversion of water from the Wisconsin River into the Fox. Such a scheme, all agreed, would be suitable for everyone, for it would provide much needed aid to manufacturers without sacrificing the interests of navigation.[2]

At no time did the river's pollution become an issue. Although the waters of the Fox were obviously contaminated, there was no public demand for an end to industrial waste, no outcry against the threat to fish and wildlife, and no apparent worries over the impact on people's health. Even the river's terrible smell drew little attention. Instead, the debate remained focused entirely on the waterpower and restoring the vitality it provided to manufacturers. Editors at the Appleton *Crescent* were stunned by the public apathy. "The freakishly fantastic phase of the whole matter," stormed the paper, "is that all Appleton submits tamely to drinking fouly poluted [*sic*] water that is sometimes not even strained, say nothing of filtered." That local citizens could be so indifferent to the water they consumed seemed "an amazing thing" to the *Crescent*'s editors. But even the paper had little to say against pollution itself. Rather, its editors simply argued that local government should obtain the city's water from artesian wells instead of the Fox. Few people questioned the use of the river to dispose of waste.[3]

This lack of public concern over the pollution of the Fox River in 1895 was emblematic of a basic fact of material life in the valley. Most people maintained a working relationship to the region's natural landscape, including the river, and were thus inclined to see its use by industry as entirely appropriate. Without romanticizing the unpleasant drudgery that often characterized people's interactions with nature in the nineteenth century, it remains true that the valley's landscape played a more visible role as a means of production in 1895 than it would by 1948. In the case of the Fox River, the stream was a valuable transportation route, connecting the cities along its banks to regional and national markets. The flow of its waters powered dozens of factories, from the earliest flour and lumber mills that characterized the valley's frontier economy to the subsequent emergence of the paper industry and its promise of future growth. Finally, and perhaps most regrettably, the waters of the Fox offered a seemingly natural and cost-effective means of ridding communities of their many wastes, both industrial and biological. Viewed in this light, the manufacturer's use of the Fox appeared little different than the lumberman's use of the forests or the farmer's use of the soil. The river was the literal and figurative embodiment of people's livelihood, a source of resources, prosperity, and progress for the entire region.[4]

This is not to say that valley residents were indifferent to the river's amenities. Certainly, people admired the beauty of the stream and its surrounding countryside. City officials established parks along its banks. Children swam in the river during the summer, many locals routinely went fishing, and the region's affluent citizens regularly indulged in boating excursions. "The lover of nature can find no spot more fitted to gratify his love for the beautiful and picturesque than this," promised one local booster, speaking of the Fox. But valley residents enjoyed these amenities in the ever-present context of the stream's importance to industry, and by extension to the general welfare of the region. It was an article of faith among nineteenth-century Americans that nature existed so that its resources could be extracted, transformed by human hands, and used to create economic gain. By the 1890s, the connections between people and this production-oriented use of nature were fast disappearing in the nation's maturing consumer society, obscured by powerful new technologies in mass production, marketing, and distribution. Yet even then, nature as a place of work, hardship, and resources remained a close enough presence in daily life that few people challenged its use by industry. Americans first came to the Fox River Valley in the mid-nineteenth century. They were drawn primarily by the transportation and waterpower available from the stream. By the end of the century, these qualities remained at the core of the river's identity, and they were little affected by pollution, no matter how severe it became. To understand how consumption would eventually alter this picture, we first need to explore the working relationships that characterized people's interactions with nature in the valley during the nineteenth century.[5]

Improving the River

On June 16, 1856, the steamboat *Aquila* arrived in Green Bay after journeying down the lower Fox River from Lake Winnebago. Though a small and relatively common sternwheeler, the ship's voyage had been anything but ordinary, for the vessel carried with it the dreams and expectations of the entire valley. "The Fox River Improvement is *completed*," announced the Green Bay *Advocate* in describing the event. In the newspaper's words, the *Aquila* marked "the first issue of the wedded waters of the proud old father Mississippi and Lake Michigan." The ship had traveled, not simply from Lake Winnebago, but all the way from Pittsburgh. After beginning its journey steaming down the Ohio and then up the Mississippi, the *Aquila* became the first vessel to travel successfully through the newly constructed improvements of the Fox-Wisconsin waterway. The ship began by steaming up the Wisconsin River to the town of Portage, where it traveled through a mile-and-a-quarter-long canal into the waters of the upper Fox River. It then descended the winding, 150-mile length of this stream into Lake Winnebago. There, the ship entered the lower Fox, the most heavily improved portion of the waterway, traveling 35 miles downstream to Green Bay through a series of eighteen locks that had been constructed in the effort to tame the river for transportation.[6]

For valley residents, the *Aquila*'s voyage was cause for jubilation. All along the Fox, from Menasha through Appleton to De Pere, the ship was greeted by factory whistles, brass bands, and cheering crowds. When it finally arrived in Green Bay, "the roar of cannon, the ringing of bells, and the shouts of many thousands" announced its presence. The steamer docked, and its crew joined dignitaries from every community in the valley to parade through the streets of Green Bay. The procession halted at a hotel where a program of formal speeches had been planned. "That broad and ample river, that is destined while time shall last, to bear on its capacious bosom, many a rich and generous freight, will never bring to us a more noble burden than she has this day yielded to our hearts," declared James H. Howe, a prominent local citizen and the featured speaker of the day. "As the humble representative of this glad community—rejoicing in the proud fruition of a hope long delayed—I bid you welcome."[7]

No event in the nineteenth-century history of the Fox River Valley better illustrates the relationship between people and nature than the improvement of the Fox River. Two distinct but reinforcing ideas shaped human interactions with the landscape during the era. First, the natural world was a place of constant strife for valley residents, as it was for many Americans, a source of obstacles to be overcome and hardships to be endured. "We see, this day, gentlemen, the power of a will to do," declared another speaker in welcoming the *Aquila* to Green Bay, "in removing those great obstacles to our commercial interests, which the God of Nature had placed in the Lower Fox, which in days gone by were considered an everlasting barrier to the navigation of the same." In this case, the barriers to which the speaker referred were the many rapids that once blocked passage of the lower Fox. But Americans often took a similar stance toward the landscape in general. In this view, nature was a thing to be conquered, and the greater the hurdles it presented, the more its improvement gave testament to the power of human resolve. Second, whatever changes people made to the landscape—whether damming a river, clearing the land for farming, building a factory, or founding a city—they tended to see their efforts as completing designs already inherent in the natural world. So it was that many observers of the Fox-Wisconsin Improvement believed the route had been "plainly marked out by the hand of Nature" for commercial transportation. By this logic, nature was nothing less than the material expression of God's will, a collection of raw material needing only human action to realize its potential. Consequently, to alter the landscape was not to harm or destroy it, but rather to fulfill nature's purpose and perfect it by adapting its resources to human aims.[8]

When combined as they often were in the mid-nineteenth century, these two ideas of nature—as obstacle to be conquered and manifestation of divine intent—created an ideology powerful enough to imbue almost any human "improvement" of the landscape with the mantle of progress. In the Fox River Valley, citizens viewed the transformation of the river in exactly these terms. "I know with what pride you join with me in welcoming the first steamboat to our harbor," intoned James H. Howe, explaining the great significance of the *Aquila*'s journey. "You greet her as the harbinger of a thousand such, that shall pour the wealth of this Great State into your lap." By "wealth," Howe referred to the riches of nature transformed by human hands and destined through the agency of the river to bring commercial and industrial prosperity. "Henceforth, Wisconsin shall be proud of the Fox River, teeming with commerce and life," he said. "For not only shall she bear upon her bosom bread enough to feed a starving Europe; not only shall the farmer, the merchant, the mechanic daily gaze upon it from their homes, and smile upon all its rich banks for theirs, but its cataracts shall invite the manufacturer and the hum of a million spindles shall mingle with the music of its rushing waters. The bowels of the earth obedient to its influence, shall yield up its treasures." According to this rationale, nature's wealth and the human resolve to exploit it joined together to fuel industrial progress. Such were the dreams of valley residents in 1856, and all depended on the mighty Fox River, properly improved, to make them reality.[9]

Unfortunately, the arrival of the *Aquila* in Green Bay would be one of the few shining moments in the history of the Fox-Wisconsin waterway. In subsequent years, expectations for the project were repeatedly dashed by financial panic, greed and mismanagement, political rivalry, the coming of the railroads, and nature's stubborn resistance to human control. By the 1880s, hopes for the waterway had faded completely. Yet the history of the Fox-Wisconsin Improvement is important nonetheless, for it reveals just how clearly valley residents defined the value of their river in terms of its productive utility.[10]

Nothing was more significant to the development of Wisconsin in the nineteenth century than transportation. Here, valley residents could be forgiven if they looked at the Fox River and believed it was destined to serve as a commercial waterway. Whether divinely intended or simply fortuitous, geography seemed to demand the stream's improvement for navigation. The Fox River originated in central Wisconsin, roughly 70 miles southwest of Lake Winnebago. The portion of the river above the lake, known as the upper Fox, was a slow and meandering stream. In contrast, the lower Fox fell quickly over a series of dramatic rapids toward Green Bay. Most important to the nineteenth-century residents of the valley, the headwaters of the upper Fox reached within a mile and a quarter of the Wisconsin River as it flowed southwesterly through the center of the state, making its way eventually to the Mississippi. The narrow strip of ground that separated the rivers was low-lying, flat, and prone to flooding. Sometimes during these floods, the waters of the two rivers would actually merge, allowing boats to pass between them freely.[11]

The portage, as the location came to be known, had long stood at the center of Wisconsin's history. Native Americans had used the passage from time out of mind to navigate through the region. When Europeans arrived in the seventeenth century, they learned of the route from local tribes. In 1673, Father Jacques Marquette and Louis Joliet became the first white explorers to cross the portage. The two Frenchmen traveled by canoe as they journeyed into Green Bay from Lake Michigan. They moved up the Fox River, portaged into the Wisconsin, and finally reached the Mississippi, where they continued downstream as far as modern-day Arkansas. The famous voyage marked the establishment of the French empire in the upper Mississippi, and the Fox-Wisconsin passage would become a vital tool in their effort to control and exploit the region's natural wealth. By the nineteenth century, as commercially minded Americans moved into the region, the significance of the route appeared only to have grown. If the Fox and Wisconsin Rivers were improved, it was thought, they would form a natural link between the Great Lakes and the Mississippi. Such a route, by joining together the two main outlets through which the Atlantic could be reached from the North American interior, would guarantee Wisconsin's commercial and industrial success. All that stood in the way was the portage and the few natural obstacles that blocked the rivers themselves.[12]

The man most directly responsible for advancing the idea of the Fox-Wisconsin Improvement was Morgan L. Martin. Martin was among the leading figures in the nineteenth-century history of the Fox River Valley. He served at various times as a land speculator, Indian agent, member of the region's Territorial Council, representative in Congress for the territory, president of the state's constitutional convention, member of the state legislature, and finally a county judge. Martin took up residence in Green Bay in 1827 at the tender age of twenty-two, arriving there from New York after a brief stay in Detroit. At the time, Green Bay was but a tiny military and trading outpost on the Wisconsin frontier with a civilian population of roughly a hundred. An attorney by training, Martin established a private legal practice, but his real interests lay in the budding commercial prospects of the region. Martin had been raised in upstate New York, not far from the newly completed Erie Canal. Having witnessed firsthand the remarkable success of this channel in drawing commerce to his former home, he was quick to see great potential in a similar waterway in Wisconsin.[13]

Almost immediately, Martin began to lobby for the improvement of the Fox-Wisconsin route. As early as 1829, he organized a public meeting in his office in Green Bay at which citizens petitioned the federal government for aid in improving the rivers. No help was forthcoming, and promoters were forced to seek other means of advancing their cause. Martin found a more supportive audience in the legislative council of the Michigan Territory, of which the Wisconsin region was still a part until 1836. In 1834, as a member of the council, Martin won approval of an act incorporating the Portage Canal Company to construct a canal between the Fox and Wisconsin Rivers. The act was limited in scope, making no mention of the other needed improvements along the route. But it launched the necessary first step in transforming the rivers into a functioning artery for commercial transportation. In similar fashion, two years later, the territorial legislature authorized the construction of a dam with canal and locks at De Pere, the first set of rapids encountered by ships moving up the lower Fox. Unfortunately, neither effort would be quickly completed. Try as they might, neither territorial governments nor private investors could muster the capital required to carry out such a massive construction effort. The improvement of the river would have to wait for federal help.[14]

Aid came finally in 1839. Following persistent calls from Wisconsin's citizens and political representatives, the United States Congress appropriated money for a survey of the route as part of a small package of internal improvements in Wisconsin. Captain Thomas J. Cram of the U.S. Army's Topographical Engineers conducted the survey. It was published in 1840, and its conclusions gave ample support to promoters of the Fox-Wisconsin waterway. Cram took for granted that a shipping channel between Lake Michigan and the Mississippi would be of national significance, both commercially and militarily. It would benefit states along the eastern seaboard, southern states near the Gulf of Mexico, and "the whole country west of the Mississippi." According to Cram, there were "three routes which seem to be adapted by nature for the completion of this great and desirable end." In addition to the Fox-Wisconsin passage, he described two other possibilities, both more southerly routes. The first utilized the Rock River instead of the lower Fox. The Rock flowed south into Lake Michigan from Wisconsin through Illinois, and its headwaters could potentially be connected to Lake Winnebago by canal. The second route made use of the Illinois River and various canals to link the Mississippi with Lake Michigan. Although all three routes might feasibly be completed, Cram concluded that the Fox-Wisconsin passage offered the shortest, most practical, and least expensive choice. According to Cram, the Wisconsin River was already navigable and required virtually no improvement. Likewise, the upper Fox River presented few obstacles to shipping beyond its lengthy, meandering course. Clearly, the majority of the work needed to construct the route would take place along the lower Fox. In careful detail, Cram described the succession of rapids obstructing the river, offering plans and approximate costs for the various dams, canals, and locks required to overcome each barrier. In the end, his report suggested the precise sum of $448,470.18 as an estimated price for the completed work.[15]

Armed with Cram's report and its favorable assessment of the Fox-Wisconsin route, promoters continued to lobby Congress for federal aid. Success would come finally in 1846, and Morgan L. Martin was again at the center of the effort. By this time, Martin had become the Wisconsin Territory's delegate to Congress. With the region nearing statehood, Martin skillfully used the rivalry between the Democratic and Whig parties to secure passage of a land grant in support of the waterway. The grant, which would become effective when Wisconsin entered the union, covered the entire length of the Fox River and its tributary lakes, providing alternate sections of public land for 3 miles on either side of the stream. Two years later, Wisconsin achieved statehood and accepted the grant following minor alterations in the terms of the arrangement. The new state government then created a Board of Public Works to administer the project, and by 1850 work began anew on both the portage canal and the dam at De Pere.[16]

The improvement of the Fox River then began in earnest. But the effort was not without continued difficulties. Chief among these was a lack of sufficient revenue to carry out the work. It soon became apparent, for example, that the structures first completed along the route had to be strengthened and improved before they could be of use, leading to rising costs. At the same time, land sales from the public grant were much slower than expected, leaving the Board of Public Works short of funds. In 1851, Morgan L. Martin again stepped forward to rescue the project. He struck a deal with the state to complete all construction still remaining along the lower Fox. Using his own resources, Martin raised a force of 500 men and began work immediately. Unfortunately, by 1853, this venture, too, had run aground, hampered by the same lack of revenue that scuttled the board's effort, as well as the opposition of Wisconsin's newly elected Whig governor, who raised objections to the

Democrat Martin's private arrangement with the state. As a result, management of the project was reorganized, this time passing to a private corporation known as the Fox-Wisconsin Improvement Company. The company, initially composed of leading citizens in the Fox River Valley, including Martin, soon appealed to investors from New York for additional support. Although this outside involvement meant that valley residents lost control of the enterprise, the revenue it generated allowed work to proceed. Bolstered by these new funds, the company gave public assurance that the channel would be completed as scheduled by the summer of 1856.[17]

So it was that valley residents greeted the *Aquila*'s arrival in June of that year with such resounding joy as the steamship journeyed down the lower Fox to Green Bay. But the deep sense of achievement they felt is impossible to understand without looking closely at the great physical transformation of the river that had been accomplished. Before the stream's improvement, the Fox fell sharply and powerfully between Lake Winnebago and Green Bay. Along its 35-mile course, it dropped 166 feet in a series of eight distinct rapids: 10 feet at the twin rapids of Neenah and Menasha, where the stream flowed north from the lake; 38 feet at Grand Chute; 10 feet more at Cedar Rapids; another 40 feet at Little Chute; 52 feet at the Grand Kaukauna, the largest single drop on the river; and finally, minor falls of 8 feet each at Rapid Croche and De Pere (Figure 4). For centuries, these rapids had hampered navigation on the lower Fox, but Americans had managed to overcome them in just a few years. They did so by constructing an elaborate array of structures: eight dams ranging in width from 450 to 1,750 feet; canals that stretched for several miles in total length, each 5 feet deep and roughly 50 feet wide; and eighteen locks to raise and lower shipping along the route. The structures were made of timber, stone, clay, and iron. Human hands had crafted them, moving tons of rock and soil and building walls to confine the stream. Their efforts had transformed the lower Fox from a fast-moving and unmanageable river into a calm, controllable channel suitable for shipping.[18]

Here then, bound together within the physical edifice of the waterway, were both the human resolve to conquer the landscape and the hard-earned realization of nature's promise. It was this twofold sense of accomplishment that made the *Aquila*'s arrival such a profound occasion for valley residents. "You recall the struggles that have preceded this triumph," declared James H. Howe to the gathered crowd in Green Bay. A good many of these struggles

Figure 4. Canal and dam at Grand Chute on the Fox River, 1855. Courtesy of the Wisconsin Historical Society, Image No. WHi-2683.

had been financial and political in character, but at its root, the waterway remained a feat against nature. "We will not fail to do full and ample justice to those noble pioneers who have watched by this great work from its earliest conception," Howe assured, "who rocked its cradle in its infancy, and who have to-day stood it forth in all the pride of its full grown strength." Howe turned at this moment to gesture to Morgan L. Martin sitting behind him on the stage, apparently too moved to speak. "We to-day remember you, sir, to whose constant exertions in the halls of Congress it is, that we owe the munificent grant by which it was fostered and declared what nature had made it, a National Work." By Howe's reasoning, it was nature that made clear the possibility of a waterway, and it was nature, too, transformed by human agency, that held the promise of commercial success for valley residents. "When the records of your earthly career shall pass in review before you," Howe told Martin, "the proudest monument of a well spent life shall be our noble river laden with the wealth of a nation."[19]

Sadly for Martin and his fellow valley residents, the Fox-Wisconsin Improvement would never realize this grand potential. Despite the optimism surrounding the *Aquila*'s voyage, its journey had only been possible because water levels in the Fox and Wisconsin were especially high during June 1856. Within weeks, a summer drought had lowered the rivers, and navigation through the waterway was once again impossible. More troubling still, a host of long-term difficulties combined to doom the project before it could ever be fully completed. First, the New York investors who joined the Improvement Company after 1853 proved more interested in generating profits than creating a functioning waterway. Through various appeals to Congress to "clarify" the government's initial land grant, they managed nearly to triple the acreage bestowed. Their efforts transformed the Improvement Company into a scheme for land speculation, while the construction of the channel itself was allowed to lag. Second, more progress might well have been made had it not been for the financial panic that gripped the nation beginning in 1857. In the wake of the crisis, land sales declined dramatically, and the company had little revenue with which to proceed with the work. Third, nature, too, continued to present a variety of obstacles, the most alarming of which was the unpredictable character of the Wisconsin River. Despite Thomas J. Cram's earlier assessment that the river needed little improvement, the shifting sandbars that typified its streambed made navigation unreliable and difficult. It gradually became clear that only massive structures and great expense could transform the Wisconsin into a functioning part of the waterway. Last, and most ominous of all for promoters of the improvement, was the advent of railroads in the mid-nineteenth century. Their greater speed, efficiency, and independence from weather made railroads the preferred choice of shippers throughout the United States. Several railroads established connections to the Fox River Valley in the 1860s, and their arrival signaled doom for the waterway.[20]

As a result of these problems, the history of the Fox-Wisconsin Improvement after 1856 is an ill-fated tale of failure and eventual collapse. Yet the demise of the project did not occur for lack of effort on the part of its promoters. By 1866, a bankrupt Fox-Wisconsin Improvement Company sold its assets once again, this time to a group of eastern capitalists organized under the title of the Green Bay and Mississippi Canal Company. The new enterprise began a campaign of intense lobbying, seeking additional federal money to complete the waterway by improving the Wisconsin River. As happened with earlier promotional efforts, supporters used nature to instill their appeals with an air of divine intention. "A navigable connection of the waters of the Mississippi with those of Lake Michigan by the route of the Wisconsin and Fox Rivers," argued one proponent in 1869, "has been long looked upon as certain to be accomplished, because nature has done so much in preparing the way for such a connection." The waterway, claimed another, would encourage trade between the industrial East and the burgeoning Northwest: "to both sections it would invite and retain labor for those channels for which nature has peculiarly fitted them, by enabling them to command the productions of the other at prices within their reach." To the project's supporters, the failure to complete it after so much energy had been expended seemed a tragic waste of the cheap transportation afforded by the natural landscape. "Nature has done much, by the natural channels already furnished by the Lakes and Rivers perforating every portion of our country," implored a special River Improvement Committee in 1875, of which Morgan L. Martin was predictably a member. "We need only improvements, comparatively trifling, to afford a system of water ways unequaled in any part of the globe."[21]

The intensive lobbying of the late 1860s and 1870s led to one last federal effort to complete the Fox-Wisconsin Improvement. In 1872, the Green Bay and Mississippi Canal Company reached agreement to turn over control of its dams, canals, and locks to the U.S. government for the paltry sum of $145,000. Between 1873 and 1885, Congress then appropriated hundreds of thousands of dollars annually for the investigation and completion of the work. But little actual improvement was achieved, owing to the difficulties of controlling the Wisconsin River's ever-shifting streambed. By the mid-1880s, hopes for continuing the project were effectively dead.[22]

In the coming years, some limited shipping would continue along the lower Fox, subject always to the natural whim of season and changing water levels. But the Fox-Wisconsin waterway, once destined to be the shining avenue of commerce in the American West, had, in the words of an 1899 government report, "proven to be nothing more than a cul-de-sac." According to the engineer who authored the report, many factors had combined to foil the improvement, chief among them the railroads. "It did not seem possible [before the 1850s]," he wrote, "that the great water way apparently designed by nature to connect the Great Lakes and the Gulf would be supplanted by other means of communication more rapid and satisfactory." Likewise, it remained unclear that Chicago, and not Green Bay, would become the great center of trade in the region, leaving all of Wisconsin to make do in its shadow. In the end, concluded the engineer, there was nothing left of commerce along the Fox River "except here and there a sporadic barge loaded with salt, coal, and lumber to be distributed to points along the Fox; the whole aggregated together making but a diminutive drop in the great ocean of trade."[23]

But if the improvement of the lower Fox River had failed to deliver on nature's promise of cheap transportation, then valley residents remained eager to make good on a second potential use of the stream: waterpower. Local citizens had long recognized the inherent value of the Fox as an energy source, but for many years their preoccupation with transportation rendered power a secondary issue. As early as 1853, C. D. Westbrook, an engineer hired by New York investors to survey the river, ranked the Fox as one of the greatest sources of power in the west. Yet "the very magnitude of the power," he cautioned, made its immediate commercial value extremely limited. Until the waterway was completed, bringing with it an influx of raw material for the flour, lumber, and textile industries, "the water power on the lower Fox . . . could hardly be rated as a saleable article." Such reasoning persisted even in 1872, when the federal government allowed the Green Bay and Mississippi Canal Company to maintain its rights to the waterpower sites along the lower Fox, despite giving up possession of the dams that created them. "If Congress elects to take the improvement of the company, it is for the purpose of making it a part of [the Fox-Wisconsin] through route, and for that purpose only," read the government report on the potential sale. Although engineers recognized "the immense water-power in the Lower Fox," they recommended leaving it in the hands of private owners. "In an engineering point of view it does not seem that these water-lots are needed by the Government." As long as the private development of waterpower did not impede navigation, the company was free to exploit the river's flow as it saw fit. This fateful decision set the stage for a new phase in the local use of the Fox, one that would see the river transformed into a remarkable engine of work for valley residents.[24]

Natural Advantages

In 1874, A. J. Reid, editor of the Appleton *Crescent*, authored a booklet entitled *The Resources and Manufacturing Capacity of the Lower Fox River Valley*. Reid was among the great promoters of the valley, and the pamphlet was a transparent effort to lure manufacturers, settlers, and investment to the region. "As a place of residence," he began, "the Fox River Valley presents every attraction which is at all desirable. The scenery which borders the majestically flowing stream, the variegated beauty of woodland and meadow and finely cultivated farms, the pleasant undulations of valley and hillside, the roar of the cataract"—all these things combined, he said, "to minister to the esthetic as well as to the practical wants of the people of this valley." Yet having said this, Reid then turned exclusively to addressing the so-called practical wants of his readers, devoting the remainder of his nearly 60-page tract to describing the "vast and inexhaustible" natural resources available to valley residents. Here, Reid followed a course set by town promoters throughout the United States whose many paeans of nature's bounty comprised what one historian termed the doctrine of natural advantages in the nineteenth century. Although the rhetoric of this booster literature was clearly exaggerated and meant to entice local development, its overwhelming emphasis on productive resources suggests the way most citizens at the time defined the role of nature in American life. "There are certain natural advantages which every community must possess in order to achieve any considerable distinction," Reid argued. According to the editor, the Fox River Valley was blessed "to a remarkable extent" with these advantages: good soil, abundant timber and minerals, not to mention "the unequalled water-power afforded by the Fox River." This collection of resources destined the valley to become, in Reid's estimation, "the great manufacturing center of the West, if not the entire country."[25]

Few people were as poetic as A. J. Reid in describing the Fox River Valley. But to judge by their actions, most shared the editor's faith in the productive capacity of the local landscape. Between the 1850s and 1890s, valley residents put nature's resources to work, transforming the region from a relative frontier into a prosperous landscape of homes, farms, businesses, and communities. Their collective efforts suggest again the dual role played by nature in American life in the nineteenth century: a source of obstacles and hardships to be overcome on the one hand, and a divine plan for human progress on the other. "The Fox River Valley, sooner or later, must take on the character which has been indicated, and for which nature has admirably designed it," proclaimed a confident Reid in describing the certainty of the region's future growth. That such development could not take place without improvements wrought by human hands in no way detracted from the importance of nature itself. Quite the contrary, it bound landscape and people together in what most Americans took for granted as the worthy endeavor of industrial progress. "This degree of development to which we have attained, is entirely due to western nerve, and muscle, and brains," boasted Reid. "It has been accomplished by a generation of pioneers who began with nothing . . . who recognized the advantages of the country . . . [and] who have put forth their efforts to overcome nature's resistance to man, and make her resources subservient to a higher and nobler purpose." When shared, as it was by many nineteenth-century Americans, the idea that improving the landscape fulfilled nature's promise served to elevate countless seemingly private activities to the status of public good. In the process, it also offered a convenient justification for almost any effort to make resources productive, regardless of the environmental harm that might result.[26]

In the Fox River Valley, residents looked first to the natural landscape in nearly every endeavor they pursued. Not surprisingly, chief among the advantages they found was the Fox River itself, especially the power the stream could generate. The lower Fox was a relatively small river, traveling only 35 miles through the inconspicuous lowland between Lake Winnebago and Green Bay. Nevertheless, in the eyes of many citizens, nature seemed to have crafted the Fox for the sole purpose of manufacturing. Lake Winnebago received its water from two principal sources: the upper Fox River, which flowed northeasterly in a slow and winding course from central Wisconsin, and the Wolf, which joined the upper Fox at a much faster rate from the pine region north of the valley. The lake itself was a broad, shallow body of water roughly 20 feet deep, 10 miles wide, and 28 miles long from north to south. Its meager depth notwithstanding, its presence gave the lower portion of the Fox River an unusually constant flow, a trait that proved invaluable to manufacturers. The lake acted as a natural reservoir. "Other streams are crippled in power by droughts, and rendered furious and dangerous by freshets," noted A. J. Reid. The Fox River, by contrast, experienced few of these problems, allowing producers to count on the stream under almost any conditions. "Its flow," waxed Reid, "is as ceaseless as the attraction of gravitation is constant; its supply as regular and uniform as the change of seasons."

Of course, the real power of the Fox came not from its steadiness, but rather from its sharp, dramatic fall. As already noted, the river dropped 166 feet on its winding course through the valley. Even more significant, it made its descent in a series of distinct rapids. As the river was gradually dammed and improved with canals and locks for transportation, valley residents rushed to exploit the waterpower that became available in the process. In a matter of years, each fall of the river had spawned a thriving manufacturing community: Neenah and Menasha at the twin rapids on the northern end of Lake Winnebago, Appleton at the Grand Chute, Kaukauna where the Grand Kaukauna had been, and De Pere just a few miles farther downstream. "We look in vain for such a rare combination of advantages elsewhere in this country," declared Reid. The Fox River, he promised, would always be the "faithful servant of industry."[27]

Although Reid's assessment of the Fox was certainly exaggerated, he was not alone among local boosters in his enthusiasm for the river's power. According to Alice E. Smith, a historian of nineteenth-century life in the valley, most of the region's promoters "prized the water resources of the Lower Fox and even regarded them as the *raison d'etre* of settlement." Nearly every description of the region dating from the period echoes Reid's celebration of the waterpower and the valley's industrial promise. "This magnificent water power is simply INEXHAUSTABLE," declared one promoter in touting the future of Menasha. "There is a superabundance of water," which resulted from the river's natural reservoir and ensured that the Fox would forever "sing the music of industry." In neighboring Kaukauna, residents proclaimed the city "the Lion of the Fox" and described the river as "a fountain of wealth that needs but to be tapped." Even visitors to the region seemed awed by the Fox and its industrial promise. "There can be no better location in the country for manufactures than these towns," professed a traveler from Milwaukee in 1875. "Here is a water power of almost sufficient strength to run the manufacturing industries of the whole continent," he continued. "This great water power must some day be utilized by manufactures, and as the mechanical production become more varied and important so the commercial interests of these cities will advance until they reach the zenith of prosperity."[28]

However important the power of the Fox loomed in the economic future of the valley, exploiting it required finding activities for which its energy could be used commercially. Fortunately for valley residents, the natural advantages afforded by the region did not end at the river's edge. "There still remains to be explained the resources of this beautiful valley," said A. J. Reid, "upon which the perpetual smiles of the Almighty seem to rest." During the late nineteenth century, the economy of the Fox River Valley was dominated by three industries, each of which relied on the particular advantages of the surrounding natural landscape: agriculture, the lumber industry, and the manufacture of paper. A brief look at the development of these industries suggests again the visible importance of nature's role as a means of production in local life.[29]

Among the earliest and most important endeavors in which valley residents engaged was agriculture. Almost without exception, those settlers who came to the region to farm during the mid-nineteenth century opted to raise wheat. Wheat farming was essentially an extractive enterprise, much like mining, intended to exploit the area's abundant natural resources in order to serve a more developed eastern market. In this case, the resource in question was land. According to Reid, the valley offered "the richest agricultural districts which the country affords." The "fertility of its soil alone," he asserted, "is an element of wealth that can be reckoned with the most flattering results." But more than fertility, the success of wheat growing depended on the fact that land was relatively inexpensive. In the poorly developed economy that characterized Wisconsin during the mid-nineteenth century, valley residents suffered from a shortage of labor and capital. Land, on the other hand, was readily available, largely because much of the region remained in the public domain, subject to federally mandated prices meant to encourage settlement.[30]

Under these circumstances, raising wheat offered a number of advantages to settlers. For one thing, wheat required little labor when compared with other crops. Once the land was cleared—which by itself was no easy task, especially in wooded areas—farmers had merely to sow the seed, which they typically did by hand, and then wait for harvest time. Wheat demanded very little attention during the bulk of its growing period. When the grain was ready to harvest, either in the spring or fall depending on the variety, farmers would cut the standing wheat with a scythe, rake it, and bind it into sheaves for threshing. The process was painstaking, and farmers could only harvest two to three acres per day. But relative to other kinds of agriculture, raising wheat left new settlers free to perform the many other chores required to establish their homesteads. Wheat also offered farmers a nearly guaranteed source of income, which, on the cash-starved frontier, could prove vital to a family's survival. Grain, in fact, served as a kind of currency allowing farmers to trade their crops directly to local merchants for food, clothing, and other necessities. Merchants, in turn, were eager to make these exchanges because they knew they could sell the wheat themselves. Either they could mill the grain locally to produce flour for nearby customers, or, more likely, they could ship it to distant markets in the east and overseas in Europe. Wheat was one of the few crops that could bear the cost of long-distance shipping and that could endure the journey without significant spoilage. Thus, in frontier areas where settlement remained limited and local markets poorly developed, wheat provided farmers with an exceptionally dependable cash crop.[31]

In essence, valley farmers in the mid-nineteenth century chose to spend land rather than money. "Farmers generally have but limited means," explained one observer at the time, "and are compelled to get all they can out of their lands, with the least possible outlay." Unfortunately, this practice had troubling consequences for the natural landscape upon which agriculture depended. Gustavus de Neveu, a resident of the valley, summarized the situation in an agricultural report to the federal government in 1859. It had become fairly common in Wisconsin, he said, for farmers to work a piece of land for several years until the fertility of the soil declined, at which point they simply moved on to new and better lands. The same shortage of labor and capital that led farmers to raise wheat also compelled them, said de Neveu, "to cultivate a large surface of land as cheaply and rapidly as possible, rather than a smaller surface in a slow and thorough manner." De Neveu branded this style of agriculture "loose and careless," and he lamented the waste of the nation's "so-called inexhaustible lands." Yet farmers clearly had good reason to use the soil as they did. As another nineteenth-century commentator explained, "*poor* farming was the only profitable farming, and consequently the only *good* farming." Valley residents simply used what nature and public land policy afforded, "an agriculturo-economical paradox from which there was no escape." As long as land remained cheap, de Neveu concluded, "so long will there be a lack of inducement for Western farmers to make the earth yield supplies to its utmost capacity."[32]

Despite mounting concerns about the fertility of the soil, wheat growing boomed in the Fox River Valley and throughout Wisconsin from the 1850s through the 1870s. The annual output statewide rose from 4 million bushels to more than 25 million during the period. In the valley, farmers were among the most productive in the state, turning out nearly 3,000 bushels per square mile of developed land. This production was crucial not only to farmers, but to the budding industrial dreams of manufacturers in the region, who sought outlets for both their capital and the power of the Fox River. During the mid-nineteenth century, flour milling ranked among the most important industries in the valley, especially on the region's western end in Neenah and Menasha. There, manufacturers took advantage of the cheap power, the abundant wheat production, and the growing local market for flour to create a thriving industry. The arrival of the railroads during the 1860s brought national markets within reach. By the end of the decade, the twin communities claimed fifteen mills in operation, utilizing forty-four waterwheels. Taken together, the mills produced roughly 224,000 barrels of flour valued at more than a million dollars. This output surpassed all Wisconsin cities except Milwaukee, and promoters such as A. J. Reid predicted that continued expansion would make the valley "the grand center for the converting of cereals into breadstuffs for the entire country." Although this dream never materialized, the combined influence of wheat growing and flour production in the region provided an early example of how natural advantages could be put to work in order to create a prosperous future.[33]

Taking shape alongside agriculture was a second cornerstone of the valley's nineteenth-century economy: the lumber industry. The history of lumbering in Wisconsin is usually described as a tragedy involving the exploitation and reckless waste of nature's resources. But as late as the 1880s, times remained flush in the industry, and valley residents did their best to profit from the enterprise. Here again, A. J. Reid was quick to point out the relative advantages afforded by nature in the Fox River Valley. According to the editor, nearly 40 percent of the region surrounding the lower Fox was timbered in 1874, more than enough to supply "the miscellaneous wants of the people." Yet as even Reid was forced to admit, the real wooded treasures of Wisconsin's landscape were located "beyond the limits of our beautiful valley, to the north and west of us." There, citizens would encounter "immense virgin forests where no traces of the innovations of industry are seen, and whose silence is yet unbroken, save by the voice of the storm-king in his fury."[34]

As usual, Reid was more poetic than reality justified. Already in the 1870s, the extensive forests that covered the northern third of Wisconsin had been penetrated by industrial logging. When combined, the various operations produced more than a billion board-feet per year, a figure that would nearly triple by the 1890s, the zenith of the industry's output in the state. Yet much as Reid claimed, the valley was in fact well situated to profit from the flow of this lumber, which remained part of the lifeblood of the local economy until well into the twentieth century. Like any settlers in a newly developing region, citizens in the valley depended on lumber to build their growing communities, from houses and storefronts to barns and fences. The Fox River provided power for numerous sawmills, and together with the railroads following the 1860s, was a convenient transportation artery for the raw materials and products of lumbering. Much of this production in the valley itself was connected to the region's flour industry, with a variety of firms manufacturing staves for the making of barrels. Other producers turned out buckets, churns, shingles, doors, and windows. Throughout the nineteenth century, the valley would remain outside the primary influence of the lumber industry in Wisconsin. Nonetheless, its residents enjoyed the tangible and highly visible benefit of their proximity to the great stands of trees just beyond their borders.[35]

As significant as flour milling and lumbering were to the Fox River Valley during the mid-nineteenth century, by the 1880s their influence had given way to a third and far more permanent economic base: the manufacture of paper. The rise of papermaking in the valley came on the heels of a corresponding decline in local wheat production and the flour industry. For a variety of reasons, during the 1870s Wisconsin's farmers found it less and less economical to raise wheat. Perhaps most important, the more developed Wisconsin became — with a rising population and growing cities — the more expensive land became, compelling farmers to earn a higher return per acre in order to remain profitable. Under these conditions, growing wheat in the valley ceased to be a practical option. Not only did local soils become exhausted, which reduced the annual harvest, but farmers discovered that their counterparts in the newly opened territories of Minnesota and the Dakotas were able to undersell them, largely because they could benefit from the same access to cheap land that characterized Wisconsin just twenty years earlier. As the output of wheat gradually declined in the valley, local milling operations struggled to compete with larger centers of production such as Minneapolis and Chicago. In response, manufacturers began looking for other ways to put the waterpower of the Fox River to work. They turned, in large part, to the production of paper.[36]

Manufacturing paper was not unheard of in the valley during the 1870s. The region's first mill had been built in Appleton in 1853, and it was joined by a handful of other firms during the 1860s and 1870s. Still, in 1874 when A. J. Reid authored his promotional booklet on manufacturing in the valley, the paper industry was among the few aspects of the local economy on which he remained relatively silent. The valley, he noted, was "unrivalled by any other place in the country as a location for industries of this class." Yet the full blossoming of papermaking would take place in the years to come, as wheat production and flour milling declined more rapidly.[37]

Reid's inattention notwithstanding, the Fox River Valley proved ideally suited for the manufacture of paper, in large part because of the valley's unique combination of natural advantages. Not surprisingly, once again, the valley's waterpower proved to be its most important asset. The machinery typically used by the industry relied on a uniform source of energy in order to produce paper of consistent thickness and quality. As Reid argued many times, the Fox River was unmatched by any stream in the evenness of its flow, as a result of the steadying influence of Lake Winnebago. "The practical manufacturer will draw his own conclusions as to the advantages of this arrangement," he submitted, "so admirably designed by nature." Waterpower also provided a cheaper source of energy than other means of production. By the 1870s, the use of steam power was increasingly common among industrial manufacturers. But Reid discouraged its use in the valley, where nature had provided more affordable methods. "Steam is valuable and can be appropriated to a greater variety of purposes," he admitted. "But power thus furnished and communicated to machinery involves a greater outlay than that supplied by falling water." In subsequent years, leaders in the valley's paper industry would follow exactly this advice, delaying their adoption of newer, more efficient sources of energy until the end of the century.[38]

Beyond the power of the Fox, the valley possessed two other natural advantages that facilitated the making of paper. First, because the industry required large volumes of water in the manufacturing process itself, producers needed water that was relatively pure in order to avoid discoloring the paper. Once again, the Fox River seemed well adapted to the purpose, insofar as its chemical composition was concerned. "I would not change the power in your city for any like quantity in any other place," said one manufacturer of paper upon visiting Appleton from the state of New York. "For purposes where *pure water* is required, no place can compare." Second, the valley also provided ample raw materials for the industry. Initially, manufacturers used straw or rags to produce low-quality paper for newsprint and packaging. By the 1880s, however, after the development of new methods of wood pulping, including the sulphite process, local papermakers turned to the forests of northern Wisconsin to supply their needs. Such a large quantity of trees in such close proximity to the valley gave manufacturers a new, highly lucrative reason to value their location. In the words of another local booster, "the Fox River is bound to be the Merrimac of the West, the spruce forests of northern Wisconsin, its cotton plantation, yielding enormous quantities of raw material from which will reproduce in an unending cycle, sufficient to supply the enormous consumption." Although the forests of Wisconsin did eventually prove to have limits, valley papermakers enjoyed the benefit of abundant timber for many years.[39]

By the 1890s, manufacturers in the Fox River Valley had utilized the area's natural advantages to create a powerful and thriving industry. "Within the space of twenty years a marvelous development has taken place," noted one Milwaukee reporter after touring the region in 1892. Paper had become big business, moving "from one small mill making an insignificant quantity of straw wrapping paper . . . to an industry in which more than $5,500,000 of capital is invested, and whose annual product has a selling value of over $9,000,000." However impressive these figures were, what most struck the reporter was the way in which the valley's production of paper was dependent on resources supplied by nature. "The Fox river valley would never have made a pound of paper if her conditions had not been particularly suitable," he explained (Figure 5). Above all, paper required "power, and plenty of it to drive the numerous and heavy machines." Here, the waters of the lower Fox furnished a "convenient and abundant cheap motive force. . . . The river moves thirty paper and pulp mills, making annually over 200,000,000 pounds of paper and about 50,000,000 pounds of pulp and sulphite fiber." Obtaining enough wood to produce this fiber was equally vital to the industry. Once again, the valley proved lucky to be "contiguous to the supplies of spruce and poplar wood, of which paper is now so largely composed."[40]

Yet much as with any industrial activity in nineteenth-century Wisconsin, nearly everyone realized that nature's advantages were only valuable to the extent that people could harness and utilize them for economic gain. According

Figure 5. Paper mill in De Pere, 1889. Courtesy of the Wisconsin Historical Society, Image No. WHi-24407.

to the reporter, the paper industry employed roughly 2,600 laborers in 1892 at wages totaling over a million dollars a year. The various mills that utilized the Fox River did so only by controlling and capturing its energy with the aid of dams, canals, and waterwheels, not to mention the complex machinery that produced the paper itself. In much the same way, although manufacturers were fortunate to be situated near the great forests of northern Wisconsin, the trees did not harvest themselves. Instead, papermakers relied on the lumber industry to gather wood from the forests, and the railroads to deliver it for use. From the valley alone, explained the reporter, "three lines of railway penetrate the forest, and every day in the winter season many train loads of logs are received and piled in towering truncated pyramids in the yards about the mills."[41]

It was this blending of nature and human effort that so fascinated many nineteenth-century Americans, including A. J. Reid in his 1874 booklet. "The final value of timber, like everything else, depends upon the amount of la-

bor expended upon it," he wrote. If the valley possessed all the advantages
required for manufacturing, nature's promise could only be realized through
the improvement and use of its many resources. Nowhere was the truth of
this statement more evident than in the actions of the valley's early settlers
who had harnessed the Fox River, made homes from the region's forests, laid
bare its fertile soil, and transformed its rich landscape into a prosperous industrial valley. According to Reid, nature had rewarded these pioneers "with
bounteous liberality," despite its often stubborn resistance. "The lesson of
their experience," he concluded, "is just sufficient to demonstrate how profitable the establishment of industrial enterprises in this valley may be made,
by the assistance of capital and its concomitants." The task left to the valley's future residents was to learn this lesson and continue down the path
marked out by nature. "The generation which inaugurates this development,"
promised Reid, "is one that will be well known in the history of modern
civilization."[42]

The Fading Frontier

Unfortunately, by the 1890s, nature's role in this scheme of industrial progress had become jeopardized by the heavy use to which valley residents had
put its resources. For manufacturers, farmers, and citizens in the region, the
local landscape had always seemed an inexhaustible storehouse of natural
wealth. But as the century neared an end, decades of headlong development
finally appeared to have taken its toll. "The pine timber that formerly covered
this region . . . has mostly long since passed away and shingles are no longer
regarded as Green Bay currency," lamented one local newspaper in 1893. Likewise, despite the growth of the paper industry, it was becoming clear that the
valley could hardly compete with larger cities such as Chicago, Minneapolis,
or even Milwaukee for access to resources and the profits they generated.
Even the great power of the Fox River, the most important natural asset in the
valley, appeared to have been exploited beyond its limits. Manufacturers in
the paper industry, charged one critic, had "continued to abuse [the river], by
pushing it along and exhausting its vitality, to such an extent that all of a sudden they woke up one morning only to find that their great and never ceasing
power was a thing of the past. . . . Never once," he complained, "did they take
into consideration this fact; that there was a limit to the water."[43]

Worries such as these were crystallized in 1893, when a nationwide financial panic triggered an economic depression that lasted for four long years. In the Fox River Valley, as in many parts of the United States, industry ground to a halt. "As we walked along down the water power in this city, yesterday," intoned the Appleton *Post*, "admiring the massive mills and factories that stud the banks of our beautiful river there came back to us the memory of other days when their mighty engines and powerful machinery throbbed as they were crowded to supply the ever increasing demand for their products." Sadly, the recent panic had silenced the river, leaving behind the "smokeless chimneys" of local mills and "the wide-spread desolation that must culminate in cheerless homes and distressing destitution." As the crisis deepened by the mid-1890s, people everywhere began to rethink the nation's development and its many implications. Diminishing natural resources were only part of the problem. During the thirty years after the Civil War, Americans had seen their country transformed by powerful forces. The United States, once a land of small commercial towns and rural agriculture, had become a nation of sprawling cities, mechanized factories, and giant corporations. Likewise, where formerly Americans had imagined society as a collection of producers, each freethinking and independent, increasingly they found it dominated instead by wage earners and middle managers, all constrained by the interests upon which they were beholden. Yet for many people, looming over all these changes was the troubling fate of nature in the 1890s. Where citizens had once been free to utilize a landscape of unbounded natural wealth, they now discovered that nature's resources were dwindling, along with the opportunities that came from exploiting them. Few Americans, no matter what their occupation, economic standing, or cultural identity, could escape the uncertainties of this dramatic transformation. How best to understand and resolve their doubts remained an open question.[44]

Nothing better captures the combination of profound value and deep concern that Americans attached to nature in the 1890s than the famous essay delivered by Frederick Jackson Turner, a young historian from the University of Wisconsin, before the American Historical Association meeting held at the World's Columbian Exposition in Chicago in 1893. Entitled "The Significance of the Frontier in American History," Turner's speech attempted to explain what he called "the first period of American history." According to Turner, this period had come to an end in 1890, when the U.S. Census Bureau re-

ported that it was no longer possible to identify a so-called frontier of settlement. "At present," the bureau explained, "the unsettled area has been so broken into by isolated bodies of settlement that there can hardly be said to be a
frontier line." For Turner, this was important because the frontier—or as he
defined it, "the existence of an area of free land, its continuous recession, and
the advance of American settlement westward"—had been profoundly in-
fluential in shaping the nation's development, the character of its people, and
the stability of its democratic institutions. Although Turner's argument was
mainly historical, its relevance to the future was obvious to anyone who encountered it. If America's great success had been a product of nature's wealth
and the opportunities it created, what was to become of the nation now that
the frontier was gone?[45]

For many years surrounding the turn of the century, it remained unclear
just how the country would answer this question. Yet on one point, Americans were unambiguous. For all their worries about the disappearance of
Turner's "free land," few people in the 1890s displayed any desire to return to
a time when nature presented real difficulties, hardships, and dangers. The
Columbian Exposition at which Turner had spoken was, after all, a celebration of human material progress. In the words of one historian, the fair was
intended to "open a new epoch in man's comprehension and control of nature." Organizers filled the grounds with wondrous displays of electricity and
other new technologies. There were commemorations of mass production
and numerous tributes to the power of human ingenuity. "Evidenced on every side are subordinations of the physical," said one commentator, describing the fair. "Ready at hand are all those contrivances of civilization which
help to elevate and ennoble man, to refine his tastes, enlarge his ideas, enrich
his interests, and further his deliverance from the despotisms of nature." Although critics complained that the fair's symbolic themes were often contra-
dictory in other respects, few visitors to the exposition had any doubts that
progress required even greater efforts to conquer the natural world.[46]

This kind of symbolism was rife throughout the 1890s, and Americans had
little need to attend the World's Fair to encounter it firsthand. The decade
witnessed many events that spoke of a new industrial order and the growing
desire of citizens to accommodate themselves to its requirements. The Battle
of Wounded Knee in 1890 marked the end of Indian resistance in the West,
a passing era that many white Americans quickly romanticized, yet just as

clearly welcomed. In the same vein, the violent defeats of organized labor in Homestead in 1892 and Chicago in 1894 were major victories for corporate dominance of the national economy. In the political arena, the defeat of Populism in the 1896 presidential election marked a similar trend, as voters soundly rejected the party's platform of social and economic reforms. And finally, the U.S. victory in the Spanish-American War in 1898 heralded the beginning of an international empire for the United States. With the country's newfound access to global markets and resources, few people could doubt the basic direction of its future development.[47]

Closer to home in the Fox River Valley, events such as these were far removed from daily life. But residents encountered the kind of modernization they signified nearly everywhere. Although valley communities had never experienced the dramatic growth and transformation that characterized America's largest cities in the late nineteenth century, they did nonetheless share in most of its important technological changes. By the 1890s, mechanization had become a ubiquitous force in the region, from farming in the countryside to the mills and factories of local cities. Area residents had witnessed the coming of the railroads, the telegraph, and even a budding telephone system. The progressive influence of industrial development was especially noticeable in the region's cities. There, streetcars carried passengers along bustling commercial avenues where shoppers could purchase almost anything they needed, from the latest in New York fashions to basic dry goods, furniture, and supplies for the home. Valley residents enjoyed a large selection of foods, including Chicago beef, canned vegetables, and fruits shipped in through the railroads from all parts of the world. The infrastructure of local cities was no less impressive. Beginning in the 1880s, most communities had established gas and electric service, public water systems, and a network of sewers to dispose of wastes. Taken together, the growing array of conveniences and amenities available to valley residents made the difficulties of life on Wisconsin's frontier an increasingly distant memory.[48]

Yet for all the ways in which the valley's development made life easier by taming the landscape, residents had ample reason to desire even more development, not less. If the frontier had begun to fade by the 1890s, at least in terms of its material hardships, it had yet to disappear entirely. Nature's role as a place of obstacles and resources remained an ever-present reality for local residents, no matter what their station in life. Even in the cities, despite their modern amenities, people daily confronted the natural environment as an adversary. Local gas and electric service, for example, was notoriously unreliable, and its use was typically limited to providing illumination only. For heat during the winter, many people burned firewood or shoveled coal into stoves or basement furnaces. Each fall, local newspapers were filled with adds warning citizens to prepare for the coming cold. "If you want coal cheap for winter, order now," suggested one Green Bay dealer. Much the same regimen applied to cooking all year round. People's dependence on open flames in their households, whether for lighting, warmth, or cooking, posed a constant danger of fire. In 1895, a valley farmer named Fred Grant was wiped out by a fire that started when he accidentally tipped over a lantern into some straw. "His house, two barns, granaries, wagon house, all this year's crops, household furniture, three cows, hogs and straw stacks were burned," the local paper reported. Such fires were common throughout the period.[49]

Valley residents in the 1890s had yet to experience the industrialized wonder of home appliances that washed laundry automatically, vacuumed dirty floors, and cooked meals without open flames. These conveniences were still years in the future, leaving residents to rely on more traditional ways of living. Each winter, for example, a thriving local ice industry sent teams of men onto the Fox River to harvest ice for the summer, allowing families to preserve food and taverns to provide cold beer. According to the Appleton *Crescent*, the city had at least three ice companies in business in 1895. One of these, a local brewery, "not only fills its own ice houses but . . . cuts for all the cheese manufacturers, saloon-keepers and farmers for a distance of 15 miles." As the article reported, a second company had recently invested in a newfangled machine to create ice. But this remained a rare exception. For the most part, people depended on winter to supply their ice, creating yet another visible link between humans and the natural environment (Figure 6). "The cold snap of the past few days is just what ice men have been praying for," noted the *Crescent*. If nature failed to provide ice, as sometimes happened in warmer years, then local citizens had to make do without.[50]

In much the same way, despite the growing infrastructure that characterized urban areas in the valley, citizens received only marginal protection from the various material hardships of life. Even in the 1890s, many of the most heavily traveled streets in local cities had yet to be paved, creating a dusty hazard when the weather was dry and a muddy quagmire when it rained.

Figure 6. Typical winter ice harvest, ca. 1900. Courtesy of the Neville Public Museum of Brown County, Image No. 8347.

Likewise, the urban waterworks and sewer systems that most communities had constructed offered little in the way of treatment, either of the water they extracted from rivers and wells or the wastes they discharged into the environment. Garbage collection was unheard of in the valley, and city health officials issued annual warnings urging residents to dispose of their refuse more carefully. As late as 1897, Green Bay's Health Officer lamented "the habitually filthy condition of the alleys and . . . back yards," and he urged the city council to create "some uniform but inexpensive mode of garbage disposition." Citizens worried constantly about the impact of this waste on water supplies and public health. The spread of infectious diseases was a looming concern throughout the period, and local outbreaks of scarlet fever, diphtheria, smallpox, and typhoid became headline news. Although these diseases were not solely the products of unsanitary environments, for most residents, they remained powerful reminders of the dangers posed by nature in the absence of proper management and human controls.[51]

Diseases were not the only natural organisms running free in valley cities during the 1890s. Like urban areas throughout the country, local towns were often populated with a wide assortment of animals. Despite regulations that discouraged the keeping of livestock, many citizens owned chickens, pigs, and cows to supplement their diets. Local butchers routinely housed cattle in the middle of town. Horses were by far the most numerous animal residents. In an age before automobiles and gas stations came to dominate the urban landscape, people relied on horses to provide their transportation. Under the best of circumstances, horses were a troublesome and unhealthy addition to already crowded cities. Not only did they deposit tons of manure and thousands of gallons of urine annually on urban streets, but they also required residents to tolerate the presence of stables in their midst, which were invariably smelly, noisy, and plagued with insects. Even more bothersome, horses, like any creatures, could become unruly. In September 1894, a passing train spooked one farmer's team in Appleton, which then bolted down a busy street. The wagon struck another team, causing "a mad race" and landing a farmer, his wife, and their son "in more or less confused heaps." Runaways of this sort were commonplace in the late nineteenth century. Although newspapers often described their occurrence as lighthearted distractions from the normal routine, the injuries they caused were frequently serious. Here was yet another vivid metaphor for the persistence of untamed nature in the 1890s.[52]

Whatever difficulties urban residents encountered during the era, the situation was even more arduous for the valley's rural citizens, the great majority of whom were farmers. In the absence of gas, electricity, public water, and sewers, the farmer's life could often seem little different than it had been a half century earlier when the valley was in fact on the frontier of American settlement. Their heat came from burning wood, their water from wells or nearby streams. Transportation proved one of the greatest hardships. During the late nineteenth century, Wisconsin's rural highways were notoriously bad. Mostly unpaved and poorly maintained, they were difficult to travel under the best of conditions. During spring and summer, rain could make getting to town impossible. In winter, by contrast, the lack of precipitation was just as disastrous. "The winter thus far has been the worst kind of one imaginable," noted the Appleton *Crescent* in January 1895. "There has been no snow and scarcely cold enough weather to make good ice roads." Without snow, lumbermen struggled to haul logs from the forests, and urban merchants endured a season of poor sales to rural customers. But the farmer's lot was unquestionably the worst. Trapped in the countryside, unable to get into town, rural citizens hoped for nothing more than greater efforts to eliminate these natural obstacles.[53]

Given the persistence of such hardships and nature's resistance to being tamed even in the 1890s, it should not be surprising that few valley residents questioned the industrial use of the Fox River, no matter what the effect on its waters. When the rains failed in Wisconsin during the spring of 1895, especially in the midst of a depression, all eyes turned immediately to the dwindling power of the Fox while little attention was paid to the cleanliness of the water. Manufacturers desperate for energy blamed many things for their dilemma. Foremost on their list of culprits was the federal policy of protecting navigation on the Fox, which had little economic value compared with the production of paper. "The present absurd situation whereby thousands of dollars are lost to manufacturers in order that dimes may be saved to a spindling navigation interest will condemn itself the moment existing conditions are known," railed one local editor in supporting the plan to convene a conference of politicians in Green Bay. Other critics pointed to the paper mills, noting that manufacturers had failed to install more dependable sources of energy, such as steam power, that did not depend so heavily on the river. Still, as the year progressed and the weather turned hotter, manufacturers could do little but look plaintively toward the skies. "If the summer months continue as dry as the past spring months it may take 60 days to fill [Lake Winnebago]," noted one observer in May. Unfortunately, the drought lasted even longer. Manufacturers and citizens alike were left to endure their losses and to consider how best to prevent similar disasters in the future.[54]

In the wake of their experience in 1895, manufacturers in the valley's paper industry would never again be so vulnerable to their dependence on natural resources. Even in the midst of the drought, they began to install steam engines that, although still relying on the river, were far more efficient and produced greater amounts of energy with less water. In the years to come, the industry would move to consolidate its control of the Fox, joining together to monopolize the flow of its waters and use its power to generate steady profits as well as energy. By the 1920s, producers had even begun to construct their own electric plants, both to supplement their growing demand for power and to reduce their dependence on local resources. Much the same situation applied to the industry's use of the forests. By the first decade of the twentieth century, the supply of timber from Wisconsin's lumber industry had begun to falter. Manufacturers in the valley responded by hiring chemists to search for new, more efficient methods of producing paper and for specialized products that generated higher profits. The result was a transformation of the industry's production in the valley, from basic newsprint and wrapping paper to a series of dedicated, high-end commodities such as fine writing paper, facial tissue, sanitary napkins, surgical dressings, and a variety of containers ranging from waxed cartons to cardboard boxes. With these crucial changes, by the 1930s, local mills managed to survive the overuse of the region's waterpower and its forests alike. In the modern era, it seemed, the valley's economy would no longer rely so directly on the use of its natural advantages.

But if manufacturers seemed to have grown independent of nature after the 1890s, the appearance was deceptive. In fact, in the years to come the valley's paper companies relied more than ever on natural resources. What changed were the lengths to which they would go both to collect the material they needed and to utilize these resources to the fullest possible extent. In other words, the industry learned to use nature more intensively, a lesson that was applied by nearly every producer in every segment of the nation's economy during the early twentieth century. Here, in the dramatic industrialization of the early twentieth century, was America's answer to Frederick Jackson Turner and the closing of the frontier. In a world where land was no longer "free" and nature's wealth was not nearly so abundant, the United States would not be forced to curtail its development—just the opposite: the nation could achieve new heights of material progress and prosperity enough for the masses. Rather than limiting their use of the natural landscape, Americans would seek to control its resources more tightly than ever in order to maximize their returns on what was left. In the Fox River Valley, it was the remarkable success of this renewed industrial effort that finally completed the evolution of a consumer society, with all its paradoxical implications for the natural environment.

3

The Renewal of Progress

Typically, when historians consider the turn-of-the-century effort to reform America's use of natural resources, they point to the conservation movement. In May 1908, President Theodore Roosevelt made conservation a national priority. He convened in the White House a conference of the nation's governors to discuss the issue. "Every step of the progress of mankind is marked by the discovery and use of natural resources previously unused," suggested the president. Echoing Frederick Jackson Turner's ideas on the importance of the frontier to the country's development, Roosevelt explained that nature had bestowed upon Americans a supply of material wealth unparalleled in its variety and abundance. Then, again like Turner, he argued that the great pace and scale of this development now confronted the United States with a troubling uncertainty, in this case, that the country's riches might soon become scarce. "The time has come," asserted Roosevelt, "to inquire seriously what will happen when our forests are gone, when the coal, the iron, the oil, and the gas are exhausted, when the soils shall have been still further impoverished and washed into the streams." Only conservation offered Americans a way to renew the nation's progress. In the president's view, the movement had become the moral duty of every citizen, an obligation "to protect ourselves and our children against the wasteful development of our natural resources."[1]

In Wisconsin, as in many states, lawmakers took up Roosevelt's challenge. Among their first responses was to organize the Legislative Committee on Water Powers, Forestry, and Drainage to investigate the development of the state's rivers and streams. Not surprisingly, the committee's first stop was the Fox River Valley. For three days in August 1909, members toured the valley's western end, visiting the waterpowers in Neenah, Menasha, Appleton, and Kaukauna and holding a series of meetings with manufacturers. What they found in the valley was a picture of wasted resources and dissatisfaction that mirrored almost perfectly the crisis outlined in Washington a year earlier. At the time, waterpower on the Fox was controlled by two principal groups: the federal government, which had possession of the majority of dams along the river; and the Green Bay and Mississippi Canal Company, which still owned the rights to the bulk of the stream's waterpower. Manufacturers were less than happy with the arrangement. Unfortunately, under the terms of the 1872 agreement in which Congress had purchased the physical improvements of the Fox, neither the federal government nor the Canal Company was obligated to further develop the power they generated. Federal officials were only required to protect navigation, and they refused to concern themselves with power. Meanwhile, the Canal Company was left to reap the profits from dams that it neither owned nor built in the first place. "As I understand," said one astonished member of the committee, "the Green Bay Company gets in early here, they have all these dams built for them, [and] they turn it back to the Government and charge rent for it?" The result was a waterpower on the Fox River that manufacturers deemed insufficient, especially during the summer and early fall when the annual reduction in water levels forced the paper mills to use more expensive steam to run their machinery.[2]

What to do about the problem remained an open question. Members of the Committee on Water Powers appeared to favor the idea of transferring control of the dams from the federal government to the state, thereby allowing Wisconsin to develop the sites beyond the requirements of navigation. But manufacturers were skeptical. "I don't see that it would help the situation a particle," cautioned one industry spokesman. According to producers, the majority of the power sites along the Fox had already been fully developed, making it impossible to improve the river by building additional dams or expanding those currently in place. Instead, they supported the construction of a reservoir system on the nearby Wolf River, which emptied into the lower Fox at Lake Winnebago. Expanding the storage capacity of the Wolf would not increase the maximum power of the Fox, they admitted. But the scheme was vital nonetheless because it would eliminate the annual threat of sum-mer droughts, making the power of the Fox substantially more uniform and therefore more useful and valuable to manufacturers.[3]

The brief visit of the Committee on Water Powers to the Fox River Val-ley illustrates two important and familiar points about conservation in the United States at the turn of the century. First, as many historians have noted, the movement was governed by an elite group of scientists, businessmen, engineers, and politicians, all of whom were primarily concerned with pro-tecting the ability of producers to utilize nature's wealth. Like many con-servationists, members of the Committee on Water Powers believed that in safeguarding people's access to resources, they acted to preserve democracy itself by ensuring the equality of opportunity among Americans. Yet as part of this belief, they also maintained a wary skepticism of the general public, a paradoxical stance that was common among leaders in every branch of conservation. "We are coming to recognize as never before the right of the Nation to guard its own future in the essential matter of natural resources," proclaimed Theodore Roosevelt. But having said this, one of the principal dangers against which the president urged protection was the common "de-mand for unrestricted individualism." By this logic, conservation was a task best left in the capable hands of experts authorized to work on behalf of the nation's citizens, without necessarily consulting them in the effort. Only these professionals, trained in a variety of disciplines, would possess the needed skills and knowledge to ensure that resources were developed efficiently and democratically. As a result, in the Fox River Valley the inquiries of the Com-mittee on Water Powers remained essentially private conversations between lawmakers and manufacturers about how best to structure the state's role in overseeing its waters. There was little interest in soliciting opinions from ordinary citizens.[4]

Second, although the Committee on Water Powers had arisen out of con-cern that Wisconsin's natural resources were being exhausted, its members had no intention of withdrawing these resources from use. Instead, they ar-gued for utilizing the wealth of nature more intensively in order to achieve the maximum possible yield from increasingly precious raw materials. Here again, Wisconsin's lawmakers echoed the priorities expressed by conserva-tionists throughout the United States. According to Theodore Roosevelt, the goal of conservation was to protect "against the wasteful development of our natural resources, whether that waste is caused by the actual destruction of such resources or by making them impossible of development hereafter." In other words, simply failing to use a resource was in itself an act of waste. Consequently, when the Committee on Water Powers visited the Fox River Valley, there was no discussion of reducing local demands on the stream. Although lawmakers and manufacturers disagreed about how best to accomplish their aims, both groups believed that the region's progress would depend on the expanded, more intensive, and efficient development of the river.[5]

The Committee on Water Powers did not begin Wisconsin's effort to conserve its natural resources, nor was it the only reform the state pursued. Between the 1880s and 1920s, lawmakers revolutionized their approach to the use of Wisconsin's resources, transforming their often careless oversight into a comprehensive program of management, planning, and supervision. Beginning in 1909, the effort was led by the state Conservation Commission, which was gradually reorganized and expanded over the years to include a variety of activities: forestry, the maintenance of state parks, fish and game management, the regulation of streams, and—after the creation of the Committee on Water Pollution—the reduction of industrial wastes. By the late 1920s, there was ample cause to rank Wisconsin's conservation movement among the most important political developments in the state's short history.[6]

Yet understanding the full significance of Wisconsin's effort to improve its use of resources requires looking beyond conservation itself. The movement's issues, institutions, and political reforms in fact comprised but a small part of a much broader impulse during the era to utilize nature's wealth more effectively and with greater care. In the Fox River Valley, dramatic changes in the structure of business, the role of government, and the influence of science and technology brought unparalleled discipline, efficiency, and productivity to the management of the area's natural resources. As a result, producers in nearly every segment of the local economy were able to deliver remarkable levels of convenience, reliability, and comfort to the people who utilized their goods and services. By the 1920s, this rapid industrialization brought a renewal of progress to the region that included higher wages, greater free time, and the general improvement of people's standard of living. Although these changes were in part the result of exactly the kind of intensive, carefully managed use of nature that conservationists championed, they had little to do with the political movement per se.

By far the most important aspect of this broad industrial progress, at least for this study, was its paradoxical influence on the role of nature in the daily experience of valley residents. Put simply, the more control producers gained over their use of natural resources, the less dependent on nature consumers seemed to be. During the nineteenth century in the Fox River Valley, natural advantages such as fertile soil, stands of timber, and the available waterpower were imperative to the region's development. By the early twentieth century, in contrast, industrialization had created new forms of energy and transportation, new industries and occupations, and new opportunities for people to thrive and earn their livings, none of which appeared to rely as directly on using the local landscape. No one better understood this peculiar aspect of industrial progress than President Theodore Roosevelt. Speaking to the conference of governors assembled in the White House in 1908, he noted that "the rise of peoples from savagery to civilization" was nearly always accompanied by steadily increasing demands on the natural world. "And yet, rather curiously," he explained, "at the same time that there comes that increase in what the average man demands from the resources, he is apt to grow to lose the sense of his dependence upon nature. He lives in big cities. He deals in industries that do not bring him in close touch with nature. He does not realize the demands he is making upon nature." According to Roosevelt, this tendency had created a dangerous apathy among Americans, a growing indifference to the country's resources and their importance. "Our position in the world has been attained by the extent and thoroughness of the control we have achieved over nature," he declared, "but we are more, and not less, dependent upon what she furnishes than at any previous time of history."[7]

This chapter examines precisely this aspect of industrial progress. It describes the development of three cornerstones in what became the modern economy of the Fox River Valley: electric energy, highway transportation, and the rise of the dairy industry. Between the 1880s and 1920s, producers in each of these areas found new and powerful means to harness the natural resources upon which they depended. In turn, the more control they gained over nature, the more efficiently and productively they could utilize their raw materials. Finally, the more productive they became, the more they contributed to the prosperity, convenience, and comfort of the consumers who purchased their goods and services. Yet ironically, although producers in each case relied more heavily on natural resources in the 1920s than they had in the 1880s, local consumers became less and less aware of their own dependence on the material world. Much as Theodore Roosevelt predicted, in the dawning industrial age, nature's role as a means of production would gradually fade from view. By the mid-twentieth century, it required a conscious act of will for most Americans to see the connections between their prosperity and their ever-increasing use of natural resources.

Extending the Current

Electricity arrived in the Fox River Valley, appropriately, in the dark of night. On September 30, 1882, a small group of men worked into the evening attempting to connect a new Edison dynamo to a waterwheel in the Appleton Paper and Pulp Company. At first, their efforts failed. "It looked like the thing wasn't made to run," recalled one of the men. "We'd try the wires this way and that way, sort of trial and error," but nothing seemed to help. Finally, a dull red glow appeared in the two small lamps that had been connected to the generator, and the men gave a cheer. They eased up the power, and slowly, the tiny mill room was filled with a steady, white, radiant light that shone "as bright as day."[8]

This simple yet magical event marked the dawn of the electrical age in Wisconsin. Three weeks earlier, Thomas Edison had begun operations in his Pearl Street station in New York City, the first centralized electrical power plant in the United States. Appleton's new powerhouse was the second. Although its service area was initially limited to two paper mills and a single residence, its successful beginning held the promise of greater wonders to come. "Verily this *is* a progressive age," proclaimed one local newspaper. Electricity was merely the latest in a series of modern technologies encountered by valley residents in the late nineteenth century. Although some people remained wary of its mysterious qualities, promoters looked boldly ahead to a world of possibilities. "It would fill a volume to state at length all the practical advantages which this development of electricity has opened up already," said another spirited observer, "and more than a volume to state all that it may be expected yet to accomplish."[9]

In the decades since electricity arrived in the United States, historians have filled dozens of such volumes describing the technological, economic, social, and political impact of commercial electric power. Yet for nineteenth-century Americans, the technology's most remarkable achievement was something that later generations, more accustomed to its use, would forget: the way it liberated people from their immediate dependence on nature for energy. At the time of electricity's introduction to Appleton, the city's factories were bound physically to the Fox River by the system of waterwheels, shafts, and belting required to harness its flow. Area residents were equally tied to the landscape because they often relied on muscle power, whether human or animal, to perform much of the labor of daily life. The new utility, by contrast, promised to break these bonds. Unlike earlier forms of power, electricity could be transmitted over great distances. In the early 1880s, this distance was limited to a few city blocks. But electricity's reach would grow quickly in the years to come, spanning dozens, then hundreds, and eventually thousands of miles. In a sense, Appleton's new dynamos could literally extend the current of the Fox River, converting the water's flow from mechanical to electric energy and then transmitting this new power wherever it might be needed. For many observers of the day, this kind of spatial flexibility seemed the ultimate realization of nature's industrial promise. "The power for work can be generated by any ordinary means, and any place where the means exist," explained the editor of the Appleton *Post*. "The tide on the shore can do work inland; the stream in the mountain gorge can do work on the hilltop; the windmill on the eminence can do work in the valley." Best of all, this miracle could be enjoyed with essentially no effort on the part of electricity's users. "This new servant which science has supplied us with is the most docile of menials," declared the editor. "A touch of a lady's finger will bring into action a power which a thousand men could not resist; another touch will stop its action or reverse it in a moment."[10]

It was this remarkable convenience that gave electricity the appearance of being independent from nature. Yet for all the ways in which electricity freed its consumers from the hardships of extracting energy directly from the landscape, the creation of electrical power remained fundamentally a product of natural resources and their use by manufacturers. In effect, commercial electric power made it possible to separate the production of energy from its ultimate consumption, an industrial transformation that was only possible through the unprecedented manipulation and control of the material world. During the fifty years following its humble beginnings in Appleton, electricity spread gradually to the valley's factories, homes, and farms.

People used it in countless ways, from lighting the nighttime darkness to performing household chores and operating industrial machinery. As the number and variety of its applications grew, local utilities struggled both to meet and encourage the greater demand. Doing so required achieving new levels of mastery over the resources they used and the techniques by which they generated commercial power. By the 1930s, their efforts had yielded a vast infrastructure of energy production, including a network of power plants and substations, thousands of miles of transmission lines, and homes and businesses wired to accept electricity. Much as Appleton's original powerhouse depended on the Fox River to generate energy, the great networks of power that eventually took shape in Wisconsin continued to rely on natural resources, not to mention the hours upon hours of labor required to exploit them. Yet for those who merely consumed electricity, its use seemed far removed both from the industrial infrastructure that produced it and from the natural landscape upon which it still depended.[11]

Understanding the profound environmental consequences of electrification requires looking closely at the efforts of utilities to expand their control of nature. In 1882, and for many years after its introduction in the valley, electricity seemed little more than an extension of people's traditional use of waterpower along the Fox. It was no accident that the man who first brought electricity to the region was a manufacturer of paper. H. J. Rogers was an Appleton industrialist who presided over the Appleton Paper and Pulp Company as well as the local gasworks. With his long experience using the power of the Fox in his paper mills and his involvement in Appleton's gas lighting business, the decision to bring hydroelectricity to the valley was an understandable leap of faith. As part of his agreement with Western Edison, Rogers received two dynamos, each with a capacity of roughly 12.5 kilowatts. He also bought the services of an electrician from Chicago who traveled to Appleton to help set up the machines. Installation of the first dynamo took place in just six weeks during August and September, and the second shortly thereafter. Rogers initially had the dynamos placed in two of his company's paper mills. Both factories along with his private residence were then wired for electric lighting. Service was less than reliable. Because the dynamos were connected to waterwheels, which also ran other machinery in the mills, the speed at which they operated tended to vary, causing the lights in the circuit to dim or brighten accordingly. At times, the voltage was so high that all the

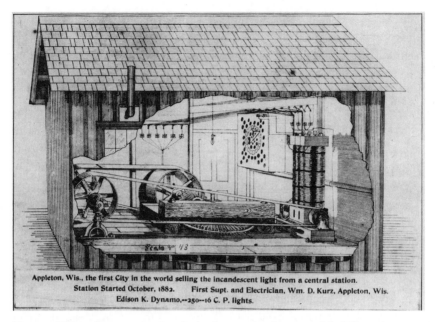

Appleton, Wis., the first City in the world selling the incandescent light from a central station.
Station Started October, 1882.   First Supt. and Electrician, Wm. D. Kurz, Appleton, Wis.
Edison K. Dynamo,--250--16 C. P. lights.

Figure 7. Vulcan Street power plant in Appleton, 1882. Courtesy of the Wisconsin Historical Society, Image No. WHi-28333.

lamps burned out. Company officials quickly attached the dynamos to their own waterwheels, but even this arrangement proved unsatisfactory. Finally, in November they constructed a small shack halfway between the paper mills to house the generators. This Vulcan Street plant, as it was eventually known, became a fully functioning central station, and by December, the tiny power-house was supplying commercial electricity for lighting to three houses, five mills, and a blast furnace (Figure 7).[12]

Although few people understood how the new power plant worked, its dependence on the Fox River gave electricity a familiar appearance to local residents. According to the *Post,* "the plan of generating the incandescent electric light, although a great scientific triumph and a high product of inventive genius, is comparatively simple." Water from the Fox was diverted through a sluice under the plant, where its movement turned a waterwheel connected by a shaft directly to the dynamos. Valley residents had seen similar arrangements up and down the Fox in local paper mills. But in this case, the waterwheel was attached to the armatures of two dynamos and used to rotate their conducting coils through powerful magnetic fields. As the mechanism turned, explained the *Post,* "the shaft upon which the coil of wires revolve is continuously charged with electricity. Touching this shaft, upon either side, are metallic brushes which receive the electricity and impart it to the wires, leading in every direction." At the other end of these transmission lines were the electric lamps, whose construction and operation also appeared straight-forward. As the *Post* described, "the electric lamp consists of a pear-shaped glass, exhausted of air, into which is sealed a filament of carbonized bamboo, slightly thicker than a horse hair." Much like the dynamo, the light bulb, too, could be easily compared with existing technologies. "This filament," continued the paper, "becoming incandescent by the passage of the electricity through it, emits a beautiful soft light, absolutely steady and constant and equaling in intensity, or exceeding if desired, the illuminating power of a gas jet of the best quality."[13]

Yet no matter how hard people tried to understand electricity in traditional terms, the principles at the heart of the Vulcan Street plant were beyond the reach of most citizens, a reflection of the growing dependence of industrial progress on scientific and technical expertise. The development of commercial electricity was the product of decades of systematic investigations into the characteristics and manipulation of electrical forces. Earlier systems of conveying power had been the work of practical mechanics using trial-and-error methods. In contrast, the transmission of electric current relied on a theoretical understanding of mechanical and electrical energy, and the means by which one could be converted to the other. During the nineteenth century, people such as Michael Faraday, Charles Brush, Thomas Edison, and Elihu Thomson began to apply this knowledge. They fashioned a mounting collection of devices with which electricity could be harnessed, manipulated, and used. This included both the Edison dynamos and the incandescent lamps now being installed in Appleton. The very existence of such technology was evidence of the growing human ability to make use of the natural environment.

Unfortunately, despite the knowledge and tools supplied by these pioneers of electrical engineering, electricity itself proved a remarkably difficult force of nature to harness. In the spring of 1883, the owners of the Vulcan Street plant formally incorporated their new firm as the Appleton Edison Light Company. Business initially was slow, primarily because several difficulties of transmitting electricity had yet to be resolved. Chief among these was the persistent recurrence of short circuits. Most of the copper wiring used during the company's early days was either bare or poorly insulated, leaving the system vulnerable to interruption. According to A. C. Langstadt, one of the plant's workers, "a little windstorm, or anything out of ordinary" could create problems along the lines. "A branch falling off a tree would fall against these wires and short circuit them," he remembered, "and then the company shut down the plant, as it had no fuse protection, and all hands had to go out and find where the trouble was." In such an event, the power could be out for hours or days while the problem was painstakingly tracked down. Lightning presented similar difficulties. During thunderstorms, the entire system had to be turned off for fear that a lightning strike might create a dangerous power surge. Even when the system did function smoothly, service remained erratic. With no voltmeters or ammeters and no regulators of any kind, plant workers judged the amount of power being generated by eyesight alone, using the intensity of a few "pilot lamps" as a guide. "If the operator's eyes were good," said Langstadt, "no particular complaint was made by the customers."[14]

From these shaky and unreliable beginnings, the evolution of electrical power in Appleton followed much the same path as it did throughout the United States, a story chronicled in many now classic histories. The details are only worth repeating to make clear the remarkable environmental achievement that large-scale electrification represented. During the early years of the electric industry, its growth was hampered by numerous economic and technological problems. Of least significance to this environmental history were the many economic hardships faced by utilities. Providing commercial electricity was such a new enterprise in the 1880s that company managers had little understanding of the unique economics that governed central stations, especially the tremendous cost in fixed capital required to provide electricity. Unlike most commodities, which could be made and sold to consumers who were then free to use them whenever they chose, electric power had to be used as it was generated. Thus, Appleton Edison was required to maintain enough capacity in its production facilities to meet the maximum possible demand of its customers, even though the actual power in use at any given time would likely be much less. The ratio of actual demand to greatest possible usage came to be known as the load factor, a quality that company managers sought to maximize. Throughout the 1880s, the utility's load factor remained extremely low. During daylight hours especially, the waterwheels, dynamos, and transmission wires maintained by Appleton Edison sat idle, unable to earn money on the substantial investment needed to keep them in working order. Complicating this problem was the volatile state of technology during the era. Because the machinery of power generation changed so rapidly, with improvements and innovations coming every year, company officials were forced to replace outdated equipment frequently, cutting into the bottom line. The result, both in Appleton and throughout the country, was frequent bankruptcies and reorganizations among utilities, as managers learned the economic terrain of the growing industry.[15]

Of much greater significance to the environmental history of electrification were the numerous technological improvements that facilitated the industry's expansion, many of which were designed to increase the utility's ability to control and manipulate nature. Some innovations were obvious and fairly minor. Fuses and insulated wires helped to reduce the number of short circuits caused by storms and fallen tree limbs. Likewise, the installation of meters allowed the company to move from flat-rate charges to fees based on the amount of power actually used by consumers. But during the 1890s, two more substantial upgrades had a dramatic impact on the industry, significantly increasing the distance over which electricity could be sent economically.

The first was the shift from direct to alternating current. During the fledgling years of commercial power, direct current had served the electric industry well. But its limitations also became apparent. In particular, utilities found that the amount of energy wasted during transmission rose exponentially with the amount of direct current being conveyed, leaving them with a costly and difficult problem. In Appleton, A. C. Langstadt estimated that as much as a third of the power generated by the Vulcan Street dynamos was lost before reaching consumers. The company might have used thicker wires in order to deliver greater quantities of energy, but the cost of doing so was prohibitive. As a result, potential customers who lived more than a mile away from the plant remained beyond the reach of Appleton Edison. Even more important, the utility was also effectively prevented from utilizing the geographic flexibility that electricity seemed to promise. In Wisconsin, the state's network of rivers offered many ideal locations for the generation of hydroelectric power. But these sites were often far removed from major cities, and until the inefficiencies of direct current transmission were overcome, they remained unavailable for exploitation.[16]

As it turned out, alternating current offered an elegant, economical solution. Though experimenters had initially viewed its fluctuating electric pulse as a nuisance, they soon discovered that alternating current possessed one critical advantage for power transmission: its voltage and current could be easily and efficiently manipulated using a device called a transformer. In essence, transformers provided an efficient method of increasing, or "stepping up," the voltage of alternating current before its transmission. Stepping up the voltage brought a corresponding decrease in the current. By transmitting electric power in this high-voltage, low-current form, utilities could dramatically reduce the loss of energy taking place along the way, meaning that power could be delivered over far greater distances than had been possible using the steadier but less flexible direct current. At the other end of the line, another transformer could then be used to step down the voltage and raise the current to whatever level was appropriate for use in factories and homes. The shift from direct to alternating current would take place gradually during the 1890s and early 1900s. But its impact was dramatic. Alternating current opened a new world for electric central stations, allowing them to expand their reach over miles and then hundreds of miles, sending power to new groups of consumers.[17]

The adoption of alternating current in turn paved the way for a second important set of innovations in the transmission of electric energy: the improvement of generating facilities. Since the industry's inception, valley utilities had relied primarily on waterpower and steam engines to drive their dynamos. Both functioned well, especially in tandem, because steam provided a useful supplement to waterpower during times of drought. The demand for electricity grew slowly during these years, and utilities managed to keep pace by simply adding dynamos and increasing the size of their engines. Moreover, as long as the inefficiencies of direct current prohibited long-distance transmission, companies had little incentive to increase the power of their generators. By the 1890s, though, the adoption of alternating current promised to end such restrictions. At the same time, the capacity of the traditional steam engine reached its practical limits. Together, this combination of factors pushed utilities to seek a means of increasing their power production.[18]

Once again, they found a solution in a simple, yet remarkably efficient, new technology: the steam turbine. While conventional engines worked through the pressure of steam forcing the movement of a piston, the turbine functioned by passing steam through a series of rotor blades attached to a shaft. First perfected in Europe, the steam turbine made its initial appearance in American central stations in the mid-1890s. Its use spread quickly as engineers recognized its obvious advantages. For one thing, where the steam engine had long been plagued by wide variations in temperature and subsequent heat loss, the turbine allowed steam to expand gradually, thereby maintaining a nearly constant operating temperature and dramatically improving efficiency. The turbine also proved capable of handling much greater variations in its operating conditions, a significant asset for central station electricity where fluctuations in demand were both frequent and large. What's more, because turbines operated at higher speeds than steam engines, they allowed utilities to use smaller generators whose compactness and durability made for much greater efficiency. By the early decades of the twentieth century, manufacturers were even producing so-called turbogenerators, in which a turbine and generator were coupled together. Arriving as it did alongside alternating current and improvements in the generation of steam, the turbine made it possible for utilities to deliver electricity over hundreds of miles with unprecedented efficiency, economy, and reliability.[19]

It was in the midst of this transmission revolution that utilities throughout Wisconsin began a period of sporadic but persistent expansion. With larger generating capacities and the ability to transmit power over longer istances, utilities were finally freed to expand in whatever ways the market for power allowed. The resulting competition for territory among utilities together with the quest for greater efficiencies led to the rapid consolidation of the industry following the turn of the century. In little more than thirty years, the Appleton Edison Company underwent a variety of transformations bankruptcy and reorganization in 1896; purchase by a larger Milwaukee utility in 1901; absorption into a national holding company in 1923, and finally a further reorganization and merger in 1927. The end result was an enterprise known as the Wisconsin Michigan Power Company, a subsidiary of the North American Company, a large holding company with utilities throughout the Midwest. In 1908, central station power in Appleton served roughly 1,200 people. The company used a combination of waterpower and

Figure 8. Appleton's electric utility, 1922. Courtesy of the Wisconsin Historical Society, Image No. WHi-28473.

steam engines to drive two 1,000-kilowatt generators, but the system was rapidly growing obsolete (Figure 8). Although the city's utility was owned by
a Milwaukee-based firm, it continued to operate as an independent unit in
isolation from any larger network of energy. By 1930, in contrast, the newly
created Wisconsin Michigan Company was connected by high-voltage transmission lines to several neighboring North American subsidiaries. This in-
terconnection, together with the installation of new, more powerful steam
turbines, gave Wisconsin Michigan unprecedented freedom to route electricity quickly and efficiently wherever it was needed. It also dramatically
enhanced the quality and reliability of service, improvements that brought a
growing demand for power. The company now served 26,000 customers in
cities, small towns, and increasingly, throughout the countryside.[20]

The growth of electric service in Appleton was paralleled throughout Wisconsin during the early decades of the twentieth century, as vast systems of
power evolved from the consolidation and systematization of small-scale regional utilities. In 1917, some 300 electric central stations were in operation in
the state, most providing only limited service within localized areas. A dozen
years later, the number of utilities had fallen by two-thirds, with 90 percent
of Wisconsin's electric service now under the control of just nine major companies. In the Fox River Valley, two systems predominated: Wisconsin Michigan in the region surrounding Appleton, and the Public Service Corporation
in neighboring Green Bay. Although the number of utilities declined, the
service they provided increased at a remarkable pace. Production grew from
400 million kilowatts per year in 1917 to well over 2 billion kilowatts annu-

ally by 1930. During the same period of time, the number of people receiving this power climbed as well, rising from less than 200,000 total customers to 630,000, including over 75 percent of all homes in the state. Electricity had become a nearly pervasive aspect of life.[21]

On September 30, 1932, the citizens of Appleton marked this achievement, celebrating fifty years of electric service in the community. At a civic pageant attended by 3,000 people, the opening of the city's original Vulcan Street plant was reenacted. Using a dynamo similar to the one initially placed along the banks of the Fox River, Wisconsin Michigan constructed a replica power plant as a permanent monument to the company's origins. As darkness fell, floodlights illuminating the tiny shack were extinguished and the pageant began. William Kurz and Edward O'Keefe, two of the plant's original care-takers, approached in a horse and buggy. Townspeople dressed in period cos-tumes awaited their arrival, shaking their heads and voicing doubts that elec-tricity might ever replace kerosene or gas lamps. Ignoring these skeptics, the two men entered the plant and carefully prepared the dynamo for operation. When all was ready, Kurz turned a small hand wheel as if to release the wa-ters of the Fox underneath the machinery. "The wheels turn! The belts move! They gain speed," exclaimed a reporter covering the scene. A dull red glow appeared in the tiny glass bulb connected to the generator and slowly grew brighter. Electricity had arrived in the valley once again.[22]

Taking place as it did against the backdrop of the nation's worst economic depression, the pageant offered citizens an opportunity to reaffirm their faith in American industry. "No age in all the history of mankind has seen such tremendous progress as has been made since that eventful day in Septem-ber of 1882," declared the editors of the *Post-Crescent*. Though people at the time had looked to the Vulcan Street powerhouse with a sense of promise, explained the paper, "not even the most prophetic mind could envisage the mighty industry that sprung from this tiny plant." By 1932, the landscape of the Fox River Valley was crisscrossed with a complex web of electric trans-mission lines, a network that connected homes, businesses, and factories throughout the region with the numerous power plants and substations responsible for generating "the magic current." Electricity was a marvel of modern technology. "Our city now is the center of a far-flung system of elec-trical lines that reach for hundreds of miles and carry power and light into scores of communities," boasted the paper. Even in the midst of depression,

Americans could still celebrate the wonder of electric power, an industrial triumph that had "revolutionized civilization."[23]

In large measure, the growth of electricity in the Fox River Valley was a result of the local utility's increasing control of nature. Each phase of Wisconsin Michigan's operation had been subdivided and carefully planned in such a way that the production of power came under the direction of human authority. Unlike the Edison dynamos of the original Vulcan Street plant, generators in 1932 relied less directly on the variable flow of the Fox River. The modern facility was still equipped to use waterpower, but it now supplied most of its electricity through a series of steam turbines and boilers powered by the combustion of coal. In the same way, Wisconsin Michigan went to great lengths to improve the coal it used in the production of steam. Coal arrived at the Appleton plant on barges which had traveled up the Fox River from Green Bay. As the coal was unloaded, it was passed through a magnetic screen to eliminate metallic impurities and then sorted by hand to remove wood and other foreign material. The coal was then fed by conveyor belt into a mechanical crusher where it was pulverized to a uniform size, dried, and then blown through a network of pipes into storage bins. This kind of processing ensured that the coal would burn in a predictable fashion with the maximum possible combustion. Much the same was true of the company's handling of water, which it drew from the Fox River. Workers first softened this water through the addition of lime. It was then pumped into the boilers where the waiting coal was burned to produce steam with a precisely controlled temperature. This steam, in turn, passed through one of four large turbines where its energy was converted to electricity with an average flow of 4,400 volts. A substation in the plant's east wing received this current, and there, a series of large transformers stepped up the power to as much as 33,000 volts. It was in this form, finally, that electrical energy was distributed throughout the region. But here, too, Wisconsin Michigan worked to maintain its precise control of the process. In 1882, power had been transmitted unaltered from the plant's generators along bare copper wires. Fifty years later, it now traveled along insulated power lines, its voltage repeatedly adjusted in order to minimize losses, and its flow protected from the hazards of wind and weather by fuses, reinforced poles, and other devices.[24]

It was this growing ability to control and manipulate nature that allowed commercial electricity to expand so rapidly during the early twentieth century. Between 1902 and 1939, the nation's electric utilities increased the amount of energy they produced from each ton of coal by more than 80 percent, an achievement that would have pleased any conservationist. Such gains were possible through the carefully managed use of the industry's raw materials. For utilities such as Wisconsin Michigan, the company's growing ability to manipulate the production process allowed it to maximize its return on limited resources while at the same time providing dramatic improvements to the quality and reliability of electric service. For those citizens and manufacturers who increasingly consumed electricity, on the other hand, the company's ability to harness nature brought increasing freedom. Valley residents had once been responsible for generating the bulk of their energy, using their own muscles and resources to draw power from the local landscape. But with the advent of electricity, much of this labor now fell on the corporate shoulders of Wisconsin Michigan, with its turbines, transmission lines, and expanding production facilities. The availability of cheap, dependable commercial power changed the character of productive labor in the valley, allowing people to perform more work in less time and with less physical effort than ever before, thanks in part to the industrialized control of nature achieved by the region's utilities.[25]

But this kind of progress came with costs as well. By the 1930s, there were fewer and fewer people who took any direct part in the difficult work of energy production, meaning they lost sight of a significant link between themselves and the natural landscape. As one newspaper noted in 1932, the majority of customers in Wisconsin Michigan's service area "cast only a casual glance at the miles of poles and high tension wires which span that vast territory." The company's employees, on the other hand, knew every inch of the system firsthand. To them, the miles of power lines that crisscrossed the countryside were "monuments to years of pioneering and back breaking toil." Constructing the system had required a tremendous amount of labor. Engineers and "cruisers" carefully surveyed the landscape, studying "streams, waterfalls, valleys, and the possibilities of building dams." They searched for the best routes over which transmission lines could be laid, paying attention to swamps, rivers, and "prominent points exposed to lightning, wind, trees and forest fires." In the process, they developed a working relationship with the valley's landscape, learning to know the region as a place of production, a storehouse of resources from which they could generate and transmit electric energy. Theirs was an understanding of the material world that few ordinary citizens possessed. "They may be engineers by profession," commented the paper, "but it is only a short time before the most of them are experienced archeologists, botanists or geologists."[26]

Certainly, there were not many people in the Fox River Valley in 1932 who regretted this lost understanding of nature. By separating the production of electricity from its eventual consumption, the growth of commercial power eliminated much of the toil and drudgery that once characterized everyday life for valley residents. Freed from the burden of supplying their own energy, people were able to indulge in other pursuits, increasing their productivity in the workplace and enjoying greater convenience and leisure time at home. Yet the growing disconnection between people and natural resources is crucial to understanding the changing place of nature in the valley's emerging consumer society. The more widely available electricity became, the more detached its use appeared to be from the material landscape. During the nineteenth century, electricity, like other forms of energy, was unambiguously a product of nature and the difficult work required to manipulate its resources. In contrast, by the 1930s, electricity arrived almost magically wherever it was needed, at the flip of a switch and seemingly without effort. The more dependent local residents became on the infrastructure of energy production—now industrialized, highly technical, and far removed from consumers—the less likely they were to encounter nature as a place of hardship, obstacles, and physical labor.

The Flow of Traffic

Electricity was not the only new technology in the early twentieth century to restore people's faith in industrial progress. Just after sunrise on the morning of September 14, 1922, a motorcade embarked on a 180-mile, day-long journey along State Highway 15 from Wisconsin's southern border through Milwaukee to Green Bay. Much as happened decades earlier with the voyage of the steamship *Aquila,* the caravan heralded the arrival of a new mode of transportation—in this case, paved highways. Highway 15 was the state's latest and most impressive stretch of concrete road. The northernmost third of the route traveled through the heart of the Fox River Valley on a course that roughly paralleled the river's. Local residents had worked for weeks planning their role in what one newspaper called the "general jollification" surrounding the road. All along the highway, communities lined the route with flags and bunting, businessmen decorated their storefronts, bands rehearsed musical numbers, and civic groups prepared automobiles to join the procession. When the appointed day arrived and the motorcade rolled into the valley, the celebration took place without a hitch. A parade of cars nearly 120 vehicles long reached Neenah just after one o'clock, a scant twenty-five minutes behind schedule. Despite threatening skies, it was met there by cheering crowds and two locomotives stationed at the edge of town with whistles blaring in welcome. Participants then drove to the city's Riverside Park, where they enjoyed a box lunch with local residents. After speeches from city officials and dignitaries riding in the caravan, the troupe moved down the valley. The motorcade traveled through Appleton, Kaukauna, and De Pere, growing in length with each stop, until finally some 200 automobiles rumbled into Green Bay that evening to complete the journey. There, at a city park along the shores of the bay, nearly 1,000 people took part in a banquet and dance to round out the day's festivities.[27]

Among the evening's many prominent speakers was Arthur R. Hirst, chief engineer of the state Highway Commission and the man principally responsible for improving Wisconsin's roads. For Hirst, the completion of Highway 15 offered the people of Wisconsin a chance to congratulate themselves on an unprecedented public achievement (Figure 9). Just fifteen years earlier, Wisconsin's rural highways had been a loosely organized collection of dirt and gravel roads, most of which were crudely constructed and maintained. Highway 15, by contrast, was part of a modern network of paved state roadways. Although the road was only 9 feet wide over most of its length, it nevertheless composed but a single link in what was then one of the longest continuous concrete highways in the nation. It stretched like a ribbon across the face of the earth from Green Bay to Milwaukee, through Chicago, and all the way to St. Louis, a distance of over 500 miles. Such a road, Hirst told the crowd, "could never have been built had it not been by the community action of the entire people."[28]

But Hirst was also worried. The state's new roadways made transportation so convenient that citizens might easily forget how much work was involved in the effort. For Hirst's state Highway Commission, this forgetfulness could translate quickly into lagging public funding and legislative support.

*Figure 9. Driving between Appleton and Green Bay, before and after concrete.
Courtesy of the Outagamie County Historical Society, Appleton, Wis., Image No. 1
988-46-1.*

"We are entering upon the greatest construction the world has ever known," he explained. By the time the last section of Highway 15 was paved, the road had come to embody a remarkable amount of labor, natural resources, and money. Contractors had moved 450,000 cubic yards of earth in constructing the highway, roughly the same amount of dirt that would be excavated in digging a canal 8 feet deep, 20 feet wide, and 8.5 miles long. To mix the pavement, they had required 190,000 cubic yards of sand, 375,000 cubic yards of stone and gravel, and 665,000 barrels of cement, enough material to fill some 19,000 railroad cars. The great work of extracting and utilizing these resources was reflected in the road's $4 million price tag, an unprecedented public expenditure at the time. Most impressive, Highway 15 was merely one of dozens of similar concrete roads then under construction by the state Highway Commission. For Hirst, the celebration of its completion served to remind citizens both of the service they derived from the road and of the tremendous labor involved in the effort. Given a renewed public commitment to the enterprise, Hirst assured, within five years motorists could "start for any village or hamlet large enough to have a name" and 20,000 miles of highway would guarantee their arrival. "When that day comes," he concluded, "the people of Wisconsin will be living in the Great American commonwealth."[29]

The irony in Hirst's concern was exactly the one noted by Theodore Roosevelt in 1908. Specifically, the more industrial progress relied on controlling the natural world, the less dependent on nature its beneficiaries seemed to feel. Paved highways, much like electricity, made it possible to separate the production of energy—in this case, for transportation—from its ultimate consumption. In the nineteenth century, the act of moving from place to place in the valley was often a personal struggle to overcome various obstacles in the landscape. The average road—whether dirt, gravel, or even macadam—did little to help with the effort. By comparison, Highway 15 was an industrial achievement that seemed nearly impervious to the influence of the natural environment. The road was an avenue of human control carved into the valley's landscape, within which the forces of nature were held at bay. On either side of the highway, natural obstacles reigned supreme: rocks, trees, and rivers continued to obstruct the passing traveler, rain still washed away soil, and snow often buried the landscape. But inside the narrow, paved boundaries of Highway 15, nature's influence was diminished, and people were freed to move from place to place with remarkable ease. "Every American understands what the automobile has done for the human race," one commentator affirmed. "It has made men FREE by making them independent of distance and time." Although automobiles received much of the credit for this transformation, the new-fangled machines were all but useless without good roads on which to travel. "Today one might say that the streets of St. Louis run to Chicago and northward to Green Bay," said another observer of the new road. Driving along Highway 15 still involved a struggle against nature, but it was a struggle that motorists themselves did not have to wage. In effect, paved highways tamed the wilderness, transforming a landscape of natural obstacles into the smooth, controlled, and human environment of the open road.[30]

Highway 15 resulted, first and foremost, from a dramatic reorganization of the system by which roads were built and maintained in Wisconsin. Before the turn of the century, road construction had been strictly a local matter. Wisconsin's own constitution prohibited state government from funding internal improvements, including highways. Roads were thus relegated to an antiquated system of management in which town supervisors maintained responsibility for raising the needed money for all highway construction and appointing overseers to collect the taxes and organize the work. In practice, the system proved disastrous for the quality of roads. State law permitted citizens to pay their road taxes in labor rather than in cash, and farmers in nineteenth-century Wisconsin preferred this option almost exclusively. Given proper direction, they might have been capable of maintaining the roads. Unfortunately, town officials tended to select overseers from the ranks of their own communities, leaving them with individuals who had no more knowledge or training in the principles of highway construction than the neighbors they were intended to supervise. As a result, the annual parties of local residents organized for the spring roadwork often degenerated into social gatherings, and little improvement to the highways was ever accomplished. "Did you ever watch the process of working out the road tax from the stand point of a practical business man?" asked one critic in 1887. "I cannot," he answered, "without thinking it the most ingeniously devised system to accomplish nothing ever invented."[31]

Such inefficiency eventually prompted Wisconsin's lawmakers to create a new state Highway Commission in 1911. The agency had much in common with the recently established Conservation Commission. It was a quintessential progressive institution: a small but powerful, centralized administrative bureau, staffed by university-trained engineers, experts in the principles of science and rational management with the know-how to build roads properly. In creating the commission, the legislature also established a new highway fund, earmarking $350,000 of state tax money to be used for the improvement of roads throughout Wisconsin and requiring both town and county governments to match whatever state funding they received for local projects. Lawmakers granted the commission full authority over the fund, including the ability to withhold support from local governments that failed to conform to the agency's regulations. In this way, the experts of the Highway Commission were able to maintain effective control over the planning, construction, and maintenance of all highways built under the aegis of the state.[32]

As already noted, Arthur Hirst served as the commission's first chief engineer. Hirst was a near embodiment of the progressive values and goals that underlay the commission he headed. Trained in civil engineering at the

University of Maryland, from which he graduated in 1902, Hirst spent several years practicing his craft, first as a construction engineer with the Pennsylvania Railroad and later in various capacities with the highway departments of both Maryland and Illinois. In 1907, he came to Wisconsin to join the state's Geological Survey, which had been assigned the task of formulating a plan by which the state could begin funding new highway construction. For Hirst, the goal was simple: "The big idea in the Wisconsin system," he would later explain, "is to provide transportation service." The practice of road building was, in his words, "a profession and a business"; and as such, it should be conducted according to business principles, with economy, efficiency, and an eye toward the public good. These values would serve to guide the commission for the next fifty years.[33]

Under Hirst's leadership, the commission quickly developed a substantial bureaucracy with an elaborate division of labor. In 1913, the agency divided the state into seven districts, each of which was assigned its own division engineer with supporting staff and a Ford automobile to monitor local road conditions and oversee construction. The counties of the Fox River Valley became Division 3, with headquarters in Green Bay. Hirst also partitioned the commission itself along functional lines. By the end of its first decade, the agency was staffed by five full-time engineers in addition to Hirst and one assistant, each with primary responsibility for overseeing one particular facet of the state's road-building effort: design, construction, maintenance, materials, and equipment. There was even a chief accountant to supervise the bookkeeping. This division of labor helped the commission to maximize the expertise it was able to marshal in managing the highways: the narrower the specialization of an employee's role, the greater his knowledge and ability were likely to become. "Consider the small matter of crushing our road gravels," Hirst explained in a 1921 speech before the state legislature. "We have had an experienced man working for a year on practically nothing else but the problem of cheaply fine-crushing gravel so as to make it most suitable for highway use." Likewise, Hirst sought to develop specialists in all facets of highway construction, from maintenance to administration. The greater the collective knowledge embodied in the commission, the better the roads would be.[34]

By 1922, when Highway 15 was completed, the state Highway Commission was little more than a decade old. Yet in that short time, the agency managed to revolutionize the practice of road building in Wisconsin. Nowhere was the transformation more evident than along the nearly 200 miles of Highway 15. At first glance, the road looked to be a simple creation: a narrow strip of concrete built atop the surface of the earth. In function, it differed little from earlier dirt, gravel, and macadam roads. In appearance, it looked essentially the same. Yet Highway 15 was actually a remarkably complex piece of artifice, part of a vast industrial system whose construction and maintenance required a massive coordinated effort—not simply the hard physical labor involved in clearing the roadbed or laying the pavement, but also the less physical but equally demanding work of engineering and administration. Improving highway design, managing traffic flow, selecting routes and obtaining rights-of-way, securing the needed financing from state and local governments—all these tasks were part of the herculean effort that made Highway 15 function. The road embodied this labor, physical and administrative alike, with the sole underlying purpose of eliminating natural obstacles to travel.

In Wisconsin, private contractors hired by the state Highway Commission performed the actual labor of constructing the roads—moving the dirt and laying the pavement. The firms worked on a project-by-project basis, often completing only small sections of the commission's various routes. In the case of Highway 15, at least eight different companies built portions of the road in the Fox River Valley, primarily in 1- to 3-mile segments. Despite its reliance on these private companies, the commission maintained strict control of all work performed through the specifications it issued to contractors. Each year, under various titles, the agency published a standard manual of regulations. The manuals comprised a kind of bible of highway construction, governing everything from the manner in which trees and vegetation were initially cleared from the roadbed to the way in which signs had to be painted and placed on the highway once the pavement was finished. The standards were compiled under the guidance of the federal Bureau of Public Roads, whose engineers and researchers worked constantly to improve methods of road building. In addition to these general guidelines, Wisconsin's commission also issued more specific plans covering each project for which contracts were let out by the state. The plans illustrated the proposed route of each section of highway in precise detail. Engineers used plat maps to show the exact geographic location of the road by tracing its so-called center line in relation to a series of benchmarks of known position and elevation. They also drew the highway in profile to illustrate where the landscape had to be filled in or cut away in order to produce a smooth surface. Finally, they provided cross sections of the roadbed at each benchmark to show how the surface of the road should be shaped under various conditions. In low-lying areas, the roadbed might need to be elevated with steep slopes on either side to facilitate drainage. Likewise, if the highway turned sharply, the roadbed was often tilted in the direction of the curve so that vehicles could handle the corner safely at greater speeds. Together, these plans and specifications provided contractors with all the information they needed to build Highway 15. At the same time, they gave the commission an invaluable tool by which to maintain its control of the roads.[35]

But the commission's many rules and regulations were more than just a means of supervising its contractors. They also symbolized the agency's power over nature. If Highway 15 was to function properly, it had to withstand not only the heavy pounding of traffic, but also the natural erosion caused by rain, snow, wind, and the constantly changing temperature. In essence, the road had to exist as much as possible in isolation from the landscape through which it passed. The commission's guidelines served to instruct contractors on how to accomplish this feat. Beneath their bureaucratic abstraction and frequently numbing detail lay a vast accumulation of knowledge, an understanding of material things such as soils, drainage patterns, cement, and reinforced concrete. This knowledge was the ultimate source from which the commission's engineers derived their authority. It was an understanding of nature drawn from the work they performed in building roads through the landscape. The more they understood, the greater their ability to manipulate this landscape became.[36]

The eventual completion of Highway 15 demonstrated just how adept the commission had grown by the early 1920s. The first step in the process was mapping a path for the highway. "Everything else being equal, the most desirable route is a straight line," advised Harry D. Blake, an assistant engineer with the Highway Commission, in one of the agency's early manuals on surveying. But everything was rarely equal. Before the creation of the state Highway Commission, town and county governments had laid out their roads based solely on local needs and conditions. There was little thought given to the priorities of the state as a whole. According to Arthur Hirst, this practice resulted in a terrible waste of resources. Roads in Wisconsin were poor, he argued, primarily because the state had constructed its highways "without having in mind the building of any definite system." In contrast, Hirst concentrated the commission's efforts on the state's most important highways, the selection of which would be accomplished by "disinterested engineers," professionals with enough detachment and breadth of vision to balance the needs of the state against narrow local concerns. Thus, in 1918, the commission laid out a so-called state trunk system of highways, a 5,000-mile assemblage of roads designed to connect every county seat in Wisconsin and each community with a population greater than 1,000.[37]

Highway 15 was born a member of this system, and the selection of its route illustrates the complex web of social and environmental constraints into which the road had to be integrated. It did anything but travel in a straight line. Highway 15 was intended to provide transportation between Milwaukee, the state's largest city, and the Fox River Valley, one of its most productive agricultural and industrial regions. Consequently, the road's social and economic significance played a far greater role in determining its course than any geographical consideration. Rather than routing Highway 15 directly between Milwaukee and Green Bay, for instance, engineers chose to move the road to the west, looping it around the far side of Lake Winnebago before allowing it to turn northeast, where the road then followed the lower Fox River down the valley to Green Bay (Figure 10). In this way, the commission managed to connect not only the two major cities at the ends of the highway, but also Fond du Lac, Oshkosh, Neenah, Menasha, Appleton, and De Pere as well. The longer route served vital social and economic functions. Highway 15 became a major avenue of travel and communication among all the towns through which it passed. Equally important, it quickly became one of the principal outlets for the combined production of the entire Fox River Valley.

Of course, nature did play a role determining a route for Highway 15. "Every highway engineer should be a thorough student of geology and physical geography," advised Harry Blake. "He ought to learn the drainage systems, the direction of streams and their relation to each other, the location and extent of marshes, the general trend of ridges and divides, and the best stream and ridge crossings all of which have an important bearing on the selection of the ultimate route for a highway." In the case of the Fox River Valley, several

Figure 10. Aerial view of State Highway 15, looking south from Appleton toward Menasha and Neenah, ca. 1925. Lake Winnebago, on the left, and the Fox River are also visible. Courtesy of the Outagamie County Historical Society, Appleton, Wis., Image No. 1989-426-32.

environmental factors influenced the commission. Most generally, the nearby supply of raw materials favored the construction of highways through the valley. Several local quarries were in operation in the region, and they helped to provide limestone, gravel, and other supplies at the lowest possible cost. Likewise, the character of the valley's soils may have influenced the route. Much of the region was covered in heavy, reddish clay that offered a firm, reliable foundation for the construction of roads. Unfortunately, the steep limestone ridge that formed the valley's eastern boundary left much of the land along that side of the Fox heavily gullied, poorly drained, and marshy. The western side of the valley, on the other hand, tended to be dryer, more level, and therefore much better suited to the construction of permanent roads. Thus, through most of the region, the commission chose to place Highway 15 along the western side of the Fox, except for a brief stretch between De Pere and Green Bay, where the highway crossed the river in order to reach the two communities.[38]

Once a route for Highway 15 had been determined, contractors began to clear and prepare the roadbed. This act created a kind of beachhead in the valley's landscape within which they could fashion a more permanent surface for the highway. If the road was to carry traffic—particularly automobiles—it required a surface that was level and almost perfectly smooth. Thus, the roadbed could not simply follow the ragged, bumpy, uneven contours of the natural landscape, even in areas where the land was essentially flat. Instead, road builders had to clear a path for the highway, removing all rocks, trees, vegetation, buildings, and other obstacles, then level that path, making sure that no hill was too steep, no dip too severe, and no corner too sharp for safe driving. The Highway Commission was very particular about how this work was accomplished. In clearing the roadbed, no tree stump could be left within 3 feet of the finished surface to prevent the wood from rotting and undermining the highway. Likewise, when contractors hauled in dirt to shape the roadbed, they had to be careful to ensure the highway's stability. "Embankments shall be constructed in successive layers of not more than one (1) foot in thickness," read the commission's standards, "each of which shall extend entirely across the embankment from slope to slope and be properly compacted." All stones larger than 3 inches in diameter had to be removed from the embankment's topmost layers, and no logs or brush could be left behind at any depth.[39]

In conducting this work, contractors used an increasingly powerful array of machinery to manipulate the landscape. At the turn of the century when most of Wisconsin's highways were still unpaved, the tools required for their construction and maintenance remained uncomplicated. In one of the state's earliest instructional pamphlets, Arthur Hirst had described how to make a useful road drag, a device typically pulled by a team of horses and used to smooth and shape dirt roads to ensure their drainage. "A simple stick of timber or piece of railroad iron" would do, he said, but the best drag could be built by fastening together two parallel halves of a split log 7 to 9 feet long. With this device, county laborers and even farmers could easily keep the average road in proper working condition. As Wisconsin began to build increasingly sophisticated highways, however, such makeshift tools gradually lost their usefulness, and contractors required more elaborate equipment. Throughout the early twentieth century, horse-drawn implements were replaced with a variety of steam- and gas-driven machinery. By the late 1920s, tractors, dump trucks, motorized graders and rollers, steam shovels, and mechanical loaders became commonplace at construction sites. These tools allowed road builders to move as many tons of earth in several hours as might before have taken days.[40]

With the roadbed constructed, contractors then began laying the pavement. As part of the state trunk system, Highway 15 was intended to be a workhorse carrying the largest volume of traffic at the greatest possible speed. Of necessity, it had to be paved with concrete, which provided a hardened, smooth, and long-lasting surface that could withstand the pressure of heavy usage. Just as important, concrete also served as one of Highway 15's primary defenses against weather and erosion. Where earth and gravel roads had once been reduced to muddy tracks during heavy rains, concrete remained firm under the worst of downpours. But joining pavement to earth was no easy task. First, contractors went over the cleared roadbed with a heavy roller in order to compact its surface and create a firm, level subgrade for the highway. Because soil by itself could not support the combined weight of pavement and traffic, road builders next placed a layer of broken stone or concrete atop the roadbed to serve as a foundation for the pavement and to help distribute more evenly the weight it would carry. Finally, the pavement itself was laid atop this foundation. Here again, the Highway Commission placed exacting standards on the process, especially the all-important composition of the concrete. Concrete was produced by combining Portland cement with sand, gravel, and pebbles of various sizes, depending on the density of the pavement desired. Engineers from the Highway Commission routinely inspected shipments of cement to ensure its quality, and they also tested the physical and chemical properties of the stone aggregate to be added to the concrete. Sand that contained too much silt was excluded, as were stones that were deemed too large. Likewise, the presence of even small amounts of organic matter in the aggregate was enough to prevent its use. When at last the concrete was ready to be poured, regulations required that a state inspector be on hand to make sure it was done properly. The foundation had to be moist—not too dry, not too wet—before the pavement could be laid. Once the concrete was in place, the road had to be covered and kept damp for at least a week while the pavement was allowed to harden.[41]

This attention to detail was essential to protecting Highway 15 from the natural elements. But concrete by itself could not prevent the road from eroding, especially under the destructive influence of water. Rainwater, run-off, streams, seeping groundwater—the source was unimportant. All were equally dangerous if allowed to linger in the roadbed. "'Keep the water moving away from the road,' is the primary rule of the road builder," cautioned Arthur Hirst in the state's very first highway pamphlet. Hirst had been talking about earth roads at the time, but what was true then for dirt was equally true for the concrete surface of Highway 15, and engineers used a variety of tactics to keep the highway safe. Bridges allowed drivers to cross the Fox River as if the river were not there. Likewise, contractors were careful to crown the road's pavement in the middle so that water falling on its surface would run off, thus preventing the formation of puddles that might damage the concrete. Engineers also required the construction of drainage ditches along the sides of the highway wherever the natural slope of the land tended to move water toward the road. In particularly wet areas, simple ditches would not suffice, and engineers had to facilitate drainage by installing drainpipes underneath or alongside the highway. They also placed concrete culverts within the roadbed itself to move water from one side of the road to the other. Whatever the method used, the idea remained the same: to channel water as quickly as possible away from, through, or beneath the roadbed without damaging the pavement.[42]

Snowfall created similar difficulties for road builders. In the early 1920s, local governments did what they could to plow the roads. But the amount of snowfall they had to move was often overwhelming, and most rural highways became difficult, if not impossible, to use. "The state of Wisconsin has many millions of dollars invested in good roads," complained the *Wisconsin Motorist* in 1920. "Is it not about time that some plan be devised by which this investment may become usable and productive for the . . . two or three months [of winter]?" Officials at the Highway Commission agreed, acknowledging that people's growing dependence on automobiles necessitated "open roads during the entire year." Yet because the counties maintained full responsibility for the costs of snow removal under state law, there was little the agency could do. This situation would remain unchanged until 1931, when the state legislature finally approved the commission's request to assume the full costs of snow removal. With a new law in place, the agency quickly expanded its war against the elements. Snow removal entailed more than just maintaining a fleet of plows. A variety of winter defenses could be built into the highways themselves. Roads could be situated and graded to encourage the wind to blow away as much snow as possible. Embankments could be heightened and lined with hedges or fences to prevent drifting. Roadbeds could be widened to facilitate plowing, and pavements could be treated with salt to resist icing. Although none of these measures would ever fully succeed in protecting highways from heavy snowfalls, they ultimately made winter driving a safer, more reliable proposition for valley residents.[43]

Given the labor, resources, and administrative effort that went into building Highway 15, it is no wonder that thousands of citizens paused to celebrate when its final section was paved in 1922. In contrast to Wisconsin's earlier network of roads, the new concrete highway seemed a miraculous achievement. "The good roads movement, together with the automobile . . . have revolutionized American life," proclaimed the Milwaukee *Sentinel* in a special edition commemorating the grand opening of Highway 15. "It has been a peaceful, beneficent revolution, but a revolution none the less." According to the newspaper, concrete roads provided more than just a better means of transportation. Calling the new road "a milestone of progress," the *Sentinel* went on to make glowing predictions about what Highway 15 would mean to the people of Wisconsin. Farmers, claimed the paper, would find the task of getting to market "no longer a difficult problem, to be faced only when imperatively necessary and at a sacrifice of time and strength." They could visit more often with friends and neighbors and travel to town whenever they pleased, enjoying "the advantages and pleasures of city life without its attendant discomforts." Urban residents, in turn, would also benefit from the highway. Merchants would find their trading areas expanded, for they could now do business with farmers who had once been out of reach. And much as farmers might come to the city routinely for shopping and entertainment, city residents could just as easily go for drives through the countryside. Good roads would allow them "to spend week ends and holidays amid refreshing rural scenes and to enjoy healthful and pleasurable experiences denied [them] a few years ago." For their part, newspapers in the Fox River Valley echoed the *Sentinel*'s enthusiasm. "This investment by Wisconsin of millions in good roads is one of the chief guarantees of our future as a state," declared the Appleton *Post-Crescent*. "It will have as much to do with the happiness, contentment and prosperity of our people as any one activity in which [the state] can engage."[44]

Yet as already noted, according to Arthur Hirst, the very success of roads such as Highway 15 threatened to jeopardize the future work of the state Highway Commission. So carefree had traveling become that motorists could easily forget the constant effort still involved in keeping the highways open. Speaking at a joint session of the state Senate and Assembly in 1921, Hirst aired his complaints to legislators. "The ordinary man observes a few yards of gravel placed, a concrete or gravel road built here or there, and a few bridges or culverts under construction, and he thinks that each is a simple operation which can be done in a few minutes time." But as Hirst reminded lawmakers, the reality was far different. During the next twelve months, he reported, the Highway Commission would build some 3,000 miles of new roadway. The work would include constructing several hundred bridges, placing thousands of culverts, and marshaling enough manpower and supplies to continue the maintenance of what would then comprise a 12,000-mile network of state highways. It would be, noted Hirst, "the largest construction enterprise ever attempted in the history of the state," requiring the movement of roughly 8,000,000 cubic yards of earth, not to mention a host of other technical and administrative tasks, from scientific research to basic accounting. This long list of duties, he said, combined to create a problem that "defies exaggeration."[45]

Hirst's protests notwithstanding, the state Highway Commission proved more than capable of solving exactly this problem. Much as predicted by the Milwaukee *Sentinel*, good roads revolutionized American life. During the first half of the twentieth century, driving became a defining element of modern society as people took to the highways in ever-increasing numbers. As early as 1916, the Highway Commission noted the remarkable proliferation of cars in Wisconsin. From less than 1,500 automobiles registered in 1905, the year the state began licensing vehicles, the number had soared to more than 130,000. Although impressed by the trend, officials predicted that car ownership would reach a "saturation point," once the collective income of Wisconsin's citizens failed to permit the purchase of additional automobiles. But such a point never arrived. In 1922, as residents in the Fox River Valley celebrated the opening of Highway 15, the area's 200,000 residents owned 29,077 vehicles, or one car for every 6.8 people. By 1930, the rate of ownership had roughly doubled, reaching one car for every 3.6 residents, a pattern that showed no signs of reversing. In the midst of this seemingly unending expansion, even the Highway Commission was forced to admit its own bewilderment.

"It seems true," said one report, "that the majority of the population has the same desire for the possession of two automobiles that it originally had for one."[46]

Yet much as Hirst had worried, the better the roads became, the easier it was for motorists to forget that driving remained fundamentally an act of controlling nature. In constructing Highway 15 through the Fox River Valley, the engineers and contractors of the state Highway Commission carried out a remarkable transformation of the region, forging the road's nearly smooth surface from the ragged, uneven terrain that composed its natural landscape. Maintaining this surface was no easy task. Each day following the highway's completion, crews of repairmen worked to undo the damage caused by natural erosion and the pounding of traffic. Their efforts were crucial to keeping the road in working order. Unfortunately, few motorists ever witnessed this effort firsthand, let alone took any part in it. From their perspective, seated comfortably behind the wheels of their cars, driving along Highway 15 became a simple, almost effortless act with little apparent connection to the landscape through which they traveled.

A Land of Milk and Money

On July 9, 1924, a distinguished group of more than a hundred farmers, bankers, businessmen, editors, and agricultural agents from the states of Kansas, Missouri, and Oklahoma arrived in Wisconsin's Fox River Valley for a tour of the region. At eight o'clock in the morning, they rumbled through the city of Appleton in a caravan of some forty automobiles and headed into the countryside. They had come to Wisconsin on a six-day mission to see how the state had become the nation's leading dairy producer — the "land of milk and money" as they called it. The valley was among their principal stopping points. The group spent the day visiting local farms, inspecting the regional highway system, and touring some of the area's numerous cheese factories. Toward the end of the afternoon, they even paused at one farmer's residence to take part in a friendly milking contest.[47]

No aspect of life in the Fox River Valley better illustrates the impact of industrial progress on the human use of nature than the transformation of agriculture at the turn of the century. Between 1880 and 1920, farming in the valley and throughout Wisconsin underwent a dramatic shift from wheat growing to dairying. The rise of dairying, like other products of industrialization such as commercial electricity and paved highways, brought new levels of prosperity to the region's citizens. According to the delegation of western visitors, dairying had created a standard of living in Wisconsin that was unmatched in their own home states where wheat growing still predominated. "Almost every farm boasts of a good modern house, large barns, silos and other improvements," they noted in a later report of their findings, "all painted and well kept, indicating a commendable degree of pride taken in comfortable and pleasant surroundings." The influence of dairying was evident not just in the countryside, but in urban areas as well. On their brief tour of Wisconsin, the delegation encountered dozens of small, thriving communities, each with "cheese factories and creameries . . . and milk condensers in the larger towns . . . , good schools and churches [and] gravel and concrete roads in every direction."[48]

But what most struck the western visitors as they explored Wisconsin's dairy industry was the way in which it appeared to have liberated farmers themselves from a crude reliance on nature. By the 1920s, farming in Wisconsin had become a full-fledged industrial enterprise, every bit as dependent on efficient production methods, scientific advances, and aggressive marketing as it was on soils, climate, and other natural conditions. "The thing that impressed me most," said one Kansas banker after the trip, "was the fact that a people could take a wilderness which nature has not caressed with as kindly a hand as she has our own Kansas, and out of it hew such a country as we saw, fill it with fine homes, and become within a few years an apparently contented and prosperous people—this with the milk cow" (Figure 11). An Oklahoma businessman expressed much the same opinion. Wisconsin's landscape, he said, reminded him of his own native region. "The only difference is that Southeastern Oklahoma is the God-made country, while sections of Wisconsin that we saw were made through the energy and agency of man." Again and again, members of the delegation commented on the remarkable coordination that made dairying in Wisconsin so successful. Farmers, bankers, manufacturers, businessmen, university researchers—all were dedicated to achieving "the intelligent and scientific management of the dairy cow" for the sole purpose of earning a profitable living from its many products.[49]

Ironically, what the western delegation perceived as independence from nature was in fact the more intensive, systematic management of natural

Figure 11. Typical dairy farm near Appleton, ca. 1925. Courtesy of the Outagamie County Historical Society, Appleton, Wis., Image No. 1989-426-32.

resources. A brief look at the people and institutions which brought about the rise of dairying in the Fox River Valley illustrates once again the paradoxical influence of industrialization on the local use of nature. On one hand, dairying was possible only by exerting ever greater control over the material resources on which farming in the valley depended. The reformers who led the campaign were not a part of Wisconsin's conservation movement per se. Nevertheless, they were guided by the same faith in science, technology, and expertise, large-scale organization, and efficient management that were so important to conservationists. What's more, their efforts helped to reduce dramatically the careless use of land that once characterized farming in the region. On the other hand, the more elaborate, complex, and successful the institutions of dairying became, the more they obscured the role of nature in producing useful commodities. By the 1920s, the practice of agriculture had become so highly industrialized that its ultimate dependence on natural resources grew less and less visible, even to the farmers who daily put them to work.

The evolution of dairying began in the Fox River Valley during the 1870s and 1880s at roughly the same time that wheat growing in the region was becoming less practical. Faced with the rising price of land in Wisconsin and the falling price of wheat on the national market, farmers had to alter their practices. Rather than using the land wastefully, farming until the soil was exhausted, then moving on to better ground, they began to invest in the lands they had, spending money to improve soils, rotating crops, and searching for a more diversified form of agriculture. They turned, for the most part, to dairying. But the shift was anything but simple. It required farmers to master an entirely new body of knowledge and practices, and to industrialize thoroughly the movement of product from landscape to market. Farmers had to invest heavily in their land, converting fields from wheat to pasturage and the raising of feed crops, constructing barns to house their cattle, building silos to store feed, and promoting the extension of highways and electric power lines into the countryside in order to facilitate production. By the 1920s, even the simplest bottle of milk was, in reality, a complex blending of nature and the human effort to control and utilize its resources.

The best way to appreciate this industrialized blending is to examine the various ways in which producers manipulated nature in the practice of dairying. It would be hard to imagine a product more natural than milk, which derives from the ordinary life cycle of the dairy cow. Like all mammals, cows produce milk in order to nourish their young until they are old enough to consume solid food and rely on their own immune systems. But cows in particular are able to do so with remarkable efficiency and in large volumes. During periods of lactation, the average cow uses less than half of its ingested nutrients for its own maintenance. Instead, the bulk of its intake is either consumed as energy to produce milk or transferred into the milk itself. This "miracle of surplus lactation" occurs through a series of physiological changes that take place following the birth of a calf. Each cow possesses four distinct mammary glands, all contained within the udder, which is held suspended from the rear abdomen by strong ligaments and muscles. Millions of tiny alveoli, or cavities, comprise the bulk of the tissue in each gland, and it is here that milk production takes place. When a calf is born, a series of hormonal signals causes cells lining the alveoli to begin producing the various components of milk from nutrients drawn from the blood. Thin membranes surrounding the alveoli then squeeze the milk through a network of ducts and into a central cistern, where it collects until the calf is ready to suckle. In the absence of human intervention, a cow's milk production typically increases during the first several weeks after giving birth, reaching a peak at about two months. From there, output slowly declines, but milk production at lower levels can continue for as long as a year and a half.[50]

Thus, the turn-of-the-century rise of dairying in the Fox River Valley had its roots in a fundamentally natural process. Yet in order for dairying to be commercially successful, this process had to be industrialized. It was first subdivided into various stages, from the feeding and breeding of cattle through lactation to the production of milk and its related commodities. The many variables that affected each stage were then identified and analyzed by trained professionals using a variety of new tools and techniques created specifically for the industry. Finally, with this knowledge in hand, each variable in the process could be adjusted in order to raise the efficiency and quality of production to high enough levels that everyone involved in the industry could profit. In Wisconsin, the actual progress of this industrialization was chaotic, uneven, and much less certain than this brief summary implies. Nevertheless, in nearly every respect, the underlying goals of producers remained consistent: to bring the natural process of lactation in the dairy cow under the disciplined control of human hands.[51]

Among the greatest obstacles to be overcome by dairy farmers was the provision of feed to their cattle. Supplying food in the proper amounts and nutritional value was essential to maintaining the cow's ability to lactate, and by the 1920s, producers would go to great lengths to control this aspect of the dairy industry. At its foundation, the raising of livestock was dependent on the same natural resource that supported all farming: fertile soil. During the mid-nineteenth century, while promoters of lumbering and the paper industry were busy extolling the valley's natural advantages, advocates of dairying, too, found reason to sing the region's praises. "All crops that have been tried here have succeeded well," reported one valley resident in 1851, "yet the soil seems more expressly adapted to grazing." It was the soil, in particular, that agriculturalists noticed. Like much of eastern Wisconsin, the Fox River Valley had long ago been inundated by the expanded glacial waters of Lake Michigan, which left the region with a thick layer of heavy, reddish clay underlying the topsoil. The advance and retreat of several ice sheets had worked over this clay, adding deposits of limestone and other material and creating a rich till. Over the centuries, the soils in some parts of the valley had grown slightly acidic, as rainwater gradually leached lime from the surface layers. But in general, by the 1850s when farmers began clearing the forests and turning over the soil, they found a moist and fertile landscape that called to mind the rich grasslands of the older eastern states. "The vernal grass upon the Schuylkill, near Philadelphia, is world-renowned for its nutritious properties," conceded one valley observer, "but there is a similar semi-native grass here that comes in almost unbidden as soon as the forest is removed, of nearly, or quite equal value, and well adapted to mowing or pasturage." The local climate would permit farmers to raise wheat, rye, oats, and many other crops, he argued, "but grass is most natural to the soil, hence it is much better adapted to stock-raising and grazing, than it is to producing grain."[52]

But good soil, by itself, was insufficient to sustain commercial dairying. In particular, during the nineteenth century, farmers in Wisconsin found that the region's lengthy winters and short growing seasons severely limited their ability to produce milk from their cattle. In the absence of good barns to keep herds warm and dry, cows could become unhealthy, with a resulting decline in output. A more fundamental problem was the lack of adequate food. By the 1880s, it was clear that farmers could potentially extend the lactation period they enjoyed from their herds by providing a more nutritional feed. Dairymen experimented with a variety of crops, including corn, hay, turnips, beets, and pumpkins, but the results proved unsatisfactory. As a result, many farmers were prevented from expanding their operations because large herds failed to produce enough milk to pay their keep. For this reason, improving the quality of winter feed became one of the industry's top priorities.

The solution came in the late nineteenth century with the gradual adoption of silage as a means of extending the lactation of cows year round. The practice of ensilage was first refined by French and German farmers during the mid-nineteenth century. It involved the storage of green forage crops in pits or specially constructed buildings called silos made of earth, stone, and later, concrete. In a well-packed silo, the crops underwent dramatic chemical changes, the result of certain bacteria that thrived in the low-oxygen environment. Despite this transformation, the resulting fodder maintained the majority of its nutritional value, thus allowing farmers to store the wealth that nature provided in the summer in order to feed their cattle during the remainder of the year. "Imitate June" was the advice provided by one instructional bulletin. "Nature gives us a model in the month of June," when pastures offered dairy cows a well-balanced diet of succulent grasses and plenty of fresh air, sunshine, clean water, and exercise. "Taking our cue from Nature," the pamphlet continued, "we try to extend these favorable conditions throughout as much of the year as possible." When silos were introduced in the United States in the late 1870s, many farmers remained suspicious, believing that silage would poison their cows or taint the milk they produced. But the tremendous advantages of the new technique quickly won over skeptics. By the 1890s, farmers in Wisconsin were building the state's first silos, and the practice rapidly expanded. In the Fox River Valley alone, more than 6,200 silos had been constructed by 1920.[53]

When practiced in this way, dairying in the Fox River Valley represented a vast improvement over the earlier wheat producers' use of the landscape. As one historian explained, "dairying was itself an exercise in conservation." Where wheat production essentially extracted the soil's nutrients and then shipped them away to various parts of the world, dairying kept them confined on the farm. By utilizing the products of the landscape to feed cattle, farmers were able to return the great majority of this material to the soil in the form of manure. In addition, farmers were encouraged to supplement this natural fertilizer with artificial varieties, and to rotate the raising of clover, alfalfa, and other crops in order to maintain the soil's fertility. By the late nineteenth century, researchers at the University of Wisconsin had begun to investigate which forms of dairy production were best suited to various soils and what mixtures of feed produced the best quality milk for different commodities. The more farmers learned, the more closely they were able to control their use of the natural landscape, and the higher the returns they were able to earn.[54]

This kind of intensive management of nature extended quickly to the cattle that farmers used. Although lactation itself was a natural process, it could be manipulated in ways both subtle and heavy-handed. "Good dairy cows should be regarded as highly efficient animal machines for converting feed into milk," instructed one dairy primer. Like any machine, the cow required raw materials and a source of energy in order to function; it needed constant care and maintenance; its operation could be adjusted to improve efficiency; and it could be replaced by a more productive unit. Controlling the cow's diet was only the beginning of this campaign. Throughout the late nineteenth century, farmers were urged to breed their cattle selectively, eschewing any effort to produce both meat and milk from their cows in favor of single-purpose cattle intended only for dairying. Once an adequate herd was obtained, farmers could further improve its output by testing the productivity of individual animals. In the 1880s, these tests were rudimentary and involved the weighing of milk, estimating its butterfat content, and measuring the cow's intake of food. But in 1890, a researcher with the University of Wisconsin named Stephen M. Babcock perfected a simple yet accurate test to measure butterfat. The procedure, which involved placing a sample of milk in a centrifuge and adding sulfuric acid to liberate the fat, could be performed by anyone. In the coming years, farmers adopted the new procedure to cull their herds of weak-producing cows. By the 1920s, the Babcock test, combined with greater efforts to selectively breed and feed cattle, brought a new level of discipline to the practice of dairying, and even greater productivity.[55]

One final, equally important step in the industrialization of dairying in the Fox River Valley was the evolution of factory production. Prior to the factory system, commercial dairying occurred only sporadically, with farmers distributing excess milk locally or using small amounts for the manufacture of cheese and butter. Production took place on individual farms, and the quality was often poor. Beginning as early as the 1860s a handful of small factories began operations in the valley, buying milk from local farmers in order to produce cheese and butter for urban markets. The factory system brought standardized methods of production, greater efficiency, and economies of scale to commercial dairying. But its greatest attribute to farming was the pressure it created to improve the quality of raw milk. Many farmers objected to the rigorous standards and uniform practices required by the factories to which they sold. Milk had to be fresh from the farm, maintained at a reasonable temperature, and transported in clean pails or cans. Initially, farmers were paid by the volume of the milk they delivered. But after the development of the Babcock test in 1890, manufacturers began paying farmers by the amount of butterfat their milk contained. This shift created a powerful economic incentive for farmers to improve their operations. Only the healthiest herds with the best diets would produce the kind of rich milk that earned high returns at the factory.[56]

Factory production in the valley's dairy industry expanded rapidly during the twentieth century. The region's growing urbanization created mounting demands for fluid milk. Meanwhile, the dramatic improvement of public highways combined with new, more efficient methods of refrigeration to allow farmers and milk dealers to reach these urban markets. This trend, too, brought further pressure on farmers to improve the quality of their product, especially during the 1890s, when the fear of disease caused many communities to impose stringent requirements on the purity of milk distributed to their citizens. The introduction of sealed glass bottles and pasteurization helped to gradually relax these concerns during the early twentieth century. But in many ways, such anxieties were also productive, sparking new research efforts to understand the biochemistry of milk, as well as new attempts to manufacture less perishable products such as condensed and evaporated milk. In this way, industrialization brought growing diversification to commercial dairying. In 1900, dairy production in Wisconsin had been dominated by cheese and butter, which accounted for more than 80 percent of the industry's net worth. By the 1920s, in contrast, this relative value would drop by roughly a third, an indication of the increasing significance of fluid milk, cream, and their numerous by-products. Viewed in strictly economic terms, the growing variety and quality of dairy production was a mark of the industry's stability and prosperity. In the Fox River Valley, milk dealers and dairy plants of various kinds became a familiar presence in most communities. Across the state as a whole, Wisconsin's industry rose to lead the nation in total output.[57]

But perhaps most important, compared with the valley's earlier reliance on wheat production, dairying used the local landscape more efficiently and productively. In this respect, the evolution of the dairy industry would likely have pleased President Theodore Roosevelt. The nation's soil, he argued before the conference of governors in 1908, was in a class of resources along with America's forests and rivers that could "actually be improved by wise use." For Roosevelt, this was the essence of conservation: to utilize the knowledge of science, the power of new technologies, and the discipline of industrial production to "improve on nature by compelling the resources to renew and even reconstruct themselves." Once again, it is worth recalling that dairying was never a major aspect of the conservation movement in Wisconsin. Nevertheless, the industry's remarkable success—much like that of electric power and paved highways—offered clear support for the central claim of conservationists, that renewed material progress was possible given the efficient use of nature.[58]

Unfortunately, just as Theodore Roosevelt had predicted, the more industrialized commercial dairying became, the less its ultimate success appeared to depend on nature. By the 1920s, the activities of the industry's farmers, manufacturers, and scientists had grown to rely more than ever on the deliberate utilization of material resources. But their use of these resources was now so carefully manipulated, so radically divided along various lines of production, and so completely dependent on new discoveries in science and technology that the crucial role of nature in the process was increasingly hidden from view. Few valley residents who purchased milk or cheese from urban retailers ever witnessed the tremendous effort required to create these products from landscape and animals. Even farmers themselves began to see their use of resources through different eyes.

Consequently, it should not be surprising that when the delegation of western visitors toured the Fox River Valley in 1924, they were as much intrigued by the region's developing infrastructure as they were its natural landscape. "In my judgment," explained one agricultural agent to the delegation, "Wisconsin depends more upon the human factor than upon any natural resources or advantages that the state possesses." As the group learned quickly, the roads, power lines, silos, and factories that now characterized Wisconsin's landscape had become essential means of production for dairy farmers, every bit as important as good soils and favorable climates. In the nineteenth century, wheat farmers in the valley had defined their prosperity by cataloging the wealth that nature provided in the region. In contrast, by the twentieth century, local dairy farmers tended to view their own good fortunes in terms of thriving communities, comfortable homes, and the growing convenience of industrial progress.[59]

Yet if electric power lines, paved highways, and urban factories were becoming essential means of production for farmers by the 1920s, they were also symbolic of something more: each was a vital part of the burgeoning world of modern consumption in the Fox River Valley at the turn of the century. Put simply, the same technological developments that most producers saw as an expanding industrial infrastructure tended to be viewed by most consumers as rapid commercialization. Dairy farmers were caught squarely in the middle of this transformation, with a foot on either side of the widening gap between production and consumption. The more farmers came to specialize in the production of milk, the more they became consumers themselves, spending their money in local communities to supply all the rest of their needs. This kind of specialization was crucial to achieving the material prosperity that farmers sought from industrialization. "We are aiming in Wisconsin to obliterate the lines between [the] urban and rural population," one farmer reported to the western delegation in 1924. By all accounts, their efforts had begun to succeed. "The present day farm house in [Outagamie] county often excels the city home in plan, conveniences and in comforts afforded," claimed the Appleton *Post-Crescent* in the early 1920s. But the productive power of electricity and paved roads told only part of this story. Of much greater significance was the way in which these and other creations of industrial progress altered life in the countryside by promoting the flow of commerce between urban and rural areas. The gradual expansion of the valley's technological infrastructure gave farmers the means, opportunity, and incentive, not just to produce better milk, but also to consume the growing array of commercial goods and services made affordable by their newfound prosperity.[60]

In this way, by the 1920s, the proliferation of commercial relationships would bring city and country ever closer together in the Fox River Valley, remaking the two halves of the region's landscape into a single unified whole. "A remarkable change has taken place in this community during the past twenty-seven years," began a 1923 advertisement for Geenen's, one of Appleton's largest department stores. "In 1896 [when Geenen's first opened] Appleton was a distinct unit in itself; today the territory has so developed that Appleton, in a broad sense, is only a part of the greater unit—The Fox River Valley." According to the ad, it was trade more than anything that knit the region together, a burgeoning network of commercial relationships facilitated by the expanding urban-industrial world. "The automobile, the good roads . . . the growing industries, etc., all have been big factors in bringing about this change," continued the ad. "The constant demand for more and better merchandise proved to the retail merchant that the change was taking place; that his field of selling was reaching out beyond the confines of Appleton City." In the years to come, urban retailers would extend their reach even farther, making the line between city and country nearly indistinguishable. This transformation, in turn, would have profound consequences on the way valley residents understood their relationship to the natural landscape. During the nineteenth century, the Fox River Valley had been defined in large part by the use of its resources as a means of production. By the mid-twentieth century, it became a place shaped instead by consumption and the expanding control over nature that consumption made possible.[61]

4

The Consumer's Metropolis

On March 29, 1920, more than 300 of Appleton's leading merchants, businessmen, and citizens gathered in the local Elk Hall to form a chamber of commerce. According to organizers, the chamber would function, much like highways and electrical power systems, as "an agency of progress" for local residents. John Conway led the effort to establish the new commercial group. Conway was proprietor of the Sherman House, Appleton's largest hotel. He had been instrumental in bringing paved roads to Outagamie County. Now, he believed, the same spirit of improvement could be brought to bear on the region as a whole. "The modern method of attacking problems is by concerted action through organization," he told the crowd. "The Chamber of Commerce is the ideal way of solving perplexing questions which confront a community." Among the list of problems citizens hoped to address were traditional economic concerns such as attracting new industry to Appleton and drawing customers to downtown stores. But there were other issues as well: the need for better housing, improving local parks, fostering health and sanitation, and promoting greater efforts in education and city planning. A new chamber of commerce, argued Conway, would make possible exactly this kind of broad community development. "We want to make Appleton not only a bigger city, but a better city to live in," he urged. In responding to his challenge, Conway found the audience receptive. By the meeting's conclusion, the assembled residents had purchased more than 660 memberships in the group at $25 apiece. Appleton's Chamber of Commerce was born.[1]

That so many people would ascribe a commercial organization with lofty social purpose reflected the growing importance of consumption in American society. By the 1920s, residents in the Fox River Valley relied on the vast flow of commercial goods and services for almost everything they did, from obtaining food, clothing, and shelter to acquiring countless other products: energy, transportation, entertainment, and health care. The list was nearly endless. People's growing dependence on consumption was the logical outgrowth of industrialization, a necessary counterpart to mass production and the division of labor. "We have grown to an age of specialization," declared Appleton's Chamber of Commerce in one of its earliest publications. The more industrialized society became, the more its various regions, communities, and citizens played individualized roles in order to maximize the overall efficiency of economic production. "So it is to the specialist in sanitation, in production, in transportation, in city planning, in housing and government that we now must turn," argued the chamber. This growing division of labor had become practically synonymous with material progress in the United States. Yet ironically, the more specialized people's roles became, the more they had to rely on each other—and on consumption more broadly—to fulfill their individual needs.[2]

For members of Appleton's Chamber of Commerce, the increasing commercialization of life in the Fox River Valley created two problems that the chamber was uniquely positioned to address. First, in the interdependent but fractured society created by industrialization, civic improvements of any kind would require cooperation. "Every city should have an organization that has as its object the furthering of the best interests of the community," urged one proponent of the chamber in 1920. By joining together retailers, manufacturers, politicians, and citizens, the chamber could facilitate exactly the kind of collaboration needed to advance the interests of everyone. Second, whatever improvements the city might pursue, its leaders would need to confront the changing priorities of local residents. According to the chamber, Appleton could no longer rely on its natural advantages and the industries they spawned. These were the priorities of an age now passed, a time when people's hard work and self-denial offered the best hope of earning a living from nature. In the dawning age of mass production, by contrast, Appleton's residents now measured the city's worth in its ability to distribute the many products of industrialization. "When 1930 shall arrive," predicted the chamber shortly after its organization, "we shall find American communities taking pride, not in the mere population or size of the town or its material wealth, but in those fundamental things that make cities really great—their collective action for the health, happiness, prosperity and the general welfare of the people." Health, happiness, and prosperity were hardly new concerns in Appleton. But the fact that so many residents now relied on consumption to attain these ends made the Chamber of Commerce an ideal organization to promote their goals.[3]

Not surprisingly, in the chamber's view, the solution to both these problems was the expansion of trade in Appleton's stores. It was commerce that could bring together divergent interests in the community, uniting everyone from rural farmers and urban housewives to city councilmen and manufacturers. It was commerce, too, that promised all citizens a chance to improve their material well-being through the purchase of goods and services. Looking back on this formula for civic advancement, it would be easy to dismiss the organization of Appleton's Chamber of Commerce as a disingenuous ploy on the part of retailers to line their pockets in the name of the public good. Yet this view would be too cynical. In the prosperous era of the 1920s, many Americans saw the accumulation of material wealth as a means to achieving noble ends, including education, social reform, and moral improvement. "The chief business of the American people is business," declared President Calvin Coolidge in 1925. This oft-quoted remark is sometimes used to epitomize the reckless hedonism of the era, especially the way it might have contributed to the Great Depression looming just ahead. But in fact, the statement more accurately reflects the common belief in the United States that prosperity could uplift the nation. For Coolidge, America's growing material wealth provided "a means to well nigh every desirable achievement," including "the multiplication of schools, the increase of knowledge, the dissemination of intelligence, the encouragement of science, the broadening of outlook, the expansion of liberties, [and] the widening of culture." In Appleton, the chamber's supporters defined the group's mission in exactly these terms. "A commercial organization's primary function is not to bring industries to a city," explained the *Post-Crescent*, "but to make the city a more desirable place in which to work and live." Urban planning, public health and sanitation, the expansion of parks and education: these were but a few of the goals that members of the Chamber of Commerce sincerely believed could be aided through the promotion of trade. By encouraging local residents to become more active consumers, the chamber intended to "arouse the dormant ability in the lay citizen, making him a factor in the city's progress."[4]

There was nothing fundamentally new about the act of consuming goods and services in the 1920s. Nevertheless, this chapter explores two aspects of consumption in the Fox River Valley that were unique to the era. First, by the mid-twentieth century, people's reliance on commercial products became a pervasive aspect of life for urban and rural citizens alike. Among the principal goals of the Appleton Chamber of Commerce was an idea it shared with nearly every industrial producer at the time, including electric utilities, the state Highway Commission, and local dairy farmers. Specifically, the chamber hoped to extend the benefits of material progress from the city into the countryside. The success of its efforts between 1920 and 1950 helped make the valley's urban and rural areas increasingly indistinguishable, at least in terms of material comforts. Second, and just as significant, was the unprecedented power of the technologies that became available during the era for purchase by consumers. The great expansion of commercial electricity and automobiles in particular gave valley residents unparalleled abilities to control and shape the material world, even in the most remote parts of the countryside.

When combined, these unique aspects of modern consumption brought the emergence of consumer society in the Fox River Valley, a world in which the productive use of the natural landscape had all but disappeared from the daily routines of local residents. The chapter concludes by suggesting the ironic impact of this transformation on perceptions of nature in the region. If industrial production obscured people's growing dependence on the use of natural resources, it was consumption that ultimately redefined the meaning of nature itself. The more valley residents relied on commercial goods and services to reduce the work, hardship, and obstacles that once characterized the natural landscape, the more nature came to function instead as a place of recreation, beauty, and escape in the seemingly artificial world that people inhabited. It is this aspect of consumption—the way it filtered out the majority of nature's unpleasant qualities while creating new windows of access to its numerous amenities—that would eventually contribute to the evolution of environmentalism in the valley.

The Boundaries of the City

In the fall of 1926, the Appleton Chamber of Commerce sponsored "Motor to Appleton Week," a six-day coordinated sale designed to draw people from the city's hinterland and bring them downtown to shop. Appleton had long been among the Fox River Valley's more important trading centers, attracting customers from as far as 40 miles away. Even so, local businessmen wanted to make these visits more frequent and to increase the dependence of area residents on the goods and services available in the community. The recent improvement of the region's highway system offered them a new and powerful means of expanding their reach.[5]

In the days before the October sale, the chamber erected 200 signs along area roadsides in a 30-mile radius surrounding Appleton. Each was a 5-foot-long arrow pointing the way to the city. To further lure distant customers, merchants placed advertisements in newspapers urging readers to "get acquainted" with local stores. "MOTOR TO APPLETON AND SAVE MONEY," declared one two-page ad. "Appleton merchants are staging this big demonstration, to show convincingly, the people of its own community and all of its adjacent territory, that Appleton is a moderate priced city — a city whose stores offer everything desired." To judge from the bargains available during the week, there was little that Appleton's shopkeepers could not provide: coats, pants, dresses, shoes, linens, curtains, soap, hair tonic, jewelry, cigars, bathtubs, stoves, washing machines, radios, percolators, groceries, and even grand pianos. The huge selection of products included merchandise with trusted brand names, everything from Pepsodent toothpaste and Lee overalls to Victor records and Goodyear tires. These well-known symbols helped to emphasize the reliability, convenience, and economy that came with every purchase. Shopping in Appleton would appeal to every consumer, rural and urban alike. "The store for the farmer, the store for the workingman," proclaimed one local retailer. "Don't fail to get here."[6]

In many ways, Motor to Appleton Week typified the efforts of the city's Chamber of Commerce to promote consumption during the early twentieth century. For local merchants, commerce provided the most effective means of solving any problem, from simple hunger or bad breath to people's growing desire for material comfort and personal fulfillment. According to retailers, there was a product to fill every need, and Appleton's stores were there to supply them. Even more important, expanding commercial trade offered a convenient way to knit the region together, giving divergent groups a common stake in the welfare of the community. This was especially true for rural farmers. "Today modern chambers of Commerce are enlarging their conception of the community and embrace not only the streets and parks of the town," argued the group, "but the roads and farms of the surrounding territory." Given the long-standing isolation of farmers from the comforts of urban life and their growing integration into the specialized industrial economy, farmers displayed a newfound interest and ability to do business in local stores. According to the chamber, the best way to encourage this trade was for merchants to uplift residents of city and country alike, and to link the well-being of each to the goods and services available in Appleton. In this way, the chamber sought to expand the boundaries of the city and make them synonymous with the reach of merchants. "Substituting the word 'community' for 'city' is the idea of advancement," instructed one speaker at a chamber banquet in 1922. Appleton, he believed, should function as "a huge plant with a 'lawn' extending for miles in every direction, and the chamber of commerce as its selling organization."[7]

Of chief importance in realizing this vision was improving the infrastructure required to bring people and commodities together. In the early 1920s, the city's principal business district was situated along College Avenue, which ran through the heart of town (Figure 12). Named in honor of Appleton's Lawrence College, the avenue was a typical main street of the American Midwest. A wide thoroughfare lined on both sides with spacious sidewalks and two- and three-story brick structures, College Avenue was home to a variety of commercial establishments. Shoppers could find art stores, bakers, bankers, beauty parlors, book stores, cigar stores, retailers of men's and women's clothing, department stores, drugstores, electric supply shops, five-and-ten stores, florists, fruit merchants, furniture stores, grain dealers, grocers, hardware suppliers, hotels, jewelry dealers, liveries and harness shops, meat markets, milk dealers, millinery stores, music stores, photographers, plumbers, restaurants and soft drink parlors, service stations and garages, sewing machine dealers, shoe stores, tea and coffee shops, and providers of fine wallpaper. This impressive collection of retailers was served by an equally extensive transportation system that included six motor bus routes, two interurbans, and four railroad lines, not to mention 135 miles of concrete highway that

Figure 12. Appleton's College Avenue, ca. 1920s. Courtesy of the Outagamie County Historical Society, Appleton, Wis., Image No. 1988-72-238.

stretched to all parts of the county. As a result, roughly 75,000 people lived within the 40-mile trading radius of College Avenue. The growing ease with which valley residents could shop in Appleton, in effect, brought "the products of all the world right to [their] door."[8]

This development notwithstanding, Appleton's Chamber of Commerce was dedicated to extending the city's reach even further. In the 1920s, bringing more shoppers downtown meant looking first to the region's highways. Given the many advantages of highway transportation, the flow of traffic through the valley came to resemble the flow of commerce itself. People used roads to get to work, buy groceries, and visit their doctors — for almost anything that required traveling from one place to another. Much the same was true for the farmers, merchants, and businessmen who relied on commercial trucking. Yet according to merchants, Appleton had been slighted by the state Highway Commission. In the early 1920s, only four trunk highways linked the city with its immediate hinterland: Highway 15 from the southwest and the northeast, and three other routes heading east, north, and west. By contrast, Green Bay had eight trunk connections, and neighboring Fond du Lac had seven. For retailers, the trunk highways were more than status symbols or emblems of civic pride. They carried real, material significance and served as tangible assets in what inevitably became a competition to win the patronage of valley residents. Green Bay was Appleton's clearest rival. In 1924, the neighboring city began promoting its own State Route 57 over Highway 15 as the best road between Milwaukee and the valley. Appleton's merchants took urgent notice. The chamber contacted cities all along Highway 15, asking them to promote the route and avoid a loss of traffic.[9]

Although such concerns were often exaggerated, few storekeepers had any doubts about the significance of highways to their trade. Unfortunately, with major construction now governed mainly by the state Highway Commission, there was little that business leaders could do themselves. Still, they did have a few ideas, the most promising of which was the placement of road signs along area highways. The arrows erected during Motor to Appleton Week served part of this function, but merchants continued to be dissatisfied. A survey conducted by the chamber in 1929 found that motorists traveling near Appleton had "no way of knowing that they were passing the city, nor . . . the size of Appleton or the accommodations offered." To remedy this situation, the chamber erected twelve billboards in strategic locations along major gateways to the city. Each was designed to advertise some aspect of the community. "You'll Like Appleton," boasted one of the signs. "25,000 Industrious People." Other billboards championed the city's "Scenic Fox River," its "Excellent Recreational Facilities," and its role as a "Home of Paper Products." On two of its largest placards, the chamber printed the slogan "Appleton: For Business, For Pleasure." In this way, merchants endeavored to inform motorists that the city could provide almost anything they desired.[10]

Road signs proved helpful. Yet they could never make up for deficiencies in the highways themselves. Consequently, members of the chamber continued to worry about the business they were losing as a result of inadequate roads. State Highway 15 posed the most difficult problem. In 1918, when the route was first laid out, the Highway Commission had placed it through the center of each of the region's towns, including Appleton. By the early 1920s, this policy was already creating problems, and experts warned Appleton's businessmen that the road would need significant changes in order to serve their needs. In particular, the growing volume and speed of traffic led to serious congestion, especially where the route traveled through the city along its principal business thoroughfare. "To be sure you have the wide and beautiful street called College [Avenue]," cautioned one city planner from the University of Wisconsin in 1921, "but you have neither adequate inlet or outlet." Consequently, traffic was forced to pass through narrow bottlenecks at either end of the city, creating frequent delays, dangerous conditions, and a less-than-ideal gateway between shoppers and the retail district.[11]

The eventual solution to the problem was a plan that Appleton's merchants initially considered disastrous: the construction of a beltline for Highway 15. The idea of a beltline was first proposed by the state Highway Commission in the early 1920s. The goal was to steer traffic around the city and away from its busy commercial district by relocating the route to the edge of town. For the Highway Commission, the change offered a means of dramatically improving the safety, efficiency, and speed of driving along the road. But in Appleton, even the suggestion that the valley's most important highway might bypass the city was enough to alarm politicians and merchants loath to risk a loss of business and prestige. These fears proved difficult for the Highway Commission to overcome. Surveys conducted by the agency showed that only 15 percent of drivers on the state's principal roadways actually stopped at any of the places through which they passed. Yet local officials remained staunch in their opposition. "Though many cities are coming to realize that traffic in transit through such cities is of slight, if any benefit," reported the commission in 1930, "many cling to the ancient prejudice against belt lines."[12]

In the meantime, state authorities did what they could to improve Highway 15 in other ways. During the 1920s and 1930s, the road was gradually widened from 9 to 20 feet. Sharp corners were straightened, railroad grade crossings eliminated, and the tops of steep hills were removed. Along portions of the road, the north- and southbound lanes were even separated and widened further still in order to accommodate rising traffic. Some improvements to the road were more symbolic than structural. Among the most significant of these was the highway's inclusion in a new national system of roadways created by the federal Bureau of Public Roads in 1925. Highway 15 became U.S. Highway 41, and its new route stretched all the way from Florida through Wisconsin into the upper peninsula of Michigan. By the mid-1930s, the Highway Commission had transformed the road from a narrow, winding ribbon of concrete into a highly regulated and efficient system of transportation, a commercial artery that increasingly carried the lifeblood of the valley's economy. Unfortunately, the more state authorities did to improve the flow of traffic, the greater the problems encountered by motorists in the cities through which the route still passed. The situation eventually grew dangerous. In 1934, a special committee of the Appleton Chamber of Commerce reported that during the past five years, eleven fatal accidents had occurred on Highway 41 along an especially narrow bottleneck north of the city.[13]

As a result of the mounting congestion in Appleton, the city's businessmen, officeholders, and residents finally acknowledged the necessity of a beltline for Highway 41. Neighboring communities followed suit, dropping their opposition to the plan. By 1939, the state Highway Commission had constructed the first sections of the new road between Neenah and Appleton. The remainder of the project would take nearly two decades to complete as, section by section, Highway 41 was moved to the outskirts of the valley's urban centers. Throughout the process, Appleton's Chamber of Commerce worked to ensure continued access to the city's business district. The effort proved difficult. In planning the new beltline, state engineers failed to include any improvements to city streets that now connected Appleton and the highway, bringing howls of protest from angry merchants. Eventually, businessmen settled on a plan to develop an alternate route through the city meant specifically for commercial traffic. The onset of war in 1941 delayed the project for nearly a decade. But the chamber eventually convinced state officials to establish a business-oriented route through downtown Appleton, to be designated as U.S. 41 but marked with yellow signs instead of white.[14]

Just as the state Highway Commission predicted, the Highway 41 beltline did little to harm Appleton's merchants. In fact, the number of shoppers driving to College Avenue grew steadily throughout the 1930s and 1940s, creating a new type of congestion despite the beltline. In this case, the issue was parking. Surveys conducted by the Chamber of Commerce revealed that many rural patrons avoided coming to the city specifically because they found it difficult to park. The potential loss of business worried local merchants. "It is certain that if other things are equal, people will do their shopping in the city that offers the most assurance of a place to park automobiles," declared the *Post-Crescent* in a 1931 editorial. According to the paper, parking was no less than a "vital necessity" to the community, and it urged politicians to act quickly to correct the problem.[15]

In the Chamber of Commerce, members wrestled with several possible solutions, the most obvious of which was simply to expand the city's parking facilities. Unfortunately, there appeared to be little available land to construct new downtown parking lots. What's more, local officials proved reluctant to spend money on the project. As a result, the chamber was left to pressure Appleton's law enforcement to step up its ticketing of parking offenders. City regulations in the early 1930s established a ninety-minute limit along the business district of College Avenue. The restriction was meant to encourage rapid turnover in parking, allowing customers enough time to complete their shopping while encouraging them to do so quickly. But the law was rarely enforced. In 1930, after merchants complained again about the lack of attention from police, the department responded. To the chamber's chagrin, the police chief reported that 50 percent of the drivers tagged on the first day were retailers themselves or their employees. Merchants responded with a "Walk to Work Club," but the problem persisted and the chamber was forced to explore other options.[16]

The most promising but controversial alternative was the installation of parking meters. During the 1930s, communities across the country installed these devices to regulate crowded streets. Much like policemen issuing tickets, the meters were intended to encourage rapid turnover in areas of high traffic. For many years, Appleton's merchants remained cool to the idea, fearing a backlash from customers who might be angered at having to pay for parking. As a result, the issue languished for more than a decade. Finally, in 1948, Appleton's mayor convinced the Chamber of Commerce to support parking meters, provided that revenues were utilized for off-street lots in which shoppers could park for free. For retailers, the plan seemed the ideal solution: a means of preserving free parking while at the same time reducing the terrible congestion on College Avenue. By 1949, a delighted chamber reported that "public acceptance of the meters [has] been very good." The city council was at work purchasing land for two downtown parking lots, and merchants looked forward to improving shoppers' access to their stores.[17]

Better highways and parking did much to improve Appleton's commercial infrastructure. But drawing shoppers downtown, especially from the countryside, depended on many additional factors, and merchants worked hard to address these as well. In the early 1920s, relations between urban and rural citizens in the Fox River Valley were less than cordial. As in many parts of the United States, the industrial transformation of the late nineteenth century had its most immediate impact in the valley's cities, causing a widening economic and cultural gap between rural and urban residents. During the early years of the twentieth century, the gradual extension of paved roads, electricity, telephones, radio, and other modernizing influences began to reach the countryside. But their jarring impact on rural life created as many tensions as it resolved. Consequently, many of the valley's farmers felt unappreciated, misunderstood, and even threatened by their urban counterparts. By 1920, rural farmers accounted for roughly half the number of customers routinely shopping in Appleton. Yet according to retailers, their seeming disaffection left them in need of exactly the kind of uplifting development that the city's Chamber of Commerce was meant to provide.[18]

Merchants took up this development with a kind of missionary zeal. As a first step, they organized a series of community dinners and picnics throughout the county. The gatherings allowed merchants and farmers to meet and discuss common interests. In particular, they helped the chamber to address a number of specific problems that sometimes kept rural patrons from shopping in Appleton. For example, businessmen learned that many farmers avoided the city because there was no public bathroom. So the chamber established a restroom in the heart of the retail district. In similar fashion, merchants helped lobby county officials for better snow removal on the highways. Opening the roads helped rural inhabitants to avoid a months-long period of isolation during the winter. It also served the interests of retailers who wished to see their rural patrons more often in their stores. Finally, the chamber worked hard to assist farmers in marketing their own commodities. Dairy farmers especially looked to urban residents as their primary customers. Unfortunately, falling prices during the 1920s combined with the general economic depression of the 1930s to create terrible financial hardship in rural areas. If merchants hoped to expand their reach into the countryside, then promoting the sale of dairy products seemed the best means of doing so. The chamber helped farmers to organize regular stock fairs, held in Appleton on the last Saturday of each month. It also coordinated frequent dairy promotions. Whether or not such events increased the patronage of farmers is difficult to measure. But the goodwill created between merchants and rural citizens almost certainly paid dividends.[19]

Without question, the chamber's most important effort to expand its reach into the countryside was the annual series of collaborative sales organized by the group. "Competition in service has taken the place of competition in price," explained one speaker at a chamber banquet in 1922. For Appleton's merchants, the task was no longer to put each other out of business. Instead, they endeavored to create greater trade for everyone. "The retailers of Appleton at present spend more than eighty thousand dollars annually to promote trade as individuals," complained H. A. Gloudemans, owner of one of the city's largest department stores. "It is my opinion that the Appleton retailers can well afford to support a small budget for trade promotion of the city as a whole." As a result, between 1930 and 1950, events such as Motor to Appleton Week became routine features of the city's retail calendar, a schedule that also included Dollar Days, the Spring and Fall Openings, Appleton Day, and the Christmas Opening. Although the names of these sales changed slightly from year to year, the idea behind them remained the same. By pooling their resources, merchants hoped to expand and stabilize their hold on the regional trading area. Annual sales proved to be among their most effective tools.[20]

Before each sale, the chamber went to great lengths to draw rural customers into the city. "The city is ready to welcome the many out of town guests who will be coming to Appleton to share in the values," promised one typical ad, this for a 1934 sale. "Don't worry about being 'tagged' for parking too long—parking time limits have been removed for visitors on that day. Restaurants will offer special menus for you who come early and make a day of it. You'll find restrooms in downtown hotels." For most events, merchants arranged for the *Post-Crescent* to include a sales insert for its rural subscribers, and to deliver the issue days in advance of the opening. Retailers also promoted their events through radio announcements, movie trailers, mailings to past customers, and ads in the newspapers of neighboring small towns. In this way, the chamber was able to design appeals aimed specifically at the rural citizen. "Fine roads and good transportation make it possible for out-of-town visitors to profit by this great event," noted one 1932 advertisement. "Appleton wants you and welcomes you as a friend and customer," urged another. Some retailers even offered special incentives to farmers. "As an added inducement to shop at this store," promised one retailer, "we will pay 17c per dozen for FRESH eggs . . . to be taken out in trade."[21]

Such appeals aside, the most obvious way to bring shoppers to Appleton was by offering low prices. In this way, retailers hoped to introduce people to the stores on College Avenue and convince them to come back routinely. "Tomorrow Begins One of the Greatest Value-Giving Events in Appleton History," declared one ad, this for a 1931 sale called, rather simply, "Trade Expansion Days." "This is no ordinary bargain event," continued the ad. "It is a conscious, carefully planned effort to improve business conditions and show definitely how Appleton dominates the retail field." Readers were encouraged to study the available bargains. Those who did found discounts on every type of commodity, with each store echoing the same message of collaboration and growth. "Join the crowds in this great co-operative trade event," urged another retailer. With so many bargains, Appleton was sure to become "the trading center of the Fox River Valley."[22]

As much as bargains helped to encourage trade, the Chamber of Commerce went still further in its cooperative endeavors. In particular, merchants sought to imbue Appleton with the kind of festive, neighborly atmosphere that stimulated spending. The idea of a program of sales, said one retailer in 1929, was continually to "draw people to Appleton for business or for pleasure." If valley residents came to the city for any reason, ran the theory, they were likely to spend money. Therefore, "it should be our object to create a friendly feeling of interest in Appleton and its activities in those people who live within its trading area." During the 1930s and 1940s, the Chamber of Commerce followed this prescription in nearly all its retail events. Sales were often accompanied by parades and pageants, contests and prizes, and special decorations and lighting. In addition, whenever possible, they were timed to coincide with other events such as teachers' conventions or farmers' institutes, which drew large numbers of people to the city. The annual Christmas Opening was especially elaborate. The chamber maintained a permanent subcommittee just for the occasion, and charged it with the seemingly redundant task of "creating public interest for Christmas." Each year in late November or early December, retailers decorated College Avenue with all the lights, trees, and wreaths appropriate to the holiday. Santa Claus made his appearance in a grand parade that featured a giant sled, a large public mailbox in which children could deposit wish lists, and an array of helpful elves dressed in costume. For the next month, Appleton's Santa Claus visited area schools, churches, civic groups, and stores, all coordinated by the chamber and all intended to create the kind of community goodwill that merchants believed would stimulate sales.[23]

As with everything the Chamber of Commerce did following its creation in 1920, self-serving economic motives partly explain its actions. Retailers used annual sales, for example, because when timed strategically, such events helped to clear their inventories of merchandise that was either out of season or out of style. Yet until the 1950s, few local residents ever challenged the chamber or its ideology of civic improvement, no matter how self-serving its efforts might frequently have been. That Appleton's merchants were allowed to shape the community with so little objection is all the more remarkable because so many of the years during this period were characterized by severe economic hardship. In many parts of the United States, the dislocations and suffering caused by the Great Depression and World War II brought labor strikes, racial and cultural tensions, and a variety of movements for economic and social reform. Wisconsin was hardly immune from this turmoil. But in the Fox River Valley, no amount of hard times displaced the idea that progress was best measured by people's ability to consume.[24]

In this respect, residents in the Fox River Valley were squarely in the American mainstream. Even in the 1930s, the growing ability of science, technology, and industry to improve people's lives was evident throughout the United States: in the great dams that brought water, electricity, and hope to the arid West; in the automobiles, radios, and power lines that reduced the isolation of rural citizens; and in the mounting array of new machinery that increased productivity in the nation's factories and households. So it was that in 1939, when the United States hosted yet another World's Fair, this one entitled "The World of Tomorrow," Americans could view its triumphant prediction of a scientific and technological utopia with hope instead of bitterness. In the wake of depression and perched on the brink of world war, the fair offered visitors the most impressive celebration of America's industrial prowess since the Columbian Exposition nearly a half century earlier. Its message was simple: if the wonders of modern industry were not yet within reach for everyone, they soon would be, thanks to the continued material progress made possible by science and technology. In the Fox River Valley, much as happened in 1893, few residents likely attended this World's Fair. Yet no one, no matter what his or her station in life, could be entirely unaware of their growing dependence on exactly the kind of development that the fair celebrated.[25]

Nothing better illustrates this dependence than a study of Appleton con- ducted by *Time* magazine at the very depths of the Great Depression. In 1931, researchers from *Time* arrived in the city to conduct a survey of retail trade. The study, which was intended for use by the magazine's advertisers, exam- ined the relationship between income levels and buying habits among Apple- ton's consumers. "How many people in each income group are replacing old radio sets?" *Time* wanted to know. "What income bracket spends the most money for low-priced cars? How many people at various income levels have built the houses they live in? What did they pay? What kind of heating equip- ment did they install? [How] many washing machines? [What] electrical ap- pliances . . . ? What is the difference between the coffee consumption of a ten-thousand-dollar-a-year family and a twenty-five-hundred-dollar-a-year family?" To answer these questions, researchers conducted dozens of inter- views, speaking with housewives, automobile dealers, grocers, bankers, retail- ers of every variety, civic groups, and local officeholders. *Time* even tracked shoppers from Appleton to Chicago and Milwaukee where investigators ob- tained sales receipts from their visits to major department stores.[26]

In all, the magazine compiled data from 1.5 million retail purchases. The information it gathered illustrates just how thoroughly consumption had permeated American life by the 1930s. According to the report, a substan- tial portion of Appleton's poorest families routinely purchased nearly every commodity the magazine examined. Dependence on consumption appeared greatest in the acquisition of food. Baked beans, flour, bread, crackers, milk, ginger ale, butter, rice, tea, sugar, canned fruit, and salad dressing: all were widely purchased in Appleton, often by 30 to 70 percent of households, with minimal variation depending on income. Much the same picture emerged in the acquisition of other necessities. By the 1930s, transportation had be- come a ubiquitous consumer good. According to the survey, poor families in Appleton could rarely purchase the newest, most expensive automobiles. Yet half of all households in the lowest income group owned at least one car, either used or a new but less expensive model. What's more, these families averaged only 20 percent less annual miles per car than their wealthier counterparts, suggesting a widespread dependence on auto transportation. In similar fashion, *Time* magazine found broad consumption of public utility service. Although wealthy citizens consumed roughly twice the amount of gas, water, and electricity as the city's poorer residents, the latter group comprised by far the largest proportion of the utilities' customer base, nearly 70 percent. This trend mirrored consumption throughout the retail market. According to the survey, water consumption was a rough indicator of people's tendency to buy soap, washing machines, and toiletries for the bathroom. Likewise, the usage of gas and electricity reflected shoppers' growing desire for radios, electric fans, water heaters, and kitchen appliances. Although these products remained out of reach for at least some local residents, the *Time* survey suggests they were moving rapidly from convenience to necessity for local citizens.[27]

In attempting to encourage this trend, Appleton's Chamber of Commerce was all too happy that its members profited from the sale of goods and services. Yet the organization remained sincere in its effort to improve the community through trade. "What becomes of a dollar spent in Appleton?" asked the chamber in a 1928 newspaper ad. "[It] may pay part of your next door neighbor's wages. It will help to lift the tax burden from your shoulders. It will help to . . . build better stores and buildings . . . , new streets for you to travel on, and parks in which you can enjoy leisure hours." In other words, according to the chamber, every dollar spent in Appleton was vital to the city's progress, contributing to "the material and cultural advancement of the community as a whole." In this way, merchants came to see the promotion of commerce as synonymous with civic advancement, an ideology that created powerful incentives for a number of related projects: improving transportation from the railroads and highways; promoting better sanitation, education, and city planning; fostering tourism; and establishing stronger commercial ties between the city and its rural hinterland. Viewed in retrospect, this formula for local development created as many problems as it solved. But the Chamber of Commerce had been founded to achieve exactly this kind of progress, and few residents at the time questioned its logic.[28]

By the late 1940s, few people could question its success as well. In simple geographic terms, Appleton's trading area remained confined to roughly the same 40-mile radius that marked its outermost reach in the 1920s. Still, the boundaries of Appleton's commercial influence expanded in other ways, thanks primarily to the rising per capita demand for goods among valley residents. During the period, the region's population increased by approximately half its original quantity, while the number of retail establishments in Appleton grew at nearly twice this rate, climbing from 220 to 418. Had consumer demand remained constant, the city's larger number of merchants would have found themselves competing for a smaller percentage of total sales. But this was not the case. Instead, the annual revenues of Appleton's merchants grew from $12 million to nearly $49 million, a fourfold increase. Hence, between the early 1920s and the late 1940s, per capita consumer spending in the region more than doubled, providing a rough measurement of people's increasing dependence on Appleton's stores for goods and services.[29]

But dollar figures alone fail to capture consumption's influence on people's interactions with nature in the Fox River Valley. The purchase of goods and services was not simply more pervasive by the late 1940s. It also gave people access to increasingly powerful technologies, a budding assortment of commercial products that dramatically reduced the hardships of life and work in the region. It is here, in the growing material comfort made possible by consumption, where the ideology of the Appleton Chamber of Commerce is most clearly revealed. For merchants, the promotion of trade was never intended literally to expand the city's boundaries. "It is not a question of making the city bigger," one speaker explained at the chamber's founding in 1920. Rather, the goal of civic improvement was to utilize Appleton's commercial establishments to extend the material benefits of urban living into the countryside, thereby encouraging a sense of affinity and collective purpose between the city and its hinterland. In this respect, the chamber's efforts at developing a single, unified community surrounding Appleton proved remarkably successful. The more rural citizens relied on consumption, the greater their ability to achieve the same level of comfort, the same independence from the local landscape, enjoyed by their urban neighbors. By the late 1940s, the Fox River Valley was still characterized by distinctly urban and rural places. But as life in the region grew ever more commercialized — with the proliferation of highways and electrical power, the mounting volume and variety of mass-produced commodities, and the growing ease of shopping in Appleton — the majority of residents were increasingly able to enjoy the benefits of life in the city, regardless of whether or not they actually lived there.[30]

The Invisible Hand of Industry

Occasionally, valley residents were reminded that consumption relied every bit as much as production on the control of nature. In the early morning hours of February 22, 1922, a storm swept over the Fox River Valley. As temperatures dropped below freezing, the clouds poured a mixture of rain, snow, and sleet that turned quickly to ice as it hit the ground. By sunrise, the entire region was encased in a crystalline blanket. In Appleton, ice clung to everything—treetops, buildings, roads, and power lines—and its heavy weight took a devastating toll. "City Cut Off from Outside World," screamed the headline in the *Post-Crescent*. Hundreds of telephone and telegraph wires had crumbled during the storm, disrupting long-distance communication. The ice rendered highways and railroads impassable. Homes and businesses throughout the region lost power. After nightfall, the situation grew even worse. Strong winds caused additional trees and utility wires to collapse, and the city's street lighting system failed to operate. Darkened roads and sidewalks became "a maze of peril," with broken poles and downed power lines strewn everywhere. Residents were urged to light their porches if possible to reduce the risk of injury.[31]

Remarkably, the only serious casualties of the storm were two railroad men injured when their engine derailed and two horses electrocuted by a fallen power line. Even so, the ice wreaked tremendous havoc, leaving in its wake enough damage to keep repairmen busy for weeks. What made the storm so severe, ironically, was not the bad weather. "There was perhaps no more snow or ice than has accompanied previous storms," reported the *Post-Crescent*. Instead, much of its impact resulted from people's growing dependence on consumption. By 1922, the purchase of goods and services was thoroughly enmeshed in the daily routines of Appleton residents. As a result, when things such as power, traffic, and commerce ceased to flow, their failure paralyzed the community. According to the *Post-Crescent*, Appleton was "exiled as never before." Hundreds of residents were left without power. Entire neighborhoods were plunged into darkness, causing a run on local stores for candles and kerosene. Factories cut production as a result of a shortage of coal for their generators, and merchants were unable to restock basic goods. The sudden breakdown in the city's commercial infrastructure made the storm a disaster in a way that it would not have been only decades earlier. As one longtime citizen told the newspaper, there had been many winter storms during the past fifty years with greater snowfalls and colder temperatures. "Sleet storms were common," he recalled, "but as a rule [they] did very little damage."[32]

For Appleton's residents, the storm was a jarring reminder that the line between civilization and crude wilderness was defined by the human ability to control nature. Most producers in the city understood this well. For consumers, on the other hand, the relative freedom of purchasing goods and services made it possible to forget their ultimate reliance on the industrialized control of nature. Their fading awareness is easy to understand. By the early 1920s, Appleton's technological and economic infrastructure had disappeared into the background of daily life. Few people noticed the miles upon miles of transmission lines that carried power to homes and businesses, so routine was their presence. Trainloads of coal entered the city daily without drawing attention. Paved highways, though relatively new, were fast becoming mundane, as was the steady stream of traffic and commerce they carried to local retailers. Maintaining these systems was a constant struggle to control the material world. Someone had to extract resources from the landscape, convert them into energy, transportation, products, and services, and then deliver them for use by consumers. Yet the bulk of this labor remained invisible, as did the many entanglements with nature that such work required. So it was that employees of the local utility, the state and county highway departments, and various commercial establishments worked in anonymity, with little recognition from the thousands of citizens who benefited from their efforts.

Then came the ice storm. For a brief moment, the harsh reality of confronting an untamed natural landscape became glaringly apparent, as one by one the various mechanisms that once controlled its influence in Appleton failed to operate. Poles and power lines fell by the hundreds, becoming headline news. People waited anxiously for shipments of coal to area factories. The flow of traffic on local highways ceased entirely, and store shelves in the city's retail districts went briefly unstocked. As long as the city's technological and economic infrastructure functioned smoothly, no one noticed the constant effort that maintaining its systems required. When it failed, however, people's dependence on nature and those who conquered it grew suddenly and powerfully clear. Thus, in the storm's aftermath, residents followed daily reports on the efforts of engineers, linemen, and road crews to restore power and transportation. Overnight, their once invisible labor became heroic.[33]

The attention was short-lived. In the wake of the storm, Appleton's residents were freed once again to enjoy the security and comfort provided by local producers without giving these things a second thought. In many ways, this level of service had become a defining quality of life in the community, a measure of progress in the region. Thirty years earlier, in the 1890s, people endured a more adversarial relationship with nature, even in the city. Their difficulties were evident in the dependence of manufacturers on waterpower from the Fox River, in the hardship of moving from place to place across the landscape, and in the labor involved in heating a home, washing clothes, cooking a meal, or disposing of waste. By the 1920s, in contrast, Appleton's growing commercial infrastructure brought the discipline of human control even to these vestiges of untamed nature. Occasionally, the natural world would escape this control, as happened briefly during the ice storm. But the more developed the city's infrastructure grew, the more these incidents became exceptions to the rule.

In the coming years, such moments would grow rare indeed. By the late 1940s, the continued expansion of electric power, highways, and commerce brought new levels of convenience and reliability to the service enjoyed by local residents, both in Appleton and its surrounding countryside. In effect, the region's commercial infrastructure functioned as a kind of invisible hand, allowing citizens to participate in taming the wilderness without having to do any of the work involved in the effort. The more powerful this infrastructure became, the more it shielded consumers from their own use of the natural landscape. As a result, the productive roles of nature and industry alike gradually disappeared from view.

Commercial electric energy offers one of the best examples of the way in which consumption helped people to tame the natural landscape. In the nineteenth century, the act of converting resources to energy had required individual and often arduous labor on the part of valley residents. But as the use of electricity spread during the twentieth century, the entire region was knit together in a seamless web of power. By the late 1940s, most inhabitants of city and country alike were mere consumers of energy, acquiring their power with the flip of a switch. The remarkable ease of using electricity gave valley residents unprecedented power to shape the world around them.

People gained the ability to extend the useful hours of sunshine, to control the flow of water through their homes, and even to adjust the climate. In every case, the use of electricity tempered people's interactions with the material landscape by eliminating the inconvenience that once characterized these experiences. As a result, homes, offices, farms, and factories throughout the valley became increasingly regulated environments in which the variable forces of nature were controlled and bent toward human ends.

In the Fox River Valley, as in other parts of the country, electricity made its earliest and most dramatic impact on manufacturing. Speaking in 1932 at the fiftieth anniversary of Appleton's Vulcan Street power station, F. J. Sensenbrenner, president of the Kimberly-Clark Company, summarized electricity's impact on the paper industry. "Fifty years ago, and for many years hence, paper machinery was driven by water wheels connected directly with the equipment," he said. But as the industry's demand for power increased, the river proved inadequate. "The high speed machines required a more efficient power source. The space occupied by the large number of water wheels was valuable, and could be used to better advantage by the process end of the business. As the quality of paper was improved it called for closer regulation than could be had with the old wheels." According to Sensenbrenner, electricity offered the means of overcoming these difficulties, and its adoption brought tremendous success to papermaking in the region. "Today throughout the valley, the old water wheel is being replaced by the steam turbine," he concluded. Although most mills maintained their own generating facilities, increasingly they supplemented their power with energy provided by Wisconsin Michigan, the corporate descendant of Appleton's original Vulcan Street plant. The growing partnership between the city's utility and its numerous papermakers offered a vivid example of what electricity could mean for the industrial progress of the region.[34]

Understandably, given the context of the celebration, Sensenbrenner oversimplified the process by which manufacturers in the Fox River Valley adopted electricity. For many years after its introduction, electric power was used for lighting only. Then, once the mills began to utilize electricity for manufacturing, they often preferred to supply their own energy and avoid the need to depend on central stations. Yet if Sensenbrenner failed to convey the full complexity of electricity's adoption in the paper industry, he nonetheless captured the importance of the transformation. Electricity allowed factories to tailor their application of power to a variety of needs and individual machinery rather than being forced to structure their production methods around a single driving force. The more precise they became in employing energy, the higher the quality of the goods they produced. The compact size of electric motors permitted better use of space on factory floors, not to mention easier and less costly maintenance of machinery. As a result, between 1900 and 1924, the use of electricity in America's paper mills climbed from virtually nothing to more than 800,000 horsepower, or roughly 40 percent of the industry's overall consumption of energy. In the Fox River Valley, as elsewhere, electric power would become a standard tool in local mills, both as a means of lighting and as the primary force behind the operation of the industry's sophisticated machinery. What's more, much as Sensenbrenner suggested, manufacturers would increasingly turn to commercial utilities to supply their growing need for energy. The more electricity they purchased, in turn, the less they had to concern themselves with extracting power from the region's landscape.[35]

During this same period, electricity also began to transform domestic life in the Fox River Valley as people wired their homes to perform a growing array of tasks. Much as happened in the paper mills, electric power was initially used for illumination. In fact, residential consumers were even slower than manufacturers to adopt the varied applications of central station energy, a pattern that held throughout the United States. In 1929, electric appliances such as flatirons, vacuum cleaners, refrigerators, and washing machines were readily available in the national marketplace, yet less than 25 percent of all homes owned more than two such devices. Many people, of course, had yet to receive electricity in any form, especially in rural areas. But even among residents who used electric lighting, few people had the wherewithal to afford more than one or two additional appliances. Not until after the 1930s, when a series of New Deal programs brought modernized housing within the reach of millions of people, did the purchase of home appliances become commonplace. Yet in the Fox River Valley as elsewhere, the countless applications of electricity in the household were obvious, and local residents would seek to adopt its use more widely throughout the period.[36]

Not surprisingly, it was local utilities and merchants who most aggressively trumpeted the convenience of electric appliances. Valley newspapers in the 1930s and 1940s were filled with advertisements heralding the labor-saving potential of the electrically wired home. Most of these ads were aimed at women, who bore the brunt of the nation's housework. Cooking seemed especially well suited to benefit from electricity. According to a 1931 ad, owning the new Hotpoint range from General Electric was "like having a maid to watch the baking only it is more dependable than any human can be." People could place their dinners in the oven, set the timer, then simply walk away, and the Hotpoint range would do the cooking for them, turning itself on at the appointed hour, heating to a precise temperature, and then turning itself off when the meal was complete. "It keeps you out of the kitchen, this modern miracle way of cooking," promised the ad. In much the same way, electric power held the potential to revolutionize laundry, saving countless hours of back-breaking labor. "Like magic! Washday Is Done, You're Ready for Fun," declared one ad for an automatic washing machine. With precise timers, powerful agitators, and quick, reliable pumps, the modern washing machine could finish the family's laundry in no time and with little effort on the part of homemakers. "Monday hardly seems like washday," another retailer assured. In all, local advertisers promised a new world of convenience for consumers, a life made free of its burdensome labors by electricity and the machines it powered. Refrigerators, blenders, vacuum cleaners, sewing machines, space heaters—the list of appliances grew longer with each passing year. And in every case, the improvements they offered were the same. "Convenience," explained one simple ad from Wisconsin Michigan. "Electric service is the 'heart' of a modern home!"[37]

In large part, what made the electrified home so modern was the way it allowed its occupants to improve the household environment by controlling the vagaries of nature. Among the earliest and most basic ways that electricity accomplished this feat was by turning night into day. Human beings have a long history of burning things to make light, but electricity performed the task in such a way that natural resources became nearly invisible in the process. Ordinarily, when a fire burns, it consumes its fuel at the site of combustion. Thus, people can see a piece of wood being destroyed by the flames in a stove. Light is often a by-product of burning, but for obvious reasons, an open flame is difficult to control and poorly suited to illuminating a home or business. Over the centuries, technological advances such as the candle and the oil lamp began to separate light and fuel, moving combustion to a wick that served as a conduit for the material to be consumed. Flames in these devices were safer, brighter, more easily controlled, and portable. Yet still, they burned with a seemingly natural fire. Electricity, by contrast, placed unprecedented distance between light and fuel. Power generated by the flow of a river or the burning of coal could be transported into homes and businesses dozens and later hundreds of miles away, where it was then used for illumination. There was no recognizable flame within the electric lamp, and little need ever to think about the energy consumed. Taken together, the various generators, transmission lines, and lamps used to produce electric lighting comprised a kind of industrialized flame, a technological recreation of a natural phenomenon whose constituent parts were carefully isolated and manipulated in order to maximize their usefulness. "Electric light is the safest, most economical, cleanest and best light there is," declared the Appleton Electric Company in a 1920 advertisement. Its widespread adoption by the mid-twentieth century allowed valley residents to extend the useful hours of daylight with unprecedented ease, and without regard for the sun itself.[38]

In much the same way, later applications of electricity did even more to reduce the hardships of nature in local homes. Before the advent of electric power, the hearth and fire had been the center of many households, providing heat, light, and a means of cooking to generations of families. But electricity, along with gas, made the open hearth irrelevant by permitting the industrialization of its many functions. Space heaters and furnaces offered warmth in the winter without the need for wood or coal. The electric range allowed residents to prepare meals in the same way, confining the heat of cooking to gleaming metal cabinets that more closely resembled furniture than a working fire. "So perfectly insulated is a Hotpoint oven," promised one valley utility, "that when the heat is 350° inside, ice water set on top keeps cool." Refrigeration, too, became increasingly convenient. Like many Americans, alley residents had once used iceboxes to preserve food by retarding its decomposition. But electric refrigerators accomplished this same task more efficiently, and without relying on the wintertime harvesting of ice from rivers and lakes. Finally, no technology better illustrates electricity's ability to control nature than air conditioning, a twentieth-century convenience that owed its existence to affordable electric power. Before the advent of electricity, people cooled their homes by taking advantage of natural fluctuations in temperature throughout the day. During the morning and evening hours, they opened windows to allow the cooler air inside, while in the afternoon they closed the windows tight against the heat. Air conditioning, by contrast, required that windows be shut permanently in order to establish a firm line between the inside and the outside worlds. The engineers who pioneered the technology hoped for nothing less than a system of "man-made weather," an indoorclimate in which nature was controlled by human hands. The eventual popularity of window air conditioners fell short of this dream. But the new appliances nonetheless allowed people to enjoy a more comfortable existence, insulated by electricity from the harshest elements of the natural world.[39]

Without question, the influence of electricity in the home was felt most dramatically in the valley's rural areas. As in most of the United States, farmers were the last of the region's citizens to receive central station power. Even in the 1920s, most private utilities still declined to extend service beyond their urban boundaries. With rural populations scattered, the cost of building transmission lines across miles of open landscape seemed prohibitively high, leaving farmers isolated from the benefits of modern energy. Into this situation stepped President Franklin D. Roosevelt and the helping hand of the New Deal. In 1935, Roosevelt issued an executive order creating the Rural Electrification Administration, a large-scale effort designed to extend electricity into the impoverished American countryside. The REA operated as a lending institution, funneling money to states, municipalities, and utilities to help defray the costs of electrification. Like many New Deal programs, the REA failed to perform exactly as it was intended. The sudden involvement of public officials in a formerly private industry caused mistrust between the agency and commercial utilities. As a result, the two groups did little to work together, and the majority of REA money went to local cooperatives. In the Fox River Valley and throughout eastern Wisconsin, REA cooperatives played only a minimal role. In the western half of the state, by contrast, settlement was more scattered, and the agency's impact was greater. But even the threat of federal competition spurred the valley's utilities to action, bringing a gradual extension of service to the region's rural customers. Much the same was true throughout the United States. In 1935, only one in ten American farms had been wired for electricity. By the mid-1950s, on the other hand, over 92 percent received dependable central station service.[40]

Electricity brought dramatic improvements to life in the valley's countryside. Before the extension of power lines, farmers maintained a fairly traditional working relationship with the natural landscape. Rarely had they enjoyed the kinds of comforts to which urban residents were long accustomed. Automobiles and paved highways did much to end this isolation, but it was electrification that brought the countryside fully within the urban-industrial world. The advent of electricity provided farm families with an array of modern technologies, including lighting, refrigeration, and a house full of small appliances. With electric pumps, even indoor plumbing became a reality, complete with flush toilets, washing machines, water heaters, and kitchen garbage disposals. More than any single appliance or machine, the radio best symbolized the growing urbanization of the countryside. Radio gave farmers access to all that civilization had to offer: entertainment, news, education, and commerce. Powered initially by batteries and tuned to the ephemeral airwaves, it was a novel and nearly magical device. "The finest in radio reception, with flawless FM, and with AM 'reach' that puts the world at your fingertips," promised one local retailer. The cultural implications of electricity were important. But what many farmers truly valued was its ability to save them labor. "Electricity has not only banished kerosene," explained one local paper in a 1948 editorial, "but [it] provided a dependable flow of vital energy that can be turned on or off at will to perform many of those formerly muscular tasks that on a modern farm would compel a man to be in more than one place at the same time." Farmers could utilize small, versatile electric motors for any number of chores, from milking cows and lifting hay to cutting wood and sharpening tools. By the mid-1950s, productivity on the farm had grown substantially, with output per man-hour of labor rising by roughly 92 percent. Much of this productivity undoubtedly came from the increased use of tractors, trucks, and fertilizer. But electricity played a crucial role in reducing the physical effort required to farm.[41]

Here then, in the growing material comfort made possible by electricity, was the essence of its influence on people's interactions with nature. Whether consumers used it to cook, vacuum, cool their homes, pump water from a well, or run their farms, they did so without lifting a finger to extract energy from the natural landscape. Generating electric power required the exploitation of resources. But so far removed from this task were the customers who actually used it that the average citizen experienced little of the heat, hardship, and toil associated with its production. Almost magically, electricity converted this labor into push-button convenience, eliminating a once vivid material connection between humans and the natural landscape. Consequently, for the majority of consumers, electricity became a wonder of the modern era, a creation of science and technology with little apparent connection to nature. Its use helped to fashion a new, more comfortable world for valley residents, gradually transforming the homes, factories, and farmsteads of the region into rationalized islands of human control set apart from the surrounding landscape.

In this respect, the influence of electricity was mirrored almost exactly by the expanding network of paved highways surrounding Appleton. In the early 1920s, the Chamber of Commerce bragged about the county's 135 miles of concrete roads. Thirty years later, the system had grown to just under 520 miles, not including an additional 890 miles of local roads and city streets. Together, this network of paved highways connected every town, village, home, and business in the region with a web of commercialized transportation. Roads provided local citizens with a convenient means of getting from place to place, no matter where they lived. Highway 41 carried the bulk of the traffic passing through Appleton. At any point along the route, at any time of year, between 2,000 and 3,000 vehicles could be expected to pass in a given day. To watch this stream of traffic was, in some ways, to take the pulse of life in the valley: the daily rush of people driving back and forth to work; the surge of weekend outings during the warm summer months; the steady flow of goods and produce traveling to market.[42]

Yet for most motorists, by 1948 the experience of driving on Highway 41 had become mundane. Arthur Hirst, the Highway Commission's first chief engineer, had been accurate in his prediction nearly thirty years earlier: the better the roads became, the less people had to think about the effort required to build and maintain them. By the 1940s, if drivers considered this work at all, they likely did so as taxpayers noting the agency's ever-increasing budgets. In 1949, the commission spent nearly $7 million managing the highways in Division No. 3, an area that encompassed the Fox River Valley. The money purchased a variety of things: 330,000 square yards of pavement, 1.3 million pounds of structural steel, the maintenance of 1,500 miles of state-controlled roadway, and the labor of almost 900 men. These expenditures seem abstract in the neatly recorded tables of the commission's budgets, but the work they describe was real. During the winter of 1948 and 1949, for example, the commission spent just under $175,000 to battle ice and snow in the valley—money that paid for the men, machinery, and materials needed to keep the highways open. Local citizens might have seen the occasional snowplow that winter or witnessed the spreading of salt, but few people were forced to clear the roads themselves. Instead, they enjoyed the commercialized convenience of paying someone else to do it for them.[43]

Electricity and paved highways were merely two examples of a much larger consumer economy, each aspect of which promised to create new levels of material comfort from the formerly untamed world of nature. Here, a second look at the efforts of retailers in the Fox River Valley can be instructive. No theme is more evident in the ads of local merchants than people's ability to control their personal surroundings simply by consuming. "Be comfortably cool," declared a retailer of electric fans. "Have hot water during all 12 months of the year," said the same distributor in selling its automatic water heater. "End garbage problems forever," promised a retailer of the new Hotpoint disposal. Often, these appeals focused on the way consumption could minimize the burdens of daily life. "It's the closest thing to magic you've ever seen," boasted one Sears ad for a new Kenmore washing machine. "Just put in the clothes, add soap . . . set two little dials . . . go away and forget it." The washer performed every task automatically, making laundry "fun, not work." With fewer burdens to weigh them down, consumers were freed, in the view of merchants, to enjoy all that life could offer. "Life's lots more fun with plenty of hot water all the time," assured one retailer. "From the first thing in the morning, when that plentiful supply of steaming hot water eases you through your daily shaving struggle," continued the ad, "'til you finish off a tough day with a care-easing hot shower or a steamy soak in the tub . . . your water heater's right in there, making life a lot easier to take." By this logic, the world of the modern consumer was not just more convenient. It was more authentic because people were liberated from much of the drudgery that once prevented them from pursuing their own fulfillment.[44]

In this way, consumption empowered shoppers to change their lives in almost any way imaginable: they could adjust the climate inside their homes, eat whatever they wished, travel whenever and wherever they pleased, listen to the music of their choice, and dress in any manner they desired, simply by making the necessary purchases. "Get what you want for yourself, your family and your home," advised one ad in 1931. Power, individual freedom, and authenticity—according to merchants, these things, too, were included with every sale. Whether or not consumers accepted these appeals is an open question. The text of commercial advertisements must be read with caution. They typically reveal as much about the aggressive efforts of retailers to shape consumer behavior as they say about shoppers themselves. Nevertheless, by the 1940s, the sheer number and variety of goods available to valley residents created unprecedented opportunities. To the extent that advertising illustrates even the existence of these possibilities, it offers a valuable illustration of the changing material circumstances of an increasingly commercialized world.[45]

No matter how people in the Fox River Valley exercised their power as consumers, it would be hard to overstate their growing dependence on the purchase of goods and services. By the late 1940s, the region's commercial infrastructure had become an expected, almost unnoticed part of life, far more powerful and reliable than it had been just twenty years earlier. On December 15, 1948, two days before the state Committee on Water Pollution began its hearing in Green Bay, a sleet storm once again descended on the Fox River Valley. According to the Appleton *Post-Crescent,* the region was blanketed by "a thin coat of ice that caused automobiles to skid wildly, made walking hazardous and interfered with bus and train schedules." But in contrast to what happened in 1922, valley residents experienced little hardship and isolation. Instead, life was restored to normal within hours, thanks largely to the expanded networks of power, transportation, and retail exchange that now comprised the valley's commercial infrastructure. "Both city and county highway departments began sanding last night and went back out in full force this morning," noted the paper. By 1948, it was still possible for nature to escape the authority of human control. But these instances were rare and much less disruptive when they did occur.[46]

Given the growing pervasiveness and power of commerce in the Fox River Valley, people's rising consumption of goods and services inevitably had profound consequences on their understanding of nature. It is not just that consumers lost sight of the material resources on which they depended. Even more important, they gained a newfound ability to seek out and experience nature's pleasant amenities. "Enjoy Yourself!" announced a 1937 advertisement in the Appleton *Post-Crescent.* "Have a good time in the good old summertime. This is the season to forget for a little while, the clock, the petty routine, and all the tiny tiresome tasks and obligations that, unchecked, make life a bore." Nature in the view of local merchants played a well-defined and highly circumscribed role. With the majority of valley residents no longer actively involved in the extraction or manipulation of resources, the natural landscape came to function as just another consumer amenity. In contrast to the workaday world that characterized the bulk of daily life, Appleton's retailers urged people to head for the great outdoors. There, with the help of local merchants, they could find all the enjoyment, convenience, and relaxation that nature was meant to afford. "There are steaks to broil in the woods at sunset, bikes to ride on the by-ways . . . and meadows to explore. There are long lazy afternoons to drowse away with a book." All this could be had with a few easy purchases, implied the newspaper. "Advertisers in the Post-Crescent are waiting to show you how!"[47]

By the mid-twentieth century, merchants in the Fox River Valley were hardly alone in suggesting this use of nature. So complete was the human control of the natural landscape that few people ever worried about confronting the harsh realities of true wilderness. Instead, no matter where they lived—on a farm, in a small town, or in the middle of Appleton—residents were free to enjoy the material comfort made possible by commercialization. Put another way, the valley had become a consumer society, a landscape in which the use of nature as a means of survival for local citizens had been replaced by their growing dependence on the purchase of goods and services. The very convenience of life in this commercialized world gradually altered people's perceptions of nature. In a sense, consumer society functioned as a kind of filter, a window through which people were allowed to enjoy the landscape's beauty and splendor while remaining safely protected from its threatening qualities. Yet because so few consumers participated directly in the work required to tame the landscape, they often failed to appreciate how artificial their view from this window had become.

The View from the Window

In September 1922, when residents of the Fox River Valley gathered in Green Bay to celebrate the completion of Highway 15, they were joined by representatives of Marinette, a neighboring city 40 miles up the shore of the bay and the northernmost terminus of the route. Highway 15 had yet to be paved all the way to Marinette. Nevertheless, the road had already proven valuable to the community. The city's tourist business, in particular, began to thrive with the route's improvement as people flocked to northern Wisconsin to fish and swim and enjoy the natural beauty. Local officials reported a 200 percent increase that summer alone in the number of visitors to the area, most of whom had made the trip on Highway 15. In addition to good roads, Marinette boasted of several other attractions, including a brand new automobile camp located in a 30-acre park near the center of town. The camp offered motorists all the comforts of home in a splendid setting of "virgin Norway and white pine." There were several cottages with porches in the front and back and a full complement of amenities, including "city water works and sewerage, kitchen sink, writing desk and equipment, excellent lavatory accommodations, drinking bubblers, shower baths, local and long distance telephone service, [and] daily newspapers." According to the camp's manager, the park welcomed between thirty and eighty registered guests per night.[48]

No aspect of the valley's commercial infrastructure better illustrates its influence on people's understanding of nature than highways. The better the roads became, the more drivers were able to enjoy a relaxing, scenic, and often pleasant experience while motoring across Wisconsin's landscape. Yet paradoxically, the greater the efforts of the state Highway Commission to harness nature, the easier it was for people to experience a scenic drive as if the landscapes through which they traveled were natural, and even wild. Before the advent of paved roads, the fields, forests, hills, and rivers, as well as the sheer distances that comprised the valley's landscape, had been nearly inseparable from the human labor required to move around, over, and through them. But in the age of concrete, transportation became a consumer good. As a result, traveling no longer required work, and these natural features ceased to be obstacles. For drivers, the valley's landscape assumed a new set of meanings, associations stripped of all human involvement save the passive acts of observation and appreciation. It became, in a word, scenery, an aspect of nature that may have seemed entirely natural, but was in fact partly the creation of industry.

By the 1920s, the experience of Marinette was typical of many Wisconsin communities, including those of the Fox River Valley, as people took to the highways in search of the great outdoors. In the valley itself, the tourist economy remained limited through the 1950s. But the region was well situated to profit from the growing interest in Wisconsin's natural wonders, especially among motorists. The valley stood at the southern boundary of the state's northern forests, the so-called cutover district, where lumber interests had once mined the landscape for its thick stands of pine and other trees. After the decline of lumbering in the early twentieth century and a failed attempt to encourage farming in the cutover, northern Wisconsin turned to reforestation and tourism as a means of revitalizing its economy. In the Fox River Valley, local highways provided several of the most direct links between these forests and the cities of Milwaukee and Chicago. Consequently, by the 1920s the valley began to serve as a gateway into Wisconsin's emerging tourist playground.[49]

Traveling specifically to enjoy scenic landscapes had a long history in the United States. In the 1830s, more than a few Americans bought passage on the Erie Canal solely to experience the beauty of what was then a wilderness in upstate New York. Later in the nineteenth century, the advent of railroads did even more to encourage this use of transportation. The unprecedented speed of the "iron horse" fundamentally altered the appearance of the landscape for travelers. "The slow unwinding view seen from a wagon or a horse was transformed into a sliding world that seemed to move by while the passenger sat immobile," wrote one historian. "The eye was not prepared to see these hurtling objects glimpsed in a rush, and had to learn to focus on the distant panorama." By the twentieth century, paved highways offered motorists much the same view of the landscape. But the growing ease and affordability of driving democratized these pleasures in a way that trains never had. In particular, automobiles personalized the liberty of convenient transportation. Drivers were not confined to scheduled times and predetermined routes. Highways could take them anywhere at any time—in the evening, on weekends, even for short trips over lunch. Equally important, car ownership proliferated during the first half of the twentieth century, making their influence and availability a fact of life for most Americans, regardless of wealth.[50]

In this way, paved roads and the cars they carried brought scenic nature within easy reach of most Americans. "Before the automobile came, human beings were limited to the front and back yard," declared one observer in 1923. "With the automobile the entire nation can visit the entire nation. To the edge of the sea or lake, or to the mountain top, from the heart of the city, means merely 'stepping on the gas.'" In Wisconsin, the thousands of motorists who annually went searching for nature often headed to the northern part of the state (Figure 13). In many cases, they described their journeys as both symbolic escapes from urban life and efforts to experience nature in its purest form. One typical example is W. H. Reed, a Milwaukee businessman who opened a summer camp for tourists in the cutover. In an article for the *Wisconsin Motorist,* he described his yearly journey through the Fox River Valley. "The trip itself is a pleasure," he wrote. "Northward from Milwaukee is a wonderful farming country, and for miles you skirt the shores of Lake Winnebago and up the Fox River Valley. Leaving Appleton you begin to drive into the heart of the wilderness." There, according to Reed, motorists entered a primitive land of forests, lakes, and winding rivers. "The further you go the more entrancing becomes the scenery," he reported. "Soon you are away and remote from the haunts of man . . . and everywhere, on every hand are lakes, lakes, lakes." Reed was not alone in his preference for unspoiled scenery. The pages of the *Wisconsin Motorist* were filled with articles and advertisements promising "a taste of Nature at her best," the "forests of old Wisconsin," and the "out of doors, like nature made it." According to Reed, these experiences provided a necessary retreat from the pressures of urban living. "Our modern life," he wrote, "is so strenuous that we must get a change of this character." A month spent on a northern lake, "is a renewal of youth," he added. "For a time we live instead of struggling to make a livlihood [*sic*]."[51]

In many ways, Reed and his fellow enthusiasts echoed the sentiments of another, more famous American nature lover, Henry David Thoreau. Thoreau is the great nineteenth-century romantic who once declared that "in Wildness is the preservation of the World." He, too, believed in the restorative powers of untamed nature. "Life consists with wildness," he said. "The most alive is the wildest. Not yet subdued to man, its presence refreshes him." But unlike Reed, Thoreau had little interest in the public roads of his own day. The arms and legs of cities, he called them, avenues of commerce and culture and, worse yet, politics—things that spoiled the highways for the proper appreciation of nature. "Roads are made for horses and men of business," he sniffed. "I do not travel in them much." By contrast, when Americans in the 1920s sought to explore the natural world, most often they did so behind the wheels of their cars, driving on well-paved highways at ever-increasing speeds. "The thing that has opened the eyes of the people of the middle west to the beauties of Northern Wisconsin," explained Reed, "are the improved road conditions."[52]

Figure 13. Motoring in the scenic north woods, ca. 1920s. Courtesy of the Neville Public Museum of Brown County, Image No. 568B.

But if highways helped to expose the wonders of nature, they did so only by distorting the character of the natural landscape. Very little that drivers experienced in northern Wisconsin could fairly be described as wilderness. Instead, drivers carried the hallmarks of civilization along with them wherever they went—in their preference for tourist camps and the comforts of modern living, in the roads on which they traveled, and most important, in the ways they came to use the landscape. Though paved roads allowed drivers remarkable freedom to explore the natural world, they unavoidably tamed that world in the process by transforming its beauty into a consumer amenity: in other words, by doing away with much of the toil and inconvenience that moving through wilderness had formerly entailed. "Have you been wondering where you can find a worth-while place where Nature is kind?" asked one writer in the *Wisconsin Motorist*. For a growing number of people, that place was the open road.[53]

Highways tamed the landscape in many ways. Distance, for example, had once been the chief natural obstacle to travel, but paved roads served to compact the land as if distance itself had been annihilated. The automobile, explained one enthusiast, "enables a man living twenty miles from seashore or lake front to use the lake or sea as though he lived at its edge." Such a miracle was possible only through the tremendous labor embodied in the roads themselves, not to mention the cars people drove. Motorists were literally carried along by the work that other people performed. "Every six miles or so," said W. H. Reed of Highway 15, "you will find a state [maintenance] patrolman with a badge on his hat . . . working to keep the road in condition." This work made driving possible. Without it, few people would have seen much of the landscape at all, let alone admired its beauty.[54]

This kind of security extended even to the automobiles that people drove. When cars first took to the roadways, they were little more than "horseless carriages," four-wheeled open buggies pulled by an engine instead of an animal. But as driving became more popular, manufacturers equipped their cars with an array of amenities. The closed car was particularly important. Fixed roofs were often said to appeal especially to women, but drivers of both sexes enjoyed the protection they offered from dust, rain, and the heat of the sun. "The well-built closed car affords, in summer and winter, a greater measure of comfort than is possible to obtain in the open type of vehicle," said the *Wisconsin Motorist* in 1920. "And comfort, after all, is the factor that most appeals to the present-day motor car owner." Heaters and radios, too, added much to the pleasure of driving, allowing people to transform their cars into mobile homes away from home, making the wilderness far more attractive.[55]

So too did a comfortable place for motorists to stay at night while traveling on the road. During the first half of the twentieth century, automobile camps and roadside motels became an expected feature of nearly every major American highway. The tourist business in northern Wisconsin grew to depend on just this kind of development, as well as more elaborate attractions such as tourist resorts and summer lodges. "Excellent hotels have sprung up all through this country," assured W. H. Reed, "wholesome homes with all the facilities of civilization." In the Fox River Valley, local communities rushed to create their own accommodations. By the early 1920s, Neenah, Appleton, Kaukauna, and Green Bay each had established public camp sites near Highway 15, providing picnic grounds, fireplaces, weather information, and free maps. Hotels, too, began to cater to passing motorists. As already noted, John Conway, proprietor of Appleton's Sherman House, was one of the city's most vocal proponents of good roads. He advertised in tour books of popular highway routes, calling attention to his "modern hotel" and its "desirable accommodations for auto parties," including a garage just half a block away.[56]

Much as happened with electricity and household appliances, local merchants who sold automobiles, gasoline, and other traveling accessories were quick to advertise the recreational use of nature made possible by their products. "Highways are Happy Ways," declared one ad for the Standard Oil Company. "The highways lead to lovely lands! Starred with lakes and ribboned by silver streams! To rugged mountains and lacy shores. To quaint hamlets and beautiful cities." Drivers could visit all these places with the help of Standard's quality fuel. "It's a sparkling, dynamic, volatile gasoline," assured the ad. Its purchase would give motorists a newfound independence. "You may pick the spots that strike your fancy. And follow the highways to your heart's content." Once again as with other products, consumers were sold not just cars or fuel, but power, freedom, and authenticity. With Standard's Red Crown gasoline, for example, valley residents could enjoy their automobiles as they were meant to be used. "What is your car to you?" asked the company. "A mere machine to get you around, or a friendly agent to help you get the most out of life?"[57]

Thus, as early as the 1920s, the construction of paved highways and the development they encouraged transformed Wisconsin's natural landscape into a kind of tourist playground. Places that had once been largely inaccessible, even to nearby residents, were suddenly opened to the gaze of a driving public, their aesthetic charms revealed. But if motorists hoped to find "the forests of old Wisconsin," they could hardly do so from behind the wheels of their cars, for the "out of doors, like Nature made it," no longer truly existed. This fact was never in doubt to the engineers of the state Highway Commission, who realized better than anyone the work required to make Wisconsin's natural beauty accessible. "Wisconsin is unique among its sister states for the variety of its scenery," bragged the commission. "It is bordered on two sides by great inland oceans. It contains thousands of fresh water lakes, beautiful rivers, innumerable brooks, rugged hills and cliffs, [and] wide cultivated areas, both rolling and flat." But what transformed these natural features into scenery, at least in part, was the fact that they no longer stood in the way of people's movement. "There is a close relationship between highway systems and scenery," explained the commission. "Highways are the means by which the traveler views the natural features characteristic of the state." With hundreds of miles of paved roads crisscrossing the Fox River Valley, local residents no longer had to expend their own energy to ford the region's streams, climb its hills, or drag a team of horses across its fields. Instead, people were freed to drive with relative ease over, around, and through these parts of the landscape, a liberty that made it easier for travelers to admire the aesthetic qualities of the features they passed along the way.[58]

As with many consumer goods, the more people came to appreciate the convenience, reliability, and safety of highway transportation, the more they expected. Already in 1930, state officials noted that many drivers thought highways were incomplete if they consisted only of "pavement and the necessary structures." In addition, explained the commission, "public opinion is coming to recognize and demand that a road must be beautiful as well as serviceable." With this growing consumer preference in mind, the commission launched a slow but steady campaign to beautify Wisconsin's highways. In the Fox River Valley, caring for local roadsides had long been a concern of civic groups, particularly women's clubs, which planted flowers and shrubs near intersections and worked to limit billboard advertising. But the commission's plan, predictably, was more systematic and ambitious. "A highway is beautiful largely to the extent that it has the appearance of nature undisturbed," declared the commission. State engineers had no intention of making the roads more natural. Road building, after all, was a struggle against nature, an effort to isolate drivers within an environment controlled by human hands. By this logic, beautification was merely an extension of this control, an effort to construct better scenery by masking the artifice of the roads. As one report casually noted, "highway beautification must simulate nature."[59]

Hence, the commission did what it could to create a seamless boundary between highways and the surrounding landscape. As with all its goals, the agency's first priority remained the smooth flow of traffic. "It is not the practice of this department to plant and seed for beauty only," said the commission. "All of the work done must serve some utilitarian purpose." Engineers, for example, required that every inch of land within the boundaries of roads be covered with vegetation unless otherwise paved. Planting the roadsides with trees, shrubs, and grass improved the highways' appearance, but it also prevented erosion and discouraged the formation of snowdrifts during the winter, efforts that reduced long-term costs. But the work of beautification could take more aggressive forms as well. Trees were not simply planted in rows. They were "grouped in masses at stream crossings and other strategic points" in order to create a natural appearance. Likewise, engineers endeavored to frame scenic vistas for drivers, either by locating roads to ensure the best views of local landscapes or by screening unattractive sights with stands of trees. By 1940, the commission had even begun to establish waysides along its major routes, with picnic tables, restroom facilities, and parklike grounds that offered shade and attractive views.[60]

Few valley residents would ever look at the concrete structures and speeding traffic of the region's major highways and claim that roads were natural. Yet few people realized just how unnatural their view from these roads had become as well. No matter how wild or pristine Wisconsin's scenery appeared to be, in a sense, what drivers saw through the windows of their cars was yet another illusion created by their growing dependence on commerce. Drivers had become consumers, not merely of transportation, but also of the natural beauty they viewed along the way. Highways did not create this scenery, but they did make it easier for people to see by giving them a means of passing through the landscape with little to no effort. In this respect, Henry David Thoreau had been correct in his assessment of roads. The highways were urban places, extensions of civilization, and everything that travelers did within their boundaries was shaped by the industrialized control of nature that made the highways possible.

Of course, the control of nature was hardly confined to the roads. By the late 1940s, this kind of consumption had become a pervasive aspect of life, making it easy for valley residents to enjoy nature without worrying about the landscape's unpleasant realities. The early decades of the twentieth century witnessed a boom in outdoor recreation, a widening array of activities that included fishing, hunting, boating, hiking, swimming, playing golf and tennis, hosting backyard barbecues, and of course, driving for the simple pleasure of scenery. Highways were only part of the budding infrastructure that emerged to support these pursuits. When valley residents took to the great outdoors, they did so with the benefit of deluxe hotels, state parks with modern facilities, lakes and forests stocked with game, and hundreds of stores selling outdoor accessories. Put a slightly different way, by the mid-twentieth century, the view that many drivers came to see through their windshields—of a landscape both comfortable and yet somehow wild—was fast becoming the view from consumer society in general.

5

Enjoying the Great Outdoors

On April 1, 1947, residents of the Fox River Valley joined voters throughout the state to decide the fate of daylight saving time in Wisconsin. First tried locally as a federal measure to conserve fuel during World War I, daylight saving received a second wartime trial in the 1940s. At first glance, the issue seems to have little relevance to the enjoyment of nature. By 1947, however, many valley residents had growing plans for an extra hour of summer sunshine. When lawmakers asked citizens if they wanted to make the scheme permanent, the issue sparked a lengthy public debate on whether outdoor recreation comprised a legitimate use of the natural landscape. As a result, the referendum on daylight saving offers a vivid snapshot of consumption's impact on the human relationship to nature.[1]

In the days leading up to the vote, newspapers in the Fox River Valley were filled with angry letters from people on both sides of the question. As in most parts of the state, opinion divided along the boundary between city and country. Most proponents of daylight saving time lived in urban areas where nature functioned as a kind of garden retreat, a place of escape from the human world of work, cities, and industry. Surrounded as they were by the structures and systems of consumer society, they looked to daylight saving as a means of restoring part of an older, more natural way of life that they identified with rural areas. "I am an average city man with limited knowledge of farm life," began one letter written by a citizen of distant Milwaukee. "Here is the man on his farm operating almost as a complete unit—to a certain extent his own boss—out in the open with all beautiful nature his . . . day in and day out." According to the writer, the farmer's lot was an enviable one. Many farmers, he admitted, possessed limited means, and they often looked tired from their labors. Yet because they spent so much time in the outdoors, they maintained a certain "air of freedom," a "healthy vigorous cheerful look of a man feeling . . . happy in his work." Urban residents, by contrast, were denied these invigorating natural influences. "The city air in winter is somewhat smoke laden," he complained, "and many city people get very little sunshine." Daylight saving would provide these urbanites "an opportunity to leave their cooped up places of employment an hour earlier each evening," time they could use during the summer to enjoy their parks and gardens or to escape the city entirely for a picnic. "I have observed thousands of these inside workers," wrote the Milwaukee resident. "I have always arrived at the same conclusion—if these people could only have more time out in the fresh air and sunlight."[2]

Meanwhile, for inhabitants of the valley's rural areas, many of whom were farmers, outdoor recreation had little relevance to their daily experience with nature. At a time when electricity, highways, and the comforts of modern living were still relatively new, theirs was a world in which the natural rhythms of landscape and season defined people's labor, not their leisure. "What need does the farmer have for daylight savings time?" asked one Green Bay resident. "He is at work long before daylight, toils all during daylight, and finishes his day's work by electric light after the sun has gone down!" While city residents viewed shifting the clocks as an opportunity to escape their working lives, most rural citizens felt the change was interfering in theirs. "The farmer before, now, and always must operate by the time given him by Old Sol," insisted one opponent of the measure. "A farmer cannot afford to knock-off work at two or three hours before sundown, just because it is such-and-such a time." In this view, daylight saving was a self-serving effort on the part of urban residents to manipulate the natural day. "We still cannot get away from nature," complained another letter writer. "We still could not grow crops in winter if we called the month of January June; neither can we make hay an hour earlier by just turning the clock one hour in advance." If urban residents wanted an extra hour each evening to relax in the outdoors, then according to many rural citizens, they could get up an hour earlier. "Who benefits [from daylight saving]?" asked a third opponent. "No one but the playboys for their pleasure only." Quipped a final critic: "If you think farmers got such a nice life why don't you buy a farm?"[3]

On election day, Wisconsin voters turned out in record numbers to cast their ballots on daylight saving time. The issue was rejected by 55 percent of the electorate. Much as expected, opposition to the measure came from the state's rural districts: the less urbanized the town, village, or county, the heavier the vote against daylight saving. In the valley's Outagamie County, for example, Appleton gave strongest approval to the measure, passing the change in time by over 1,600 votes. The neighboring communities of Kaukauna, Kimberly, and Little Chute added similar support. In contrast, beyond these urban boundaries, the measure faltered badly as, one by one, the county's smaller towns and villages voiced their opposition. Seymour rejected daylight saving by a vote of 341 to 28. The citizens of Hortonville said no 228 to 92. In tiny Maine, the count was 100 to only 3. Individually, these communities were small compared with Appleton, but their greater numbers carried the day. When all the ballots were counted, Outagamie County rejected daylight saving time by a vote of 11,192 to 10,211, a pattern that was repeated throughout the state.[4]

Despite the failure of daylight saving to win approval in 1947, the debate surrounding the issue illustrates the growing impact of consumption on people's ideas of nature in the mid-twentieth century. That supporters of the measure lived primarily in the cities was no coincidence. Their emphasis on enjoying the great outdoors, and their resulting support for daylight saving, both resulted from their increasing distance from the use of nature as a means of production. This fact was not lost on rural opponents of the measure. "Aren't there enough sunshiny days for you to go shopping?" complained one resident of the countryside. "On sunny days the farmer is working longer hours than ever raising bumper crops to make more pork chops and dairy products for city residents." In the eyes of many rural citizens, to ignore the landscape's role in producing these commodities, not to mention the people who farmed it, was to jeopardize the very survival of cities. "Enjoy your daylight saving time playing golf, motoring, or what you will," warned a second critic. "What [the farmer] wants above all else is your respect and appreciation of the work he does for the city dwellers." But far from respect, daylight saving appeared to be just another elite infringement on the traditional, more natural way of life of those who produced. Here, farmers earned the support of several urban residents who identified with the importance of labor. "As for the city folks, many are now working on shifts, [and] it would not help them," one housewife pointed out. "We shall grant that some will receive more time for pleasure," declared another Appleton resident, "but for the man with the work shirt, the fellow who keeps the wheels of the mill turning, the farmer who always is rising before sunrise and the man who has put in his number of working years, this referendum is uncalled for."[5]

Clearly, at the heart of the conflict over daylight saving was an idea of nature that owed its existence to consumption. In the Fox River Valley, as in most parts of the country, consumption was an outgrowth of the region's cities and the industrial and commercial development they spawned. Where local citizens had once relied on this infrastructure to provide necessities and a few conveniences, by the late 1940s, a rising number of residents were interested in its ability to deliver outdoor recreation. The fact that most of these people still lived in the valley's urban areas was evident in the referendum on daylight saving in 1947. But their ranks were growing. Exactly ten years later, in April 1957, daylight saving time would win approval in another statewide ballot. It became a permanent fixture of summertime in the Fox River Valley, as did the mounting demands for outdoor recreation that daylight saving came to symbolize.[6]

The Conservation of Recreation

To better understand the link between consumption and outdoor recreation, it is helpful to examine once again those people who worked hardest to promote both. This chapter looks first to conservationists. Shortly after returning from President Theodore Roosevelt's White House conference on conservation in 1908, Wisconsin's Governor James O. Davidson took action. Joining legislatures and chief executives from thirty-five other states across the country, Davidson appointed a state Conservation Commission to assume responsibility for safeguarding Wisconsin's natural resources. Outdoor recreation was not on the group's agenda. In its initial 63-page report, published in 1909, the governor and various members of the commission discussed a variety of problems and potential reforms. For Davidson, the issue of greatest concern was "the undeveloped water powers of the state," which he regarded as "the most valuable of its natural resources." Other members issued reports on

Wisconsin's forests and soils. In each case, the commission focused exclusively on the economic value of these resources for manufacturers, lumbermen, and farmers. Among the only times the report alluded to recreation was in the statement of E. M. Griffith, Wisconsin's first state forester, who had been on the job since 1904. The bulk of Griffith's comments described the expansion of forest reserves and the prevention of fires. But he did note the likely influence of these policies on the recreational use of the woodlands. "As the forest reserve is increased and the lands saved from desolation by logging and fire, many more summer tourists and sportsmen will come to northern Wisconsin," he said. "The money that they will spend will benefit [hunting and fishing] guides to such an extent that they should be only too willing to co-operate in every way to save the forests, fish and game, as it will mean the building up of their own business."[7]

What Griffith predicted for the region's guides was presumably true for any resident with a vested interest in tourism. Outdoor recreation could be a means of economic development. For many conservationists in the early twentieth century, this idea would emerge as the greatest threat to natural resources in the nation, every bit as destructive as lumbering had been to the forests. "So sacred is our dogma of 'development,'" complained Aldo Leopold in 1925, "that there is no effective protest." In subsequent years, Leopold would become one of Wisconsin's and the nation's foremost conservationists, and a vocal critic of large-scale, commercialized recreation. Promoters of tourism, he claimed, had little interest in conserving resources. A park was "a tourist-getter of the first water" for these boosters, "and tourists are to be valued above all things." According to Leopold, this kind of development inevitably created pressure to accommodate tourists with better roads, hotels, and recreational facilities. "Just so does the quality of wilderness fade before the juggernaut of mass recreation." Yet despite protests such as Leopold's, conservationists in Wisconsin embraced exactly this kind of large-scale recreation during the early twentieth century. A brief look at their activities has much to reveal about conservation and the growing interest in recreation that the movement inspired.[8]

The seeds of this development were evident as early as 1915, when the state legislature created Wisconsin's first permanent Conservation Commission. Six years earlier, when Governor Davidson established his commission, the group comprised seven unpaid members whose duty was to gather facts and make recommendations regarding improving Wisconsin's management of resources. By contrast, the new agency pursued more ambitious goals. In keeping with the Progressive Era in which it was born, the commission was designed to centralize most of the existing conservation activities then underway in the state. In addition to its own duties, the revised commission would assume the activities of four distinct agencies: the state Park Board, the state Forestry Board, the Commission of Fisheries, and the Fish and Game Warden. Notably absent from this list was any effort to include the management of waterpower, which at the time was among the most hotly debated issues in Wisconsin. But the commission's expanded responsibilities were sweeping nonetheless. They included "all the closely related duties and problems of administration over forest and stream, fish and game." Although the challenges were daunting, they could each be addressed with the same attention to efficiency and careful management that governed other progressive reforms. "We have passed that stage in our industrial life when haphazard or antiquated methods will apply," explained the agency in one of its earliest reports. "We are living in an age of industrial development which surpasses the fondest dreams of our ancestors, and we are steadily moving on. We must apply the same rules to this business."[9]

The new Conservation Commission allocated its duties among three divisions: Fisheries, Wild Life Conservation, and Forests and Parks. This structure expanded quickly and became more elaborate as the agency's responsibilities broadened. But the growing influence of outdoor recreation was apparent in each section from the beginning. The incorporation of fish and game in the restructured commission steered conservationists most immediately toward the promotion of recreation. Sportsmen had long been among the strongest proponents of wildlife conservation, both in Wisconsin and throughout the United States. As a result, the commission sought to balance its efforts to protect resources with the interests of sportsmen who demanded an adequate supply of game. In Wisconsin, the regulation of hunting and fishing was among the first efforts at resource management taken up by the legislature, dating back to the state's earliest days. By 1915 there was a mounting collection of laws governing seasons, bag limits, and other restrictions on the killing of birds and animals. Enforcing these regulations was the job of the conservation warden. At the time the Conservation Commission was created, there were seventy-six wardens, each of whom had the necessary police powers to arrest violators. But the force was woefully inadequate for the state's vast territory. In the Fox River Valley, the area surrounding Lake Winnebago comprised "the most extensive hunting and fishing grounds of the state." Yet lack of manpower left the region effectively unprotected, leading to "the wholesale slaughter of both fish and game." Market hunters were a particular concern. "They figure that there is only one chance in ten of their being caught," explained one conservationist. Consequently, these individuals "had built up a profitable business [in the valley] at the expense of the law-abiding citizens." In the absence of stronger regulations and greater numbers of wardens, the problem would only grow worse.[10]

In the years to come, the commission worked toward precisely these goals, dramatically expanding its regulatory and enforcement capabilities. But the agency's developing commitment to outdoor recreation reached well beyond the protection of wildlife. In the case of fisheries, there were two major components to the Conservation Commission's management of lakes and streams: the operation of hatcheries to replenish game fish, and the systematic removal of undesirable species known as rough fish. Both had long histories in Wisconsin, and both were influenced by the priorities of recreation. Of the two activities, it was hatcheries that claimed the earliest origins in the state. In 1873, the Wisconsin legislature appropriated $500 for the propagation of fish. The effort was carried out with the help of the U.S. commissioner of fisheries, and it led to the production of 20,000 salmon released in the waters near Madison and Lake Geneva in the southern part of Wisconsin. After this successful venture, the state created its own Commission of Fisheries in 1874, and one year later established its first permanent hatchery outside the state capital. By 1915, when Wisconsin centralized its various conservation activities, there were eleven hatcheries throughout the state, including one near Lake Winnebago on the western end of the Fox River Valley. Together, these operations distributed over 246,000,000 adult fish, yearlings, small fry, and eggs. The species produced included Wisconsin's most coveted fish: brook trout, rainbow trout, walleyed pike, black bass, muskellunge, pickerel, lake trout, bluefin, whitefish, and perch. The Fox River Valley received more than 4 million of these fish, primarily in Lake Winnebago. Yet the effort was not enough. "It does not take much of an observer to see we are playing a losing game," said one conservation official in 1915. Given the growing number of fishermen, both recreational and commercial, and the daunting challenge of enforcing regulations, the commission found it difficult to keep up with mounting demands on the state's fisheries.[11]

Consequently, state conservationists continued to broaden the hatchery program. For many years, the commission focused simply on producing larger numbers of fish. Between 1915 and 1936, the number of hatcheries grew from eleven to twenty-three, plus dozens of smaller rearing ponds, some operated jointly with private groups. Production from these expanded facilities rose accordingly, reaching totals of more than a billion fish annually in the years prior to World War II. But during the 1930s, the commission began to recognize that better fisheries required a more systematic approach to their management. "One weakness in the Wisconsin program," the commission admitted in 1932, "is that practically all effort has been expended on the production of fish and little on the protection of their habitat." In response, conservationists began a concerted effort to improve lakes and streams. One method involved the installation of specially designed "spawners and refuges" in the state's waters to provide shelter, food, and protection from fast-moving currents. These artificial habitats, which were constructed of brush, logs, and boulders and submerged at strategic locations, were intended to "step up" the capacity of lakes and streams to support the propagation of fish. Even more significant were the growing contributions of science in the hatcheries. A new Biology Division, launched in 1937, became responsible for improving propagation techniques, preventing disease among fish, and tracking the behavior of various species in the wild in order to determine how best to manage their distribution. As a result of these studies, the commission even noted the growing impact of industrial pollution. Unfortunately, beyond simply refusing to distribute young fish in contaminated waters, the agency had little authority to act.[12]

A second component of Wisconsin's fisheries management was the removal of undesirable species from lakes and streams. The most common of these so-called rough fish were carp, buffalo, suckers, redhorse, sheepshead, eelpout, dogfish, and garfish. All but carp were native to the state. In some cases, rough fish were carnivores that preyed on the various species of more desirable game fish. In others, as was the case with carp, the fish ate only plant life. Yet in large numbers, schools of carp could devastate the habitat of less hardy species by destroying the vegetation along lake bottoms, stirring up sediment, and interfering with breeding. In the absence of unusual pressures on either rough fish or the game varieties, the two groups maintained a relative balance of species. Unfortunately, the growing popularity of outdoor recreation in Wisconsin upset this equilibrium. "Rough fish become exceedingly numerous in many of the inland lakes because the general public does not fish for them," the commission explained. As a result, it was left to conservationists to restore the natural order.[13]

The commission responded with a methodical campaign to remove rough fish from Wisconsin's rivers and lakes. In 1911, an early system of granting licenses for the removal of fish was replaced by the hiring of contractors. Under this more vigorous policy, teams of paid commercial fishermen utilized increasingly sophisticated netting and traps to extract and dispose of millions of pounds of undesirable species each year. Some of these fish were sold in local or eastern markets. Others were processed in a specially constructed canning plant and used as feed in the commission's fish hatcheries and game farms. In Lake Winnebago, the agency waged a particularly fierce campaign against carp and sheepshead. "Where the carp has established himself it is practically impossible to exterminate the fish," the agency lamented in 1916. But repeated efforts could limit their numbers. As a result, by the 1930s both the removal of rough fish and the production of game fish in hatcheries became growing industries in their own right, requiring the expenditure of tens of thousands of dollars each year. For the many recreational and commercial fishermen who benefited from these efforts, nature played only the most distant role in their enjoyment of the great outdoors. "Good fishing is no longer a gift of the gods," explained the commission.[14]

Much the same could be said for people's enjoyment of wildlife. In 1915, when the first permanent Conservation Commission was formed, many species of birds and animals were in trouble throughout Wisconsin. According to the agency, ruffed grouse and prairie chickens were both "on their last legs." Quail and waterfowl were recovering under state protection but still in jeopardy. Deer, too, were endangered despite the immediate benefit of a new "one buck" limit for hunters. Of greatest concern was the impact of the state's rapid development on wildlife. "The coming of the automobile has opened the remote districts where seclusion was found, and settlement is encroaching more and more upon their habitations," explained the commission. Development brought greater pressure on all game animals because larger numbers of hunters and fishermen inevitably came with rising populations. For many years, the commission's response to these problems remained limited, focusing on strengthening and improving the enforcement of Wisconsin's game laws. But in 1928, the agency established a new Game Division to apply the same principles of systematic management to wildlife that were already being applied its fisheries. The division established dozens of game farms throughout the state, including four in the Fox River Valley alone. As their name suggests, the farms were intended not just to protect animals, but to allow for their artificial propagation and distribution. By the mid-1930s, the operation had grown to include pheasants, partridges, wild turkeys, raccoons, foxes, mink, and white-tailed deer. The commission also launched a number of research efforts to count, study, and more effectively breed various species of wildlife. In addition, just as rough fish were removed from lakes, many predators were trapped and exterminated at the game farms. And much as rivers and streams were improved to propagate fish, the commission sought to restore a variety of habitats, including prairies and marshland, and to enhance the available food supply by providing winter feed. Finally, the commission worked to expand its network of wildlife refuges, setting aside several hundred thousand acres for waterfowl and deer.[15]

If human hands increasingly manipulated fish and game populations during the early twentieth century, the same was even truer for the landscapes of Wisconsin's state parks. The state legislature established its first park in northern Wisconsin in 1878, but sold half the land twenty years later for timber. It tried again at the turn of the century, joining with Minnesota to form the Interstate Park along both sides of their shared border at the St. Croix River. By 1915, there were six state parks in Wisconsin's system. This number grew to fourteen by the mid-1930s, plus three additional roadside parks intended specifically for travelers. In the commission's view, parks played a crucial role in the increasingly artificial lives of Wisconsin's residents. "The quiet lake, the running stream, the depth of the forest, the study of wild things" all these were necessary for urban residents confined "in the high pitch of industrial and commercial activities." Yet the commission provided these same parks with many industrial and commercial comforts. Devil's Lake Park in central Wisconsin offers a typical example. The region was composed of a glacial lake with high surrounding cliffs. The lake had long been a favored spot for recreation, and there were several existing inns, some of which were in poor condition. But the commission planned to enhance these attractions through "the repair of the hotel buildings and cottages...the installation of water systems, and the general improvement of all playgrounds." Reconstructing local roads was most important. By 1916, the state Highway Commission was at work linking the park with a new state trunk route that provided better access from the populated regions to the south and east. Such efforts were common in all the commission's parks, and all were intended to make Wisconsin a "natural playground" for tourists and residents.[16]

The growing emphasis on recreation by the Conservation Commission was even apparent in its management of the state's forests. As in many places, the practice of forestry began in Wisconsin in response to the rapid harvesting of trees. As early as 1867, a special committee formed by the state legislature warned that unchecked lumbering was destroying the state's woodlands. Little was done until the 1890s when lawmakers moved haltingly toward an organized policy of forestry. One of their most important steps came in 1904 when they created the office of State Forester. To fill the new position, they hired E. M. Griffith, a disciple of Gifford Pinchot, a close friend of Theodore Roosevelt and the nation's first professional forester. Griffith brought the same zeal for the efficient management of resources to Wisconsin that Pinchot and Roosevelt displayed in Washington. "The two great deterrent factors that are keeping many timberland owners from adopting forestry methods are fire and taxes," he explained in 1909. Griffith first tackled the problem of fire, establishing a network of state and local wardens to patrol the forests and monitor conditions. To curtail the wasteful lumbering practices that made forests susceptible to fire, he worked to expand state forest reserves. In addition, by 1915 Wisconsin had established two nurseries in the northern part of the state to raise and distribute various kinds of trees (Figure 14). The millions of seedlings eventually produced each year were used to rebuild the forests, both in the state's expanding reserves and parks as well as on private property. In the latter case, citizens were hindered from restoring their lands by Wisconsin's punitive tax law. "Forests are a crop just as much as wheat or corn," said Griffith, "and when the private owner is forced to pay an annual . . . tax on his growing timber, it is no wonder that he cuts, and usually cuts all." Correcting this problem proved a difficult challenge. But finally, in 1927, the legislature enacted a Forest Crop Law that allowed citizens to pay a drastically reduced flat tax on lands designated for forestry. In return, the state agreed to compensate local towns for a portion of their lost revenue. The

Figure 14. Northern Wisconsin tree nursery, raising several varieties of evergreens. Courtesy of the Wisconsin Historical Society, Image No. WHi-5750.

reform helped make forestry in Wisconsin a joint venture between the state and its citizens.[17]

Although the Conservation Commission's early management of forests focused on their value as an economic resource, the agency quickly realized their broader relevance. "The basis of all conservation work lies in forestry and reforestation," explained the commission in 1928. This included the use of trees for lumbering, woodworking, and the manufacture of paper, but also their growing importance for recreation. "Without forests the condition of our lakes and streams would become such that they would not harbor the fish and other aquatic life which makes Wisconsin famous throughout the country," continued the agency. "Without forests to provide cover our game would dwindle away to the point where there would be no more hunting." Lastly, it was the forests, too, that provided "the beauty spots, recreation centers, and wonderful scenery which annually attract millions of tourists to the state." Although the commission's efforts to improve forest reserves for recreation never matched its restructuring of the landscapes in state parks, the agency did work to ensure adequate roads, trails, campsites, and sanitary facilities suitable for an enjoyable, if slightly less luxurious, woodland experience. By the late 1930s, the legislature had even authorized the creation of so-called recreational forests in the populated region between Milwaukee and the Fox River Valley in order to provide more convenient access to the enjoyment of wooded landscapes.[18]

Without question, the Conservation Commission's most explicit effort to promote outdoor recreation came in 1936 when the agency inaugurated a new division entitled Recreational Publicity. A year earlier, the state legislature appropriated $50,000 and ordered the commission to "collect, compile and distribute information . . . as to the facilities, advantages and attractions of the state . . . and to plan and conduct a program of . . . publicity designed to attract tourists." Coming in the midst of the nation's worst depression, the scheme was an obvious attempt to stimulate Wisconsin's economy. Given the Conservation Commission's familiarity with natural resources, the agency made a logical choice to encourage their recreational use by prospective visitors. For its first promotional effort, the publicity division chose a wildlife theme. "Follow the Birds to Vacation Land" was the slogan selected. "Wisconsin is a vacationist's paradise within easy reach of your own door! Wise old waterfowl make Wisconsin their summer home. Why not you?" According to the booklet, the combination of Wisconsin's splendid natural landscape and its convenient, modern facilities created unparalleled recreational opportunities for tourists. "Bathing, fishing, boating, summer sports of all kinds, beauties of nature to see and to enjoy, primitive northwoods, delightful roads to roam — you will find them all at their best in Wisconsin, where friends and nature meet."[19]

In creating the Recreational Publicity division, the Conservation Commission took its first full step as a booster of economic development through outdoor recreation. Despite an early lack of attention, facilitating people's enjoyment of nature had become a chief priority in nearly every realm of the commission's activities. Its entry into the world of mass marketing symbolized this transformation. In all, the division produced over a million "units" of publicity material in its first year of operation, more than half of which was distributed outside Wisconsin. This included a variety of advertising techniques. In addition to its primary brochure, there were colorful letterheads and picture postcards, stickers, envelopes big and small, and a Wisconsin "Fun Map," all conveying the message that Wisconsin was the ideal place to vacation. The division also placed newspaper ads in more than two dozen cities from which the state was likely to draw tourists, including nearby locations such as Minneapolis, St. Paul, Chicago, and Indianapolis as well as distant communities such as Louisville, Memphis, and Nashville. "Nature Has Been Kind to Wisconsin," read one of the headlines. But tourists would enjoy more than nature. "Travel in Comfort Over Wisconsin's 'Roads to Roam,'" said one. "There's a Lakeside Cabin Awaiting You," read another. Some even pointed to the efforts of conservationists themselves to make the state a vacationer's paradise. "There's a Reason Why Fishing is Good in Wisconsin." Finally, to supplement this print material, the division placed forty-five billboards at strategic locations along the highways of six states. Each was a 12-by 18-foot invitation to "Relax in Wisconsin!"[20]

To critics of these kinds of efforts, the systematic promotion of outdoor recreation was troubling to say the least, for it threatened the very resources that conservationists sought to protect. "We have here the old conflict between preservation and use," warned Aldo Leopold in 1921, "long since an issue with respect to timber, water power, and other purely economic resources, but just now coming to be an issue with respect to recreation." Yet in many ways, the commission's expanding involvement in recreation had been a logical outgrowth of exactly the principles upon which the agency had been founded. "Conservation may best be defined as 'the full use of all our natural resources without permanent injury to those resources,'" explained one report in 1934. Maximizing the use of resources was always the driving purpose of conservation, part of the Progressive Era emphasis on productive efficiency that led to conservation's emergence as a national movement at the turn of the century. What changed during the intervening years were the rising demands that people made on their resources, as evidenced by the growing ranks of Wisconsin's residents and visitors alike that annually spent time hunting, fishing, camping, and playing in the great outdoors. In this respect, conservation was no different than the extension of power lines, the construction of highways, or any systematic effort to manage natural resources: the more control people gained over nature, the more they expected nature to deliver. It was this kind of pressure that led the commission by the 1930s to define recreation as a legitimate, even necessary, use of Wisconsin's landscape.[21]

Much as Leopold predicted, the promotion of tourism would place enormous strain on the state's resources. "Conservation has gone beyond the point of conserving," explained the commission by 1937, "and the state faces the problem of meeting a demand that even virgin conditions of the area could not have supplied for a comparatively short time." But rather than limit the availability of outdoor recreation, the Conservation Commission responded as most industrial producers would have: it redoubled its effort to create more facilities. Here again, the agency followed the example of conservation's architects at the turn of the century. "The first great fact about conservation is that it stands for development," wrote Gifford Pinchot in 1910. According to Pinchot, there were many people who mistakenly assumed that conservation meant strictly the preservation of resources for the future. "There could be no more serious mistake," he cautioned. "Conservation does mean provision for the future, but it means also and first of all the recognition of the right of the present generation to the fullest necessary use of all the resources with which this country is so abundantly blessed." Twenty-five years later, the inheritors of Pinchot's philosophy in Wisconsin still followed his mandate. "Conservation is founded entirely on promotion of the general welfare," explained the commission. Given the public's rising interest in the enjoyment of nature, the agency could ill afford to overlook "commercial values" of any kind, including "the selling of recreational advantages that add millions to the total of state income and distribute it over the entire Wisconsin area."[22]

By the mid-1930s, however, it was equally clear that the Conservation Commission alone was incapable of expanding outdoor recreation far enough to reach even the state's own citizens, to say nothing of distant tourists. This effort would require massive investment and the combined contributions of road builders, the state legislature, city officials, chambers of commerce, and private individuals throughout Wisconsin. Above all, it needed planning.

Planning for Play

In 1934, the state of Wisconsin issued its first-ever statewide regional plan. Regional planning was a growing trend in American policy making, and Wisconsin was part of the movement, having organized a state Regional Planning Committee three years earlier. "Planning has always been a factor in government," read the committee's report, especially in cities. But the recent expansion of industrial and commercial development made the extension of planning efforts an increasing priority. The breadth of this need was reflected both in the committee's structure and the scope of its report. Although officially attached to the Highway Commission, the committee comprised representatives from nearly every important development-related agency of state government. In addition to three private citizens appointed by the governor, its members included the state chief engineer, the health officer, the commissioner of conservation, and one member each from the Industrial Commission and the Public Service Commission, which regulated Wisconsin's utilities. The committee's first statewide report surveyed the broad sweep of modern life in Wisconsin, including population growth; occupational trends; education; water and mineral resources; the conservation of soil, trees, and wildlife; electric power; taxation; and transportation from the rails, water, highways, and air. Its purpose was simple: "to outline and develop such a program for the state . . . that the resources and facilities available may be utilized to the maximum benefit for the population . . . without unnecessary permanent deterioration."[23]

In other words, state planners intended to extend the practice of conservation by applying its concern for coordination and the wise use of resources to new aspects of modern life. By this logic, if the various institutions responsible for Wisconsin's economic growth could be encouraged to work together, their collective benefit to society would rise well above what each might contribute on its own. Not surprisingly, outdoor recreation was a part of this scheme, as was its role in fostering the state's economic development. Although the planning committee defined recreation as "that broad form of land use which best contributes to man's non-material wants," the group noted quickly that supplying these wants involved "commercial transactions" with an average annual value of $120,000,000. This made outdoor recreation the fourth leading industry in Wisconsin. As conservationists had learned, its development was extremely complex. "Recreation is intimately associated with the problems of reforestation, game management, lake and stream control, health, urban and rural planning, population, taxation, zoning, transportation industry, and even unemployment." Conservation alone would not suffice. Instead, by the 1930s, developing the recreational use of the landscape was also the job of the regional planner.[24]

In 1935, the legislature transferred the functions of the Regional Planning Committee to a new independent agency known as the state Planning Board. With its membership broadened to include representatives of public and higher education, the new board set about its task. Its first major report on outdoor recreation appeared in 1939. Entitled "A Park, Parkway, and

Recreational Area Plan," the document was a model of bureaucratic and technical analysis. "As the complexities of life continue to increase, the necessity for recreation becomes greater," explained the board. According to the report, Wisconsin's former abundance of forests, lakes, and streams had gradually disappeared. "If the people are to have recreation, definite provision for the necessary facilities must be made, and at public expense." The recreational plan comprised the first step in achieving this goal. The report offered an appraisal of the state's current recreational facilities, an analysis of their relative value, an estimate of future needs, and recommendations on a course of action. "Its purpose is to present to the people of Wisconsin the opportunities afforded them by nature, and to outline a plan of procedure for the acquisition, development, maintenance and operation of a state-wide recreational system."[25]

The board began by summarizing the crisis facing outdoor recreation in Wisconsin. At the heart of the problem was the state's urban-industrial development and the resulting growth in people's interest in the wonders of nature. "In recent times, the enjoyment of outdoor recreation has increased enormously," the board concluded. In part, this was a consequence of better roads, the expansion of parks and other recreational facilities, and the new ability of public institutions to provide these services. But the board noted as well "a growing desire for relaxation and for change from ordinary living and working conditions" coinciding with "the increase of urban industrial population and the growth of large cities." It was this dramatic "change in our living routine" that seemed most responsible for the recent expansion in recreational activities: "sight-seeing, picnicking, camping, walking, fishing, boating, riding, skiing, snowshoeing, skating . . . and nature study . . . ; in other words, those forms of enjoyment requiring relatively few 'improvements' but considerable areas of varied types." City parks, playgrounds, and community centers could accommodate most forms of organized recreation such as pageants, festivals, and competitive sporting events. But for the so-called unorganized activities associated with outdoor recreation, the state would need to play a leading role. "Local communities are not in a position to acquire areas sufficiently large to supply proper recreation facilities . . . within their own boundaries."[26]

In Wisconsin, this problem was made even worse by two additional factors. First, because urban development was highly concentrated, roughly 75 percent of Wisconsin's population lived in the state's southeastern corner, a region bounded by Milwaukee and Madison in the south and the cities of the Fox River Valley in the north. Unfortunately, of the nineteen state parks that had been established by 1939, only two were located in this same region, creating an imbalance in the availability of facilities that would only grow worse as development continued. Second, Wisconsin served as a recreational outlet, not just for its own urban residents, but increasingly for thousands of tourists from all parts of the country who journeyed to the state each year. "To supply recreation for these people is one of Wisconsin's greatest businesses," the board affirmed, and it required "large areas of land and water and forest." Combined, these two trends in the state's urban-industrial development created enormous pressure on existing recreational landscapes. "Popular demand exceeds the ability of these areas to furnish the type of recreation desired," planners warned, "and the purposes for which they were originally established may be actually defeated through excessive use."[27]

In considering how best to respond to this crisis, the board offered a slightly updated restatement of the "greatest good for the greatest number" philosophy of conservation in Wisconsin. "Development of parks and recreational areas," it argued, "should afford maximum recreational facilities to the maximum number of people." In essence, this meant democratizing the enjoyment of nature by making recreational facilities more widely available to those most in need of its benefits: low-income urban residents. According to the board, nearly everyone enjoyed outdoor recreation if given the opportunity. "The main limiting factors are actually income and leisure time, and these factors, together with population density, determine *where* recreational facilities should be provided." Clearly, the greatest need was in the state's highly urbanized southeastern region. An inventory of Wisconsin's current recreational facilities revealed the stark inequity. In addition to its nineteen parks, the state was responsible for managing eight forest reserves and dozens of wildlife areas, including game farms, marshes, and a variety of animal refuges. The federal government played a smaller but similar role, supervising two national forests in northern Wisconsin, the Chequamegon and the Nicolet, which together comprised roughly 2 million acres. Likewise, town and county governments contributed to this recreational infrastructure, maintaining a variety of urban parks and small parcels of forested land. Unfortunately, when all these assets were tallied, they appeared to offer very little nature to urban residents, especially those lacking the wherewithal to travel great distances. According to the report, only three of Wisconsin's twenty-six largest cities were as close as 15 miles from a recreational area, the average driving distance for potential day trips. Only seven more were as close as 50 miles, the typical range for weekend and vacation use. In essence, planners concluded, for the low-income urban residents with the most "genuine need for the natural type of recreational area," the pleasures of the great outdoors remained unavailable.[28]

Having assessed the present condition and future needs of outdoor recreation in Wisconsin, the board offered its recommendations. Not surprisingly, the chief priority was expansion. Most of the state's existing facilities showed the potential for further development. In all, the board suggested adding nearly 6,000 acres to the current state parks, 80,000 acres to the state forests, and 350 acres to Wisconsin's five roadside parks. But this was only the beginning. The board then recommended the creation of nine brand new state parks totaling more than 20,000 acres. This included one facility on the shores of Lake Michigan in the densely populated southeastern corner of Wisconsin. For the state forests, planners suggested two areas of approximately 170,000 acres in the central part of the state, again much more accessible to urban populations. In the Fox River Valley, citizens remained isolated from much of this proposed development. But included in the board's collection of new parks was one location on the eastern side of Lake Winnebago just south of Appleton. There, a large outcropping of Niagara limestone formed a high bluff overlooking the water. Two hundred acres of land were already in the possession of the county government, and planners recommended the purchase of 800 more along several miles of shoreline. "This is the only remaining extensive stretch of shore on this lake which has not been highly developed for private use," the board reported. According to planners, the magnificent view, the stands of timber, and its close proximity to the valley's cities made the area ideally suited for inclusion in the park system.[29]

In proposing this massive expansion of Wisconsin's parks and forests, the state Planning Board also urged more attention to preserving the resources that made recreation possible. Here, design was of crucial importance. "An excellent area may be ruined and its true value . . . lost if the plan for its use and development is wrong," the board explained. Accordingly, planners made detailed suggestions regarding the structure and operation of recreational facilities. They began by classifying what was intended in each type of landscape. State parks were meant to be large, accessible, and characterized by uncommonly beautiful or unique natural features. The forest reserves, by contrast, should be larger tracts of land deemed unsuitable for agriculture, where multiple-use areas could be established for timber production, watershed management, wildlife protection, and recreation. In the operation of parks and forests, the board had numerous suggestions, including guidelines for the construction of approach roads and entrances, public roads and service areas, trails and picnic facilities, beaches, and all necessary buildings. "Any park structure is an intrusion upon an existing natural condition which is to be retained if it is to serve its purpose," planners cautioned. "They should be inconspicuous and indigenous to the region." Likewise, the use of "highly colored paint" was deemed incongruous with the natural setting. Buildings could be accented by planting vegetation, but only local species were appropriate, and planners discouraged their grouping in rows. Despite this attention to maintaining a sense of nature, the board was realistic about certain additions to the parks. Roads, of course, were a must. Pure drinking water and adequate sanitation were also important, as was the operation of concessions.[30]

Coming as it did in 1939, the state Planning Board's report on outdoor recreation was inevitably caught in the maelstrom of World War II. It would be many years before some of its recommendations were implemented. In the Fox River Valley, High Cliff State Park was finally opened in 1957, shortly after the state purchased the sections of shoreline along Lake Winnebago that the board had suggested. Yet despite these delays, the creation of the state Planning Board demonstrates Wisconsin's commitment to providing its citizens with opportunities to enjoy nature. The board's efforts, together with the gradual expansion of the Conservation Commission, had transformed the state government into a producer of outdoor recreation, just as utilities created power, road builders furnished transportation, and farmers delivered milk. Like most industrial producers, state officials relied on their growing ability to control the natural landscape in order to meet the demands of their customers.

One further example illustrates this point well. In January 1941, the State Planning Board published "A Recreational Plan for Vilas County." County officials had come to the state for assistance in formulating the plan, which attempted to implement many of the guidelines established by the board two years earlier. According to planners, the new document would allow the county "to make the most of its recreational assets." Located on Wisconsin's northern border with Michigan, Vilas County had long been a favorite destination for tourists, including vacationers from the Fox River Valley. Unfortunately, many of its best lakes and forested regions remained, in the words of planners, "undeveloped and unused." Although 60 percent of the county's land was publicly owned, and much of this had been reforested with the help of conservationists, tourism in the region relied almost exclusively on private industry. At the time, there were 123 resort hotels in the county and nearly 700 smaller cottages. Although these facilities could accommodate thousands of vacationers, local officials hoped for more. Here, the untapped recreational potential of the county's public lands offered a treasure of tourist dollars. "There are historically important places, not generally remembered," planners noted. "There are points of great scenic interest which have gone unrecognized; there are trips to be made by water that are the scenic equals of any in the country, but they are not generally known." If these resources were properly developed, the board predicted, they could "open whole new avenues in the field of outdoor recreation" for Vilas County.[31]

As planners had done in their earlier statewide report, they first conducted an inventory of the county's recreational assets. These included 38,000 acres of national forest and 40,000 additional acres maintained as a reservation by the U.S. Indian Service. Both could be improved for tourism. State forests in the county accounted for 122,000 acres of land with twelve lakeside campgrounds that offered tables, fireplaces, toilets, wells, and beaches suitable for swimming. But planners saw the potential for further development. "Between 450 and 550 people use these camps on a normal day during the summer," the board reported. "Most of them can be developed to accommodate twice their present capacity." Finally, the county itself owned 66,000 acres of forest, more than a third of which was being managed under the Forest Crop Law. Although much of the remaining lands were "situated on lakes and streams, and [had] a high recreational value," the county had yet to develop its great potential.[32]

To address these problems, the Vilas County plan recommended the establishment of five local parks, each with the necessary amenities to facilitate their enjoyment. County roads that were no longer in use thanks to the construction of bigger state highways could be converted to parkways designed for pleasure driving. Hundreds of miles of roadway were available for such development, which could be further enhanced by the construction of way-sides at scenic locations. Much the same philosophy could be applied to the county's network of lakes and streams. Planners suggested the creation of canoe routes to link the various parks and other recreational assets of the county. By posting guide markers and constructing lunch grounds along the routes, the county could provide its tourists yet another means of traveling through the region in comfort and relative security. Finally, planners recommended increased attention to winter sports. The construction of ski trails would "be of great value in extending the recreational assets of the county" by allowing citizens to reap the benefits of tourism during the entire year, not just in the summer.[33]

According to planners, among the most powerful tools available to the county for promoting development was the policy of rural zoning. The practice of zoning had a long history in Wisconsin's cities where a lack of enforceable standards could lead to fire hazards, poor sanitation, and generally illogical development. For many years, there seemed little need for this kind of regulation in the countryside. By the 1920s, however, the movement of highways, power lines, and population into the state's rural areas brought a growing need for careful planning. As a result, in 1929 the state legislature authorized Wisconsin's counties to zone their rural lands. In essence, zoning gave counties the power to control development. It allowed them to create districts in which certain uses deemed harmful to the general welfare were prohibited. During the 1930s, it was the counties of northern Wisconsin that benefited most directly from the law. Their primary concern was to restrict the spread of settlement into isolated areas where extending roads and other public services was expensive. But in the opinion of planners, zoning would also ensure the most effective use of natural resources, including their development for tourism. By the 1930s, Vilas County had enacted a system of zoning, restricting agriculture from some regions in order to promote reforestation, and designating others for recreation. But planners urged a more aggressive approach. Zoning could be utilized to remove billboards and power lines from the view of motorists on local highways, to prevent residential construction on lakeshores, and to restrict commercial development from disturbing especially beautiful recreational spots. In this way, by extending their authority over the landscape, county officials improved its recreational potential, making its features more attractive and accessible, and therefore more lucrative.[34]

By the 1940s, state planners, conservationists, and local officials had developed an impressive ability to produce outdoor recreation from nature. Tourism was an industry, and like any business, it depended on someone to identify, improve, and utilize the necessary resources from the material landscape. In the case of tourism, it was public officials who increasingly played this role in Wisconsin. As a result, conservationists and planners spoke of assets, facilities, and economic benefits, even though their goal ostensibly was to reveal the beauties of nature. In the dawning age of outdoor recreation, there was nothing intangible about beauty. It was a product of abundant wildlife, flowing rivers, and unbroken forests, not to mention comfortable hotels, convenient parks, and miles of paved roads. It was this industrial infrastructure that made nature so widely available.[35]

Yet for most residents of Wisconsin and certainly for the state's tourists, enjoying the great outdoors was a commercial experience, largely disconnected from the systematic effort required to create it. Although conservationists worked constantly to reseed the forests and fill them with game, to stock rivers and lakes with fish, and to build parks that were both beautiful and convenient, vacationers were free to enjoy these things as if they were natural. If people were conscious of the growing convenience of outdoor recreation, it was mainly through the hoards of resort owners, hunting and fishing guides, and retailers who worked to entice their business. As a result, understanding the consumer's experience of nature in the mid-twentieth century requires looking more closely at the messages they heard from these boosters.

"Wisconsin's Outdoor Living Room"

By the late 1940s, as the nation's attention shifted gradually from war, Americans were ready to relax. In the Fox River Valley, as in many parts of the United States, people turned to the great outdoors as an outlet for the spending and gratification so long delayed by the crisis. Although many local citizens followed the well-worn path from Milwaukee and Chicago through the valley into northern Wisconsin, others stayed closer to home. Here valley residents were fortunate to have one of the state's most popular tourist destinations in their own backyard. "Vacation in Door County, Wisconsin's Outdoor Living Room," proclaimed one tourist brochure published in 1945 by the Door County Chamber of Commerce. Located just north and east of Green Bay, Door County encompassed the narrow peninsula on the state's eastern border that formed the bay from the waters of Lake Michigan. According to the chamber, the region possessed "the combined charm of a rugged, fruitful land, and the cool, clear water of an inland sea." Yet as the idea of an "outdoor living room" suggested, there was little that was rugged about visiting Door County.[36]

Certainly, much of the scenery and recreational amenities available in Door County were natural. The region's climate was a major selling point. Because the county was uniquely positioned with "water on either side of its long, slender mainland," it was said to enjoy both mild winters and cool summer breezes, circumstances that made it the "Air-Conditioned Playground of the Middle West." Likewise, while visiting Door County, travelers were assured they would find "unusual natural resources of sheer beauty." These included "spacious bays [and] high rugged cliffs," abundant fish and wildlife, the "sylvan beauty" of sheltered forests, "gently sloping sandy beaches," and "uncontaminated, clear blue water." Given these attributes, tourists would find it easy to "commune with nature in ecstatic peace . . . and drink deeply of the never ending scenic panorama which makes [the] cares of man forgotten."

Although the natural splendor of Door County was impressive, for local boosters and likely for tourists, what made the region an "outdoor living room" was the fact that visitors could enjoy the same comfort and modern amenities that typified their own homes: "Your every demand finds fulfillment," assured the chamber. Door County, in fact, possessed a large and highly developed commercial infrastructure, each element of which was intended to enhance the safety, security, and convenience of vacationing in the region (Figure 15). Not surprisingly, the effort began with transportation. "Motorists will find concrete highways from Chicago and all midwestern communities running into Door County," explained the pamphlet. In addition, there were numerous railroads and two airports that served both the northern and southern ends of the county. Once travelers arrived, they could select from forty-two resort hotels, plus a variety of cottages and campgrounds for those seeking a rustic experience. During their stay, visitors could participate in any activity they fancied, all made simple and enjoyable by the county's

Figure 15. Typical Door County tourist resort. Courtesy of the Neville Public Museum of Brown County, Image No. 2001.16.21.

modern recreational facilities. Yachtsmen would find the waters of Door County "the finest cruising territory in the United States," thanks in part to the Coast Guard stations, radio beacons, lighthouses, and docking facilities that served the area. For those remaining ashore, there were two state parks in Door County, each bordering the water. "Both are laid out with roads and trails," described the pamphlet, "and [both] have facilities for camping, boating, picnicking, fishing, hiking and nature study." In one of the parks, there was even a golf course. Anglers could rest assured that game fish had been "protected by law from the nets of commercial fishermen, with the interest of the tourist at heart." Local guides provided tips on the best fishing holes. In addition, the county was home to a fish hatchery with the largest rearing pond for smallmouth black bass in Wisconsin. Finally, tourists could enjoy horseback riding at "well-equipped stables," swimming on public beaches "under the supervision of life guards," and an outdoor theater where "talented artists, some of Hollywood fame, present very fine, high class productions." Given these recreational facilities, the chamber concluded, "every day in every way, your vacation will be filled with enjoyment if you come to Door County."

Despite the obvious self-interest in such promotions, they suggest an important point: by the late 1940s, their portrayals of the outdoors as a recreational playground provided among the few remaining instances for Americans to think about nature at all. This image of the landscape was hardly new. During the nineteenth century, when boosters championed the Fox River Valley they often mentioned its natural splendor. "In autumn particularly," began one description, this by a resident of Kaukauna, "the winding Fox moving majestically along between its steep and grassy banks, the forest primeval stretching away in nearly every direction with its countless tints and ruddy hues mingling in one grand harmony of color . . . the musical roar of the water as it rushes over the rapids . . . all go to make up a scene as beautiful as a poet's dream." Beautiful perhaps, but such comments were nearly always appended to lengthy descriptions of nature's usefulness as a means of production. "The great wealth of Kaukauna must ever lie in her magnificent manufacturing advantages," explained the same writer before reciting them in elaborate detail. Resources, not recreation, sustained people in the nineteenth century. In contrast, fifty years later, there was little point in offering valley residents a catalog of the landscape's useful advantages. Most residents depended more directly on commerce than resources to secure their well-being. As a result, it took an act of will for people to think about nature as anything but a recreational amenity. Certainly, the growing assortment of modern boosters who promoted Wisconsin's great outdoors had obvious reasons to embellish. But if the image of nature as a playground seemed ubiquitous by the 1940s, this was true in part because there were few other images available. For most valley residents, the majority of the landscape's production-oriented functions were now obscured by the region's industrial and commercial infrastructure. In this respect, outdoor recreation was among the few economic uses of nature that still required talking explicitly about its qualities.[37]

Given the predominance of recreation as an image of nature in the Fox River Valley, it is all the more important to examine how this idea was constructed. In March 1948, at precisely the moment when local residents unleashed their anger at the paper industry, citizens in Green Bay prepared for a new season of outdoor recreation by attending the city's annual sports show. Sponsored by area merchants and the city's newspaper, the event was the first such exposition to be held in Green Bay since the war. Organizers promised a festival of entertainment. In addition to the twenty-five retailers displaying their outdoor apparel and equipment, customers could enjoy a live orchestra; service bars with beer, soda, and food; trivia contests with prizes for lucky participants; and expert demonstrations of archery, fishing, and dog handling. The show offered "everything that will interest the outdoor sports fan." In the process, it demonstrated the extent to which recreation had come to define people's understanding of nature by the mid-twentieth century.[38]

That such events occurred at all reflected the growing tendency in the United States to use nature as a recreational amenity. In the nineteenth century, outdoor enthusiasts typically came from America's elite, those citizens with the wherewithal to afford spending time and money enjoying the natural environment. In contrast, by the mid-twentieth century, the ranks of American nature lovers had grown considerably, a fact in evidence at Green Bay. Attendance at the two-day sports show climbed into the thousands, reaching well beyond the traditional groups of hunters and fishermen that once comprised the majority of outdoorsmen. For the show's postwar debut, organizers deliberately broadened the event "to cover all phases of summer outdoor recreation," including weekend picnics and softball games, pleasure driving, golfing, summer camping, and evening barbecues. As these activities suggest, outdoor recreation was no longer confined to privileged Americans. Instead, its appeal had widened to become a standard of middle-class living, both in the Fox River Valley and throughout the country, an expected part of people's normal routine. Most important, by the 1940s, recreation was among the few remaining means by which Americans interacted directly and self-consciously with nature.[39]

According to retailers, consumption offered valley residents the most convenient and accessible gateway through which to experience the great outdoors. "Sports are nature's tonic for longer, more enjoyable living," declared one newspaper ad for a Green Bay sporting goods store. "For more complete enjoyment of sports," the ad continued, "the emphasis is on better, proper equipment." Visitors to the sports show saw this message reinforced by the sheer number and variety of goods on display. No matter what their interest in nature, consumers found an array of products. Anglers could buy fishing rods, trout nets, tackle boxes, hip waders, and bobbers and lures of every kind. There were rifles, ammunition, and bows and arrows for hunters. Campers found all the gear they needed, including iceboxes, sleeping bags, tents, axes, and air mattresses. There were tennis rackets, baseball bats, and golf clubs for weekend sportsmen, and clothes for every activity in spring and summer fashions. Backyard enthusiasts could supply their families with mowers, seed, and fertilizer to keep the lawn in prime condition. The more adventurous among the crowd could even purchase big-ticket items such as station wagons, trailer-campers, and luxury cabin cruisers. In every case, merchants sought to link their products with the greater enjoyment of nature. "There is fun ahead next summer if you act now and arrange to buy your MARTIN OUTBOARD MOTOR," promised one local retailer. Consumption was the means by which people could best explore the great outdoors.[40]

When packaged by merchants in this way, the specific idea of nature they sold was a contradiction in terms. On the one hand, the recreational landscape was a place made safe from the isolation and perils of untamed wilderness by the purchase of sporting equipment. According to nearly every retailer at the sports show, outdoor recreation had become a "carefree" pursuit, assuming that consumers purchased the proper accessories for each activity. Buy a new Evinrude motor, promised one store, and boaters would enjoy a new standard of convenience, including "the amazing Weedless Drive that lets you through waters closed to other motors . . . gives you the all-clear through weeds and over rocks, snags, reefs . . . lets you power anywhere there is water to float your boat!" (Figure 16). By the same token, the new Karriall Kamper offered a "comfortable weather-tight room" with enough features to tame any wilderness: "sleeping bunks for four, including pillows and mattresses, a table with two chairs, cook stove, 50-lb. capacity built-in icebox, and many different sized compartments for guns, rods, food, clothes and other gear." Pulling these campers was simple with the purchase of a "Mighty Jeep." Given a full line of trucks and station wagons from which to select, shoppers were sure to find the right combination of comfort, strength, and versatility to meet their needs. Power, speed, and ease of use: such appeals were typical of retailers selling access to the great outdoors.[41]

But if outdoor recreation was best enjoyed by taming the landscape with the purchase of sporting goods, then merchants were equally clear that the experience of nature was only authentic in the absence of human intrusions. By this logic, consumption offered a gateway to real wilderness, making it possible to experience the outdoors in its purest form, unsullied by toil, inconvenience, or cares of any kind. "You can go where you please, when you

Figure 16. Recreational boating on the Fox River near Appleton, ca. 1933. Courtesy of the Outagamie County Historical Society, Appleton, Wis., Image No. A84-80-6.

please and not worry about hotel rooms, dusty highways, or overcrowding," boasted the Fox River Boat Company. The "carefree pleasure" of operating a 40-foot cabin cruiser was available for only a few hundred dollars, two weeks' pay in the average salary. "Sportsmen, Fishermen, Huntsmen!" proclaimed a dealer of campers, "Just go . . . No reservations . . . No worries . . . Lots of fun!" The idea that inconvenience was a natural part of the landscape seemed not to occur to merchants. "Relax! Go boating!" urged another local dealer. "When the great outdoors beckons you, take to the water in a FOXCRAFT." Boating was invigorating and healthful, assured the retailer, especially in a boat with lightweight, dependable, strong, and maintenance-free construction. For those people able to heed such calls, consumption promised the "more complete enjoyment of sports and that earned relaxation that contributes so vitally to rugged health." In just this way, retailers at the sports show attached authenticity to every purchase. "Bent's Big Store is the natural place to go to find the proper equipment to make your participation in sports more successful, your interest keener and livelier."[42]

Not everyone welcomed this brand of outdoor recreation. Aldo Leopold, for one, thought it a poor substitute for encountering untamed wilderness. "Then came the gadgeteer, otherwise known as the sporting-goods dealer," he wrote. "He has draped the American outdoorsman with an infinity of contraptions, all offered as aides to self-reliance, hardihood, woodcraft, or marksmanship, but too often functioning as substitutes for them." But while Leopold worried about the loss of wilderness skills, the majority of Americans embraced whatever gadgets they could find. For tourists, the great outdoors was a world of modern convenience in which they could shape their activities in any way imaginable. Typically, this meant searching for unspoiled nature, while at the same time taking with them enough tools and apparel to guarantee their relative comfort. That so few people noticed how tamed this experience really was stemmed from their reliance on consumption. Outdoor recreation was a by-product of affordable energy, paved highways, mass production, commercial development, and rising standards of living, all of which transformed the natural landscape into a world every bit as predictable and secure as the average living room. Yet because most people remained detached from the massive infrastructure that rendered nature accessible, it was easy to lose sight of just how unnatural the great outdoors had become.[43]

The landscape of the Fox River Valley was anything but pristine by the 1940s. Still, the rising appeal of the great outdoors made pollution increasingly unbearable to local residents. In the nineteenth century, the region's obvious dependence on the Fox as a means of production made pollution an acceptable cost of progress. Fifty years later, in a world where outdoor living rooms had become an expected part of every community, standards had risen. The more determined people grew to use the landscape's natural amenities—and the more equipment they bought in the process—the more pollution and other forms of industrial harm threatened them personally by spoiling the kinds of experiences they hoped to enjoy. Inevitably, their disappointment moved them to action. At the Green Bay Sports Show, net proceeds from the two-day event were divided between the Brown County Conservation Club and Ducks Unlimited, two private organizations working to safeguard the local environment. This kind of political involvement was an outgrowth of people's consumption and the ways in which it shaped their interactions with nature. By December 1948, it would lead to the first organized effort to end the paper industry's pollution of the Fox River.[44]

6

"Pollution Concerns You!"

The late 1940s were an inauspicious time for political reform in the Fox River Valley. On Tuesday, November 5, 1946, residents of the valley joined citizens across Wisconsin to elect Joseph R. McCarthy as their new U.S. senator. McCarthy was a native of the valley. Born and raised on a farm near Appleton, he eventually became a lawyer and then a circuit judge for the county. Although he had been a supporter of Franklin Roosevelt's New Deal in the 1930s, McCarthy now claimed to have changed his views. "America today is confronted with a decision," read one of his campaign leaflets. "Shall government by LEFT-WING BUREAUCRATS tell us how to live, or shall the American government be RETURNED TO THE PEOPLE?" McCarthy's answer was vaguely worded but apparently clear enough for voters. "Let's put an end to all this NEEDLESS WASTE OF TAX MONEY. WE MUST HAVE REAL AMERICANISM IN WASHINGTON!"[1]

In many ways, McCarthy's tactics in the 1946 campaign displayed the same penchant for reckless self-promotion and personal attacks that would later characterize his role in the infamous Red Scare of the 1950s. But in Wisconsin, his election was notable more immediately for what it symbolized in state politics. First, McCarthy's victory in the general election continued the dominance of conservative Republicans in Wisconsin, who looked to extend their eight uninterrupted years of controlling the governor's chair, the state legislature, and most local and congressional offices. Second, in his primary election, McCarthy had defeated Robert La Follette Jr., son of "Fighting Bob" La Follette, Wisconsin's great progressive leader. During the 1930s, Bob Jr. and his brother Phil had abandoned Republicans to establish their own Progressive Party and rally the forces of liberal reform in the state. Phil became governor and Bob Jr. a U.S. senator. By 1938, however, their fortunes had declined again as the party was swept from power in Wisconsin by a renewed conservative ascendancy. Although Bob Jr. survived for a second term in the Senate, his Progressive Party collapsed around him. Thus, in 1946 when La Follette ran for a third term, he did so as a Republican. His defeat by McCarthy in the primary made it clear that the party would remain conservative—news that was surely welcome in the Fox River Valley, where manufacturers in the paper industry enjoyed a long and friendly relationship with the Republican establishment.[2]

For all these reasons, during the late 1940s the political climate for confronting the paper industry appeared bleak to say the least. Yet just such an effort took place, and its surprising success demonstrates just how powerful a consumer-driven reform movement can be. In many respects, the campaign to rid the Fox River of industrial pollution began with a single canoe trip. In 1946, a thirty-one-year-old attorney named Donald Soquet returned home to Green Bay from the war. Soquet, the son of an avid duck hunter and fisherman, had grown up a sportsman himself, spending much of his youth exploring the local outdoors. So it was that after three and a half years in the army, one of his first acts upon returning was to journey to his family's boathouse for a canoe ride on the river and bay. What he found on the trip disturbed him. The waters of the Fox and its tributary streams were turgid and foul. Near the mouth of the river, the bay was filled with piles of floating debris. According to Soquet, the lower Fox had never been so polluted: not when he was a boy during the 1920s, when fish and wildlife were plentiful; not even more recently, just before the war. To the young attorney, the change appeared dramatic, and it made a personal impact. "Having seen [the Fox] in its more or less pristine condition, I felt terrible," he later remembered.[3]

Soquet's anger would compel him to act. At the suggestion of an acquaintance, Soquet organized a Brown County chapter of the Izaak Walton League (IWL). The league had been active in Wisconsin since 1922, when it first gained prominence throughout the Midwest as a fishermen's lobby for the preservation of rivers and lakes. For help with the venture, he turned to Virgil Muench, a well-known local attorney and fellow sportsman who worked in the same office building. Together, the two organized their chapter from the handful of friends and acquaintances whom they knew to be supporters of conservation. As Soquet and Muench would discover, by the 1940s, the idea of cleaning up the Fox River appealed to more than fishermen. According to one participant, "membership of the League was made up of business and professional men, commercial fishermen, property owners, sportsmen, and private citizens." Their reasons for joining varied. But no matter what the concern—whether for wildlife or people's health, property values or the loss of swimming, foul odors or the threat to tourism—the activists were united by "an intense desire to rid the community of its curse of polluted waters."[4]

It was Soquet's hope that affiliation with the IWL would lend credibility to a cause which he knew might be unpopular. Despite the obvious harm being done to the river, the paper industry's importance to the local economy remained undisputed in the 1940s. In addition to the twenty-one pulp and paper companies then located in the Fox River Valley, there were numerous factories dedicated to converting paper to other commodities. Combined, these manufacturers had developed a diversified line of products, including book paper, cardboard, toilet paper, facial tissue, cups, napkins, boxes, bags, stationery, milk cartons, and other packaging. Valley papermakers provided jobs for nearly 10,000 people, a workforce that comprised roughly half the region's total industrial employment. Statewide, in the twenty Wisconsin counties where paper was produced, the wages and salaries paid to workers in the industry were nearly double those earned by neighboring dairy farmers. These generous incomes fueled local economies, as did the millions in tax dollars that companies paid to city governments. "It is no exaggeration," wrote one observer in 1940, "to say that the economic welfare and happiness of 500,000 Wisconsin people residing in the 33 paper mill communities, or on the farms surrounding these communities, are to a large extent dependent on the paper industry." In the Fox River Valley, the economic value of the industry had long prevented efforts to improve the stream. While state officials took a wait-and-see approach, allowing manufacturers more time to study the issue, citizens appeared content to let the matter rest. "I think they'd come to accept [pollution] as something there wasn't going to be anything done about," Soquet recalled. "After all, the paper mills were so important."[5]

Yet within just two years of Soquet's return to Green Bay, this situation changed dramatically, thanks largely to the small group of activists that Soquet organized. Beginning in the spring of 1948 and lasting through the summer of 1949, water pollution became front-page news in the Fox River Valley and throughout Wisconsin. The Brown County IWL won election for a handpicked candidate to Wisconsin's Senate; the group forced a public hearing on the contamination of the Fox River, the result of which was an unprecedented order requiring paper mills to reduce their dumping; and its members led a fight in the state capitol to strengthen the regulation of water pollution throughout Wisconsin. In retrospect, the group's achievements inaugurated a new era in state policy toward the natural environment, a period characterized by the rising public determination to protect nature from the impact of human society. Where citizens had once seemed willing to tolerate pollution as a public necessity, they increasingly defined it instead as an unwarranted threat to the welfare of the community.

As this book has argued, understanding how a single canoe trip changed the direction of state policy requires exploring the context in which it took place. Among the most important aspects of this context was the evolution of a consumer society in the Fox River Valley and its influence on the interactions between people and nature in the region. Like Soquet, many of the citizens who challenged the paper industry in 1948 had grown up in the twentieth century. Theirs was a world in which the expanding human ability to control nature had two distinct and conflicting impacts on their encounters with the Fox River. First, industrial and commercial development brought material progress to the region, including automobiles, paved roads, electricity, and an endless stream of modern conveniences. New technologies meant less physical labor, higher incomes, more free time, and for those who desired it, new opportunities for outdoor recreation, including those available on the Fox. Yet at the same time, the use of nature had its costs as well. In the case of the paper industry, it brought rising pollution levels, the death of fish and wildlife, terrible smells, and a growing danger to public health. For decades, valley residents ignored this harm in deference to the apparent needs of manufacturers. By the 1940s, however, new forms of power and transportation diminished the industrial importance of the Fox. At the same time, the river's value to local citizens as a natural amenity increased. In this altered context, pollution no longer seemed unavoidable. Instead, it was unacceptable.

The first inklings of widespread hostility toward pollution emerged in Green Bay during the spring of 1948, at the very moment that hundreds of local residents flocked to the city's annual sports show. The cause was the

innocuous question of swimming pools. Two years earlier, area parks commissioners asked the Green Bay City Council to address the lack of swimming facilities in the community. After long months of indecision, the council opted to place a tax levy on the ballot asking residents to pay $300,000
for the construction of two public pools, the first such facilities in the city.
Unexpectedly, the issue struck a nerve among citizens, many of whom believed that pollution had spoiled their own river and bay for recreational use
(Figure 17). "Why should the taxpayers pay for a swimming pool while the big
concerns such as the paper mills in Green Bay and down the Valley as far as
Oshkosh are putting . . . this pollution into the water," one resident stormed.
"If they would clean up we would not have to have any public swimming
pools." What began as a simple question of funding a community project
broadened quickly into a fierce debate over the wretched condition of the Fox
River. "How long are the people of Green Bay going to ignore the fact that we
have an open sewer flowing through the middle of town?" asked two members
of the local conservation club. "These waters stink to high heaven," chimed
another citizen. In the end, the measure to fund the swimming pools won
approval. But the uproar makes clear the link between people's desire for
natural amenities and their determination to protect the river from industrial
harm.[6]

By 1948, this kind of consumer activism was a familiar pattern in American politics, a consequence of the changing circumstances of economic life.
During the late nineteenth and early twentieth centuries, production in the
United States became the function of large-scale corporations and technological systems. On the one hand, railroads, automobiles, home appliances,
and the wealth of goods and services that flowed from manufacturers had
a profoundly liberating influence, offering people unprecedented freedom
from material hardships. On the other hand, the road builders, utilities, government agencies, and corporations responsible for creating these opportunities became so powerful themselves that they threatened to trample the
ability of ordinary citizens to control them politically. For many people, the
obvious solution was to empower consumers and taxpayers to safeguard the
public interest. In Wisconsin, lawmakers adopted a variety of strategies to
achieve this end. In the case of utilities such as gas, electricity, and transportation, they created the Railroad Commission, later renamed the Public

Figure 17. Bay Beach City Park in Green Bay, closed to swimming during the 1940s. Courtesy of the Henry Lefebvre Collection of the Neville Public Museum of Brown County, Image No. 18.1988.5600A.

Service Commission, to regulate these private corporations. If the agencies in question were public, typically the state legislature assumed this responsibility itself, as it did in the case of the Highway Commission by controlling the agency's budget. In other instances, local government took the lead. Whatever the specific issue or strategy involved, policy making in the modern era was increasingly an effort to balance the interests of consumers against those of large-scale institutions.[7]

This was exactly the situation in Green Bay in 1948 when the question of swimming pools prompted taxpayers to grow angry at the paper industry. Four points are worth noting about their complaints and the emerging environmental ethic they represent. First, what united citizens in this case was their tendency to view the Fox River as a consumer amenity: a source of swimming, boating, fishing, and scenic beauty. "I think we have the greatest swimming (and fishing) pool right in our own backyard," said one resident, referring to the bay. "What town in all America can boast of the facilities for everything that our beach has?" Although these "facilities" were natural parts of the valley's landscape, never before had citizens appeared so angered at their pollution. "Why throw good money away on man-made swimming pools," asked another resident, "when the finest natural swimming pools we could ever wish for are merely waiting to be restored." In this way, the self-interested desire for natural amenities among consumers served paradoxically as a bond, drawing people together in opposition to the paper industry. That manufacturers appeared reluctant to address the problem seemed to critics little more than evidence of their greed and political influence. "There are laws prohibiting this pollution," one citizen stormed, "but, apparently the paper industry is stronger than the government."[8]

Second, however self-interested consumer activists may have been, they defined their opposition to pollution as an effort to safeguard the community. Here again, it was natural amenities that explained both the deep sense of loss they felt and the political stand it motivated. "Twenty years ago we caught swell perch in the Fox river," said one resident. "The river now is a death trap to fish." Given the rising significance of outdoor recreation as a middle-class standard of living, pollution threatened more than individual sportsmen. It jeopardized everyone, including future generations, by undermining people's ability to enjoy the full benefits of American progress. "What could you catch now?" asked another resident, angrily noting the decline of fishing. "You guess? That's a picture of our bay that our kids are going to inherit." In this way, the selfish desire for natural amenities served as the nucleus for an awakened sense of civic responsibility. "We have seen the pollution of the Fox river kill thousands of wild waterfowl and tons of fish," lamented one letter writer. "As good citizens, we recognized the filthy, unsanitary condition of the Fox . . . as a disgrace to our community." Even those who favored swimming pools shared the sense of loss in the local environment. "The condition of the bay water is disgraceful," one proponent admitted. "Something should be done about it as soon as possible."[9]

Third, if consumption joined people together as guardians of the public good, it also offered them a variety of tools with which to effect change. By the 1940s, local residents were better informed about the nature of pollution than earlier generations. "Many reports show the extent of the pollution," one person noted. Over the years, residents had followed these reports, marking each new discovery. The knowledge they gained played an important role in prompting at least some individuals to act. "Now that domestic sewage and paper mill wastes can be successfully treated," declared one letter to the editor, "why tolerate the shameful pollution of the historic Fox river any longer." In much the same way, citizens grew savvy about the economic power of their own consumption, and its potential impact on public policy. "Pool costs must be an operating expense of the mills," suggested one resident, "a cost to be allocated over their entire production and spread over national sales; not just locally." If neither the mills nor the government addressed people's concerns, then others urged the marshaling of public opinion. "We had a wonderful opportunity of forcing the issue of a clean bay if enough protest had been registered in the right place," lamented one resident after the "yes" vote for pools. The authority to regulate pollution had been present in Wisconsin's statutes for years. The only thing lacking had been a united popular will to use it.[10]

In these respects, consumer society played a positive role in advancing the idea of pollution control. But there was a fourth aspect of consumption's influence that was less constructive. Because most critics of the paper mills remained focused on their own use of the Fox as a natural amenity, they seemed unable to acknowledge their equal complicity in polluting the river.

Simply put, everyone used paper. Whether farmers or mill workers, retail clerks or middle managers, people from all walks of life relied on the products of the valley's leading industry. Paper had become an essential component in everything from communication and packaging to maintaining personal hygiene. Yet few critics of the paper mills assumed any responsibility for harming the river themselves. "Rarely do we read that the paper industry is vitally interested in this problem," complained one citizen, a worker at a local mill. Manufacturers, he argued, were "seriously and intensely endeavoring to improve the situation," spending "thousands of dollars on research and equipment." Unfortunately, finding a solution was difficult. It required more than a state-mandated end to pollution. "Such a directive at the present time would simply mean the shutting down of pulp mills." On this point, many people in Green Bay still agreed, including editors at the local newspaper. Noting the rising tenor of criticism from its readers, the *Press-Gazette* urged citizens to be patient with the paper industry. If steps toward improving the river had been "exasperatingly slow," this was only because of "circumstances that are unchangeable and irremovable. . . . Progress in water sanitation can never be pushed beyond the point where the industry polluting the water can keep pace."[11]

But to those who valued recreation on the Fox as a key measure of progress, such arguments fell on deaf ears. "Why should the people of any community be obliged to foot the bill for damages incurred by any industry?" asked an opponent of the pools. Time and time again, officials in Green Bay acted to prevent public annoyances, from stray animals to the burning of garbage. "Yet, we allow the contamination of our rivers and bay, and the killing of fish, as though it were nothing." This kind of criticism had never before been leveled at the paper industry. In the nineteenth century, few residents would ever have challenged the mills, particularly where the Fox was concerned. But fifty years later, industrialization now divided consumption from the production, isolating the majority of citizens from the direct use of natural resources. At the same time, the more people treasured the consumer-oriented amenities of the Fox, the less willing they were to forgive the river's pollution. "Certainly no one, not even an important industry, should be permitted to destroy natural resources," complained one resident. That the waters of the Fox might still be necessary for production seemed not to occur to opponents of the industry. "Let's see what our great paper mills have done in Green Bay," asked another person, dismissively. "Oh yes, they wrecked our swimming."[12]

It was in this climate of mounting frustration with pollution that the Brown County IWL mapped out a campaign against the paper industry. Having decided that changes in state law were necessary, the group first put forward its own candidate for the Wisconsin Senate. In the fall of 1948, Fred Kaftan, a local attorney and one-time college roommate of Donald Soquet's, agreed to run in a district that included Brown County. His campaign was built on the single issue of water pollution and his message was simple. "We are entitled to concrete action," he declared during one speech before his own IWL. "Pollution will cease only when public opinion is aroused and organized." Apparently, voters shared this sentiment. In the September primary, Kaftan secured the Republican nomination, soundly defeating his opponent. Six weeks later, he won the general election as well, edging out a longtime Democratic incumbent with a record of defending paper mills against regulation.[13]

Kaftan's victory demonstrated the legitimacy of pollution as an issue in the Fox River Valley. But his election was not the IWL's boldest maneuver. In the midst of Kaftan's campaign, members circulated a petition demanding state action to eliminate industrial waste. They collected 2,500 signatures, which they promptly handed to Wisconsin's Governor Oscar Rennebohm as he visited Green Bay on a reelection tour of his own. According to Donald Soquet, the governor seemed reluctant and uninterested. Nonetheless, Rennebohm agreed to review the issue, and one month later, he returned to hear from citizens. Their message was clear. Property owners complained about the water's stench. Commercial fishermen described pulling dead fish from the bay. "One farmer reported that water [in the Fox] was so bad that his cows were unable to drink it." In the end, members of the IWL requested an independent survey to determine the extent and causes of the river's contamination. Although Rennebohm refused to blame industry alone, he promised an investigation by the Committee on Water Pollution (CWP). "There was no question about the seriousness of the problem," he reportedly said.[14]

In late November, shortly after the governor was reelected, Rennebohm made good on his pledge. The CWP announced a hearing in Green Bay in December to gather evidence on the condition of the Fox. With the attention of state authorities now focused on the valley, members of the IWL turned their sights on fellow residents. They began a publicity campaign to draw as many people as possible to the hearing. Through letters to the editor, newspaper advertisements, and talks before civic groups, the league urged citizens to take an interest in the river. "Pollution Concerns You!" declared a three-part series of advertisements. "It's responsible for the foul odors that greet your nostrils when you're out for a pleasant trip! It will cost you the price of two swimming pools ($300,000) to replace natural outdoor facilities. It has caused fish and wildlife to virtually disappear due to the unsanitary conditions created." In bold headlines, each installment in the series pushed residents to think about how pollution detracted from the quality of their lives. "Consider these facts," said the second ad. "Pollution poses a serious threat to the health and hygiene of your family. [It] eliminates use of water as a source for drinking purposes . . . prevents commercial fishermen from earning a substantial livelihood . . . causes great loss and hardship among property owners . . . [and] hampers conservation efforts to attract sportsmen and tourists." Despite all these problems, state authorities permitted sewage and industrial wastes to enter the Fox virtually untreated. "Will the polluters clean up?" asked the third and final ad. "Only when the public demands it."[15]

On December 17, when members of the CWP finally arrived in Green Bay, they discovered quickly just how determined local residents were to make this demand. Officials had expected to remain in the city for only a single day. But the large crowd that appeared for the proceedings, both to testify and simply to listen, forced the committee first to change the venue to a bigger room, and then to extend the hearing itself several times. In the end, the CWP listened to four days of testimony taking place over two and a half weeks. Hundreds of people voiced their concern for the Fox River, both inside and outside the courtroom. Their eagerness to be heard proved the validity of the IWL's cause: valley residents were no longer apathetic about pollution. On the contrary, it worried them and they meant to see it stopped.

Without fully reviewing the issues discussed during the hearing, there are two points worth emphasizing about consumer society and its influence on the debate. First, much as happened in the earlier conflict over swimming pools, residents joined together to oppose pollution because of their interest in natural amenities. Nowhere was this link more evident than in people's growing concern for public health. Health was the cornerstone of the case presented by the IWL, and at first glance, it would seem to have little connection either to consumption or the ideas of nature it fostered. "This scourge is of vital interest to you and me from the standpoint of health and sanitation," urged one letter writer, "and not just the concern of sportsmen and conservationists." But a closer look reveals that here, too, it was the popularity of natural amenities more than rising pollution that played the key role in causing citizens to worry. In 1927, when the state Board of Health issued its first-ever survey of pollution in Wisconsin's rivers, the agency was uncertain about the dangers it posed. "Stream pollution may or may not affect the public health," argued the report. Despite significant contamination throughout the state, including in the Fox River, officials cautioned that people were endangered only where they used streams for drinking and bathing. "Pollution from industrial wastes, therefore, does not, as a rule, constitute a serious menace to public health." Although outdoor recreation, tourism, and scenic beauty were becoming more popular in the 1920s, state authorities regarded them as narrow interests only. Twenty years later, this situation had changed dramatically, as evidenced by the outpouring of hostility among citizens in the Fox River Valley. Pollution was no threat to the drinking water in Green Bay, which the city obtained from several wells. Instead, residents were angered by pollution's impact on the river's ability to support swimming, fishing, and other recreational uses. As long as the Fox remained badly polluted, then anyone who entered its waters was potentially at risk. For opponents of the mills, the river's amenities became synonymous with the issue of health, and therefore a matter of public concern. Recall how the Green Bay *Press-Gazette* characterized the debate in 1948: "There is a serious conflict between the recreational and health interests on one hand and economic advantages on the other." Recreation and health versus paper and jobs, consumption versus production—these were the dividing lines over which the question of polluting the Fox would be decided.[16]

Second, again as happened in the swimming pool debate, opponents of the mills articulated a new conception of the public value of the Fox River. For most, the issue came down to a simple question: whose demands on the Fox should state officials protect first? On one side of the issue was the handful of the private corporations who utilized the river for manufacturing. On the other side were the thousands of citizens who valued the stream for other reasons. Where conservationists had long favored the economic claims of industry, opponents now argued for a reassessment of where the balance should lie. "During the last few days the residents of the Fox River Valley have had officially established a fact that has long been noisomely apparent," began one letter to the editor, written in the midst of the hearing. "One of the most beautiful streams in the world, a potential resort paradise and fisherman's bonanza, our Fox river, is grossly polluted." For the sake of industrial profits, claimed the writer, state officials repeatedly ignored acts of pollution that were clear violations of law. No such privilege extended to private citizens. "A few months ago, in a letter to the State Board of Health, I made a request . . . to pipe effluent from a home disposal system directly into the Fox river." His application was promptly denied. Though manufacturers had sanction to use the river in whatever manner they chose, the resulting pollution prevented ordinary residents from making their own claims on the Fox. The paper mills, said the writer, "have been rapaciously neglectful of the natural fish life, of the rights of the residents who own property adjacent to the river, of the rights of all citizens to enjoy and properly use the natural recreational advantages of swimming, fishing, boating, and sight-seeing." For this writer, like most opponents of the mills, the enjoyment of natural amenities was nothing less than a public right, a claim stemming from people's shared sense of ownership of the river. "The situation boils down to this," charged the writer. "Are the great majority of residents content to permit the theft of their rights to the use and enjoyment of the Fox river by a few corporate soul-less enterprises? Are our residents to be continually exposed and perhaps injured in heath by this meandering cesspool . . . ? Are our summer visitors to continue to enjoy the spectacle of flowered, wooded banks bordering gently lapping sewage and dead fish?" For anyone who cared at all about the Fox River—about its role as a place to go swimming and boating; about its value to other industries such as tourism and commercial fishing; about the beauty of its waters and the preservation of its wildlife—the answer was no. "Write, call or talk to your legislative representatives now," urged the writer. "The sooner we act, the sooner the river will be ours again."[17]

It was this sense of ownership among citizens that finally moved the CWP to restrict the industrial use of the Fox River. Recreation in Wisconsin's rivers was hardly new in 1948. But in cold political terms, the committee realized that the people involved in these activities were fast becoming more varied and numerous, and thus, potentially powerful. At a January meeting of the CWP following the hearing in Green Bay, members discussed the situation.

All agreed that pollution control was still a matter of feasibility. Whatever decision they reached would necessarily depend on the available methods of waste treatment. Nevertheless, the group was keenly aware that Americans had become "increasingly conscious" of the pollution problem, an awareness that posed a problem for regulators. "The Committee has extended a considerable amount of cooperation to the industries," said the chairman, Edward Schneberger. But the patience of local citizens had begun to wear thin. "As time goes on," he added, "the Committee might be looked upon as protectors of the industry." Thus, in June 1949, authorities ordered thirteen manufacturers to reduce the waste they discharged into the Fox. Just days before the ruling, Adolph Kanneberg wrote the CWP in a last-ditch effort to prevent the ruling. Arguing that members of the IWL had unfairly charged his clients with deceiving the public, he asked for more time to respond. The CWP denied the request. "Industry should realize their time is running out," said Chairman Schneberger. "They have been violating the law over a period of years, and must now comply."[18]

Viewed in the context of more than a century of industrial and commercial development in the Fox River Valley, the committee's decision demonstrated the great power of consumption to unite citizens on the question of pollution. By 1948, valley residents had come to depend on the Fox as much for its recreational and scenic amenities as they did on its usefulness to manufacturers. These aspects of the river were jeopardized by pollution in a way that papermaking was not. Even more important, they gave citizens new, very personal reasons to care about the Fox and its protection from industrial harm. Taken together, the various interests that residents now expected the Fox to support—from outdoor recreation and tourism to commercial fishing and the enhancement of property values—required state officials to pay greater attention to the river's amenity value in managing the stream's use. In this way, the growing public demand for natural amenities contributed as much to the ruling by the CWP as did pollution in the Fox River itself.

Unfortunately for pollution opponents, what seemed like a victory in June 1949 was soon to become a disappointing and frustrating defeat. At the very moment that members of the Brown County IWL awaited the committee's decision regarding the Fox River, they were engaged in a statewide debate on the future of environmental regulation in Wisconsin. Their efforts and the outcome of this much broader discussion would demonstrate that the influence of consumption on environmental politics was every bit as limiting as it was empowering.

On February 15, 1949, just weeks after taking his seat in the State Senate, Fred Kaftan introduced a series of five bills before the legislature designed to widen the campaign against industrial waste. Under Kaftan's proposed legislation, it would be a crime to cause pollution in the surface waters of the state. Established manufacturers were given a two-year window in which to install treatment facilities. All new industries had to submit waste disposal plans before construction could begin. Should violations occur, district attorneys were empowered to prosecute offenders. Maximum fines for each violation were raised from $100 to $1,000. And finally, the chairman of the CWP was made a full-time, salaried appointee with increased authority to conduct the committee's work. The legislation created a storm of controversy. Over the next six months, pollution became the most discussed public policy issue in Wisconsin, as sportsmen, manufacturers, lawmakers, and citizens wrestled with the question of industrial waste. By July, the dispute was settled with victories on both sides. But the compromise did little to resolve the widening conflict between the interests of production and consumption. In the Fox River Valley, this conflict would thwart the improvement of the stream even before the cleanup could begin.[19]

At the heart of Kaftan's proposal was the belief that citizens had the same right as manufacturers to use Wisconsin's rivers. But this right was poorly served by state law. Under the present statutes, Kaftan argued, "the pollution committee has the burden of proving that there are adequate means of disposing of industrial wastes before [it] orders polluters to clean up." In every other instance, manufacturers had to seek permission to use a public resource. Commercial truckers needed approval to use the highways, shippers required permission to travel the rivers, and radio stations needed authorization to broadcast on the airways. Yet industry was allowed to pollute without obtaining the people's consent. For supporters of Kaftan's legislation, the assertion that pollution control was too expensive was merely a shield behind which manufacturers continued to profit at the people's expense. "It is our contention," wrote Virgil Muench, Arthur Kaftan, and Donald Soquet in a letter to the CWP, "that the [paper] mills . . . are duty-bound both morally and legally to extend themselves beyond the 'economically feasible' consideration." To require anything less, they argued, would force citizens to "under-write the mill's experiments and to absorb continuing losses so long as pollution continues."[20]

Unfortunately for Kaftan, because his legislation seemed to focus exclusively on protecting recreational amenities, it was exposed to withering criticism from manufacturers who argued that the greatest public value of Wisconsin's rivers was their utilization for production. Few people, after all, could survive without the goods, services, and jobs that industry provided. Yet critics of pollution appeared to dismiss this important work almost entirely. "Apparently the sporting and outdoor interests in their pre-occupation with a desire for 'virgin' fishing and hunting conditions, have no thought or interest in the general welfare," complained the Wisconsin Manufacturers' Association. In a March press release the association warned members of Kaftan's "vicious proposal," arguing that his legislation "could put virtually every factory in Wisconsin out of business." Such attacks upon industry, it said, were the products of "fanatical professional sportsmen" whose "brashness and thoughtlessness" deserved "a stinging rebuke from the people of Wisconsin."[21]

In the Fox River Valley, manufacturers took heed. Even before Kaftan announced his proposal, local paper companies launched their own public relations offensive. In a series of newspaper advertisements mirroring those of the IWL, the mills defended their efforts to end pollution. "Outdoorsmen, public officials, and industry share equally in their desire to clean up Wisconsin's waters," the first ad assured. Their only differences lay in how best to achieve this result. In carefully measured sentences, manufacturers explained the composition of sulphite waste, why they had to place it in the river, and why they had yet to discover a better solution. "Plainly, this problem is extremely difficult. To assail the industry for not having found the answer is like condemning medical science for not having solved cancer." Viewed in this light, Kaftan's legislation seemed especially punitive to manufacturers. According to the Green Bay Association of Commerce, the bills posed "one of the most serious problems that has faced the community . . . in a long time." If enacted, said the association, the program "could do more harm than good in the attempt to clean up the surface water of Wisconsin."[22]

The issue came to a head on March 24, when hundreds of people gathered in the state capitol in Madison to hear testimony on Kaftan's bills. "Applause was loud and frequent," reported the Press-Gazette, "and about evenly

divided between the two sides to the dispute." Supporters of the antipollution measures did their best to bolster the plan. Some attacked manufacturers
directly. "Every dollar made by industries through pollution is a dollar taken
from the public illegally," declared Richard Steffens, an assemblyman from
Menasha and a coauthor of the bills. According to Arthur Kaftan, the mills
would never willingly implement pollution control "until they can get back
every cent they put in." Though several techniques for reducing waste had already proven successful, he argued, manufacturers refused to act because doing so would cost them money. "They'll have to be forced to do something
about it." Other speakers took a different tack, discussing the harmful consequences of industrial waste. "The stench of the [Fox] river is unbearable
in the summer," complained one resident of De Pere. "I have a right to enjoy life at home with my family." If dollars were most important, said another
speaker, then clamping down on pollution might generate its own rewards.
"Hunting and fishing is a big business too. It ought to be remembered when
the cost of pollution control is measured." In the end, proponents of the bills
had a simple message for lawmakers: pollution was wrong, and it was time
for the state to act. "Industry has no more right to poison our waters than
it has to poison the products it puts on the market," offered one supporter.
In the opinion of Virgil Meunch, the bills created a historic opportunity for
lawmakers to improve people's lives. "This legislature must be the one that
has ended pollution in Wisconsin," he urged.[23]

Although pollution opponents were passionate in their calls to strengthen
the law, their inability to address the continued need for production left
them vulnerable to attack. Lined up against Senator Kaftan's bills was a powerful array of opponents including the state Chamber of Commerce, the state
Federation of Labor, the League of Wisconsin Municipalities, the Wisconsin
Canners Association, the Federation of Women's Clubs, local dairy organizations, and numerous city officials, all of whom feared the impact of pollu-
tion-control on industry. As they entered the capitol, they wore ribbons and
carried signs shouting, "Fish or Factories!" It was factories, they argued, that
were more important. Adolph Kanneberg once again set the tone for opponents. "The philosophy of prohibiting pollution is upside down," he suggested. "The real job is to help municipalities and industries find feasible
ways . . . to reduce pollution." According to Kanneberg, Kaftan and his supporters had "just discovered pollution" and knew little about crafting a work-

able approach to its management. "Pollution can never be abolished in toto without abolishing civilization and the good things that go with it," he said. "Knowing this fact is the first, absolutely essential step toward real progress." Other speakers echoed Kanneberg in his dismay with the legislation. "If these bills should be enacted," said one mill owner, "there is only one economically feasible known way to comply, namely, to cease manufacturing sulphite pulp." Reducing pollution was a worthy goal, opponents contended, but not at the price of destroying the state's industries.[24]

This kind of criticism stung opponents of pollution. "There are many other angles to this besides that of killing fish," complained Fred Kaftan. According to the senator, pollution damaged an array of interests, from health and conservation to outdoor recreation and tourism. Even workers in the paper mills had a stake in a clean environment. Other observers agreed, noting the growing public anxiety about pollution. "There is no escaping the conclusion that the aroused residents demand something be done," said one Milwaukee journalist of the mood in the Fox River Valley. "These men were not tub thumping sportsmen nor conservation zealots," he reported, after speaking with local merchants. "They were every day businessmen and everyone there was hot under the collar over this pollution." Although passage of Kaftan's bills seemed unlikely, many commentators realized that deep-rooted changes in public opinion were underway. "It is clear that the pollution issue is a popular one and that the sensitive legislator must recognize it," declared another longtime political columnist. Kaftan himself saw much the same trend. "If the legislature neglects the challenge of pollution today," he told his colleagues, "the public will ultimately 'rise up' and demand an even more radical program in the future."[25]

In many ways, Kaftan's warning was prophetic, foretelling as it did the later emergence of a more determined environmental movement in the 1970s. But in the immediate aftermath of the debate, its resolution marked a clear defeat for opponents of pollution. After months of wrangling, lawmakers passed a bill in July. The new legislation strengthened Wisconsin's regulation of industrial waste in several ways. Most important, the CWP would now be headed by a full-time, salaried director with more freedom and resources to concentrate on policing the state's surface waters. In addition, the legislature more than doubled the CWP's budget and set time limits on the agency's decision-making process. Yet in the end, most of the get-tough policies were removed from the final bill: the time limit for ending industrial waste, the required permits for new industries, the stiff penalties for violators. Kaftan was understandably disappointed. At the very least, he said, the CWP would now "have no excuse for [the] failure to do its job."[26]

In hindsight, the new legislation was more significant than it appeared at the time. Limited though it was, the law marked a turning point in the history of pollution control in Wisconsin. But change would come slowly. On December 22, 1949, nearly one year to the day after the dramatic Fox River hearing in Green Bay, valley residents again gathered in the city to hear testimony on industrial waste. This time, officials from the CWP had come to hear the pleas of six paper mills. Having defeated the IWL in the state legislature, manufacturers appealed again to the CWP requesting extensions of the deadlines issued by the committee. In response, members of the local IWL launched another campaign to rally citizens to protect the river. "The public has waited 25 years for these mills to end pollution," said one newspaper advertisement. "How much longer?"[27]

But on this day, the mills would have their way. Adolph Kanneberg had died the previous summer, shortly after his testimony in the state legislature. Nonetheless, according to one Milwaukee reporter who covered the proceedings, "the paper mill operators came to the hearing 'loaded.' They wheeled in their top attorneys to let down a barrage of well documented statements." One by one, manufacturers argued for more time to reduce pollution. "Technical findings in the field of spent sulphite liquor pollution are not sufficient for any mill to comply with the orders," said J. M. Conway of Green Bay's Hoberg Mills. Companies had been instructed to submit plans for new treatment facilities by the end of the year. But this goal was impossible, producers argued, without a feasible means of actually reducing waste. "We have no anticipation or expectation of making a single dollar of profit in any way out of what we do to solve the . . . problem," said Milan Boex, president of Northern Mills, "but we must avoid a loss." To impose costly treatment procedures on mills competing in a national market was too risky. Such a ruling, said another official from Appleton's Kimberly-Clark Company, would lead his firm to close. "It is a cold, deliberate analysis and not a threat," he said.[28]

Against this litany of witnesses and economic pleas, opponents of the mills once again asserted the right of citizens to enjoy the natural amenities of the Fox. "The mills have already found the most 'economically feasible known method' of waste sulphite disposal," quipped Virgil Muench in a statement before the committee. "That method is the continued dumping of sulphite wastes into the Fox River." Because manufacturers used the river as a cost-free disposal site, it was in their interest to delay any treatment expenditure as long as possible. For Muench, all claims to the contrary rang hollow. "They are either asking . . . the public to take the losses so they can continue to profit, or they are asking the people . . . to take over and subsidize the pulp industry in the erection of waste disposal facilities." According to Muench, this was fundamentally un-American, even raising the specter of communism so prevalent during the era. "Paper is an essential commodity," he admitted. "[But] does it necessarily follow that riparian property owners, the commercial fishermen, and the public . . . should suffer untold and continued losses year after year merely because the pulp mills refuse to expend the money necessary to abate their pollution?"[29]

For anyone who looked to the Fox River as a natural amenity, the answer was obviously no. But for state officials preoccupied with economic development, the pleas of manufacturers carried tremendous weight. By the hearing's conclusion, the CWP did what everyone seemed to expect, agreeing to suspend indefinitely its restrictions on valley paper companies. Yet it would be a mistake to conclude that the decision marked a complete return to the committee's traditional policies. If the lengthy debate over the Fox River demonstrated anything, in fact, it was that public deference to manufacturers was deteriorating rapidly by 1949. In the years to come, Wisconsin's lawmakers were increasingly forced to contend with ordinary citizens and their own demands on nature. A legal framework once governed by the priorities of production was now influenced just as strongly by the interests of consumption. In this changed political climate lay the most important legacies of consumer society for modern environmentalism.

Conclusion
The Meaning of Nature

Among the clearest lessons from Wisconsin's Fox River Valley is that consumer society offers a tenuous foundation for environmentalism. Although many citizens objected to pollution in 1948, they were not opposed to the basic direction of industrial and commercial development. Quite the opposite, they did what decades of material progress encouraged them to do: they demanded more. For most people, the great outdoors in Wisconsin had become anything but natural. Paved highways and automobiles made nature accessible to the masses. State parks, resort hotels, and modern accessories infused the wilderness with urban comforts. And the efforts of conservationists to replenish the forests, fish, and wildlife made people's enjoyment of the outdoors increasingly satisfying. In this context, valley residents came to expect the same level of environmental quality in their own Fox River. They wanted the stream to provide not merely production but also the full range of amenities made possible by the region's consumer infrastructure. Viewed this way, their antipollution campaign was fundamentally conservative, forging only the weakest of platforms on which to secure the protection of nature.

Yet just as obviously, environmentalists should find some hope in the influence of consumption on modern politics. Limited though their perspective may have been, the valley residents who opposed pollution in 1948 advanced the belief that progress had limits, that it might be defined in ways that moved beyond traditional production-oriented measurements such as jobs, profits, and industrial output. Even more important, whatever they lacked in terms of radical vision, they made up for in sheer numbers. Consumption and the ideas of nature it fostered touched a broad segment of local society, cutting across traditional boundaries of occupation, political party, and place of residence. In subsequent years, the enjoyment of natural amenities has grown ever more pervasive, and so too has the idea that progress has limits. In this respect, consumer society paved the way for more extensive environmental critiques of modernization, including sustainability, deep ecology, and the rights of nature.

Unfortunately, if contemporary environmentalists hope to expand on these connections, they will need to overcome the most troubling legacy of consumer society: the way it renders invisible the use of nature as a means of production. In the Fox River Valley, both the paper industry and its opponents were guilty of describing the river in simplistic terms. The manufacturer's cry of "Fish or Factories!" was a disingenuous ploy to avoid restrictions on industrial waste. But their portrayal of the river as a vital engine of economic growth succeeded in part because most opponents of pollution framed their demands as a choice between the preservation of the Fox as a natural amenity and its use by manufacturers. Neither argument was realistic. Both were shaped by the widening gap between production and consumption in people's interactions with nature in the mid-twentieth century. Since 1948, this gap has only grown more extreme, as has the gulf between the respective understandings of nature they encourage: the human world of resources, jobs, and economic growth versus the seemingly nonhuman and natural realm of wilderness, scenic beauty, and recreational pleasures. To whatever extent environmentalism becomes a choice between these mutually exclusive alternatives, it is vulnerable to the divisions caused by consumer society.

As it happens, the history of the Fox River Valley offers one useful but difficult lesson for environmentalists hoping to overcome this problem: to embrace and even celebrate the human ability to control nature. There is no aspect of modern life that does not depend, in some measure, on the industrialized manipulation of nature. Although the majority of Americans now have little involvement with utilizing resources directly from the landscape, every citizen without exception relies on the fact that society extracts these resources and puts them to remarkable use. Certainly, residents of the Fox River Valley understood this in 1948. Few opponents of pollution expressed additional, more fundamental objections to the control of nature. On the contrary, they enjoyed the improved standard of living that came with utilizing resources for agricultural and industrial development. They relished the comfort made possible by electricity, automobiles, paved highways, and convenient shopping. In confronting the paper industry, they simply argued that such comforts should include natural amenities as well, attributes that required a determined effort to protect the environment from harm. Consequently, they championed new discoveries in the science of waste management and lobbied for greater efforts to understand the complex ecosystem of the Fox River in order to improve its waters. In this way, they hoped to enhance the river's value to the larger community by preserving its viability as a habitat for wildlife and its role as a scenic and recreational amenity.

On this point, pollution opponents in the Fox River Valley bear a strong resemblance to environmentalists today, the majority of whom would never seriously urge people to return to a state of unimproved wilderness. Yet modern environmentalists have a tendency to be ambivalent, if not simply hostile, toward the industrialized control and manipulation of nature. The environment is something to be protected from human society, not subjected to its increasingly pervasive influence. Given the extent to which consumption has now disconnected Americans from their dependence on natural resources, to adopt this stance comes with great political risk. In the nation's consumer society, the central challenge of environmental politics is to remind people that using nature is the ultimate source of all their comforts, from basic necessities to lavish amenities. Too often, however, it is the opponents of environmentalism who are most eager to make this argument, and therefore are most successful at shaping the terms of the debate. Because progress depends on using nature, they suggest that environmentalism is a dangerous threat to economic growth and the jobs and prosperity it generates. Environmentalists, by contrast, remain wary of using nature. Although quick to condemn the harmful consequences of industrial progress, they often fail to acknowledge the ways in which their own lives are entangled in these same developments. As a result, their arguments become vulnerable to charges of elitism and hypocrisy.

Certainly, there are many important, even urgent, reasons for people to exercise better judgment and greater restraint in their use of the natural world.

But the basic idea that humans depend on this use should never be in doubt. Until environmentalists can celebrate the full meaning of nature — both the wonders of its untamed splendor and the equally remarkable achievements of its control — then Americans will likely continue to mistrust their pleas for environmental protection.[1]

ABBREVIATIONS

Appleton Chamber of Commerce	ACC
Appleton *Post-Crescent*	APC
Green Bay *Press-Gazette*	GBPG
State Historical Society of Wisconsin	SHSW

INTRODUCTION: A RIVER OF PAPER?

1. For a transcript of the hearing, see the Committee on Water Pollution (CWP), Records, Box 27, located in the State Historical Society of Wisconsin (SHSW) Archives. (This document hereafter referred to as "Transcript.") The hearing was cosponsored by the State Board of Health. See also "Experts Testify Paper Mill Waste Pollutes River and Bay," GBPG, December 17, 1948, 1, 6; "Pollution Clean Up Stymied by Sulphite Liquor, Testimony," GBPG, December 18, 1948, 1–2; "Rotten-Egg and Pig Pen Odors Listed at Pollution Hearing," GBPG, January 4, 1949, 1, 3; "Sulphite Liquor Elimination Key to Clean River — Martin," GBPG, January 5, 1949, 1; Paul Wozniak, "They Thought We Were Dreamers: Early Anti-Pollution Efforts on the Lower Fox and East Rivers of Northeast Wisconsin, 1927–1949," *Transactions of the Wisconsin Academy of Sciences, Arts and Letters* 84 (1996): 161–175; Paul Wozniak, "Cleaning Up the Dirty Brown Fox," *Voyageur: Northeast Wisconsin's Historical Review* 6 (Summer/Fall 1990): 18–28; and Harry Nelson Tubbs, "Pollution: The Green Bay Story," located in the Arthur Kaftan Papers, Box 1, SHSW. On the history of the Izaak Walton League, see Philip V. Scarpino, *Great River: An Environmental History of the Upper Mississippi, 1890–1950* (Columbia: University of Missouri Press, 1985), 114–150.

2. On the history of the Fox River Valley, see Alice E. Smith, *Millstone and Saw: The Origins of Neenah-Menasha* (Madison: SHSW, 1966); Charles N. Glaab and Lawrence H. Larsen, *Factories in the Valley: Neenah-Menasha, 1870–1915* (Madison: SHSW, 1969); and William A. Titus, ed., *History of the Fox River Valley: Lake Winnebago and the Green Bay Region,* vols. 1–3 (Chicago: S. J. Clarke Publishing, 1930). According to Ray Hughes Whitbeck, *The Geography of the Fox-Winnebago Valley,* Wisconsin Geological and Natural History Survey, Bulletin 42 (Madison: Published by the State, 1915), 22, the rapids of the lower Fox generated nearly 43,000 horsepower.

3. Francis F. Bowman Jr., *Paper in Wisconsin: Ninety-Two Years Industrial Progress* (N.p.: N.p., 1940), 7; and "Transcript," 55. I borrow the phrase "a river of paper" from a booklet published by a valley paper company in defense of the industry: John H. Ainsworth, *The Lower Fox . . . A River of Paper: A Discussion of Pollution, Plankton and Paper* (Kaukauna, Wis.: Thimany Pulp & Paper

Company, 1957). The population figure refers to the number of urban residents along the lower Fox River. The total population of the four-county region surrounding the river was just under 300,000 in 1950. The counties are Winnebago, Outagamie, Calumet, and Brown. *Report of the Seventeenth Decennial Census of the United States, Census of Population:* 1950, vol. 1, *Number of Inhabitants* (Washington, D.C.: Government Printing Office, 1952), 49-11 to 49-19. See also David C. Smith, *History of Papermaking in the United States, 1691–1969* (New York: Lockwood Publishing, 1970).

4. "Transcript," 4–43, 140–144; quote from 35–36. See also Ralph H. Scott, A. F. Bartsch, and Theodore F. Wisniewski, "Pollution Survey: The Lower Fox River," December 15, 1948, in CWP, Box 2, SHSW.

5. "Transcript," 51–52 and 62.

6. "Pollution of the Fox," GBPG, December 24, 1948, 8. The ruling, issued on June 27, 1949, can be found in CWP, Box 2, SHSW. In addition to waste from the paper mills, the lower Fox was contaminated with sewage from the cities lining its banks. Hence, the committee also ordered six municipalities to reduce their pollution. On environmentalism after World War II, see Samuel Hays, *Beauty, Health, and Permanence: Environmental Politics in the United States, 1955–1985* (New York: Cambridge University Press, 1987); Thomas R. Huffman, *Protectors of the Land and Water: Environmentalism in Wisconsin, 1961–1968* (Chapel Hill: University of North Carolina Press, 1994); Hal Rothman, *The Greening of a Nation? Environmentalism in the United States since 1945* (Fort Worth, Tex.: Harcourt Brace, 1998); Mark Harvey, *A Symbol of Wilderness: Echo Park and the American Conservation Movement* (Seattle: University of Washington Press, 2000); Adam Rome, *The Bulldozer in the Countryside: Suburban Sprawl and the Rise of American Environmentalism* (New York: Cambridge University Press, 2001); Andrew Hurley, *Environmental Inequalities: Class, Race, and Industrial Pollution in Gary, Indiana, 1945–1980* (Chapel Hill: University of North Carolina Press, 1995); Robert Gottlieb, *Forcing the Spring: The Transformation of the American Environmental Movement* (Washington, D.C.: Island Press, 1993); Scott Hamilton Dewey, *Don't Breathe the Air: Air Pollution and U.S. Environmental Politics, 1945–1970* (College Station: Texas A&M University, 2000); Thomas Raymond Wellock, *Critical Masses: Opposition to Nuclear Power in California, 1958–1978* (Madison: University of Wisconsin Press, 1998); Robert Easton, *Black Tide: The Santa Barbara Oil Spill and Its Consequences* (New York: Delacorte Press, 1972); Donald Fleming, "Roots of the New Conservation Movement," *Perspectives in American History* 6 (1972): 7–91; Susan R. Schrepfer, *The Fight to Save the Redwoods: A History of Environmental Reform, 1917–1978* (Madison: University of Wisconsin Press, 1983); and Rachel Carson, *Silent Spring* (Boston: Houghton Mifflin, 1962). See also Michael Bess, *The Light-Green Society: Ecology and Technological Modernity in France, 1960–2000* (Chicago: University of Chicago Press, 2003); and

Ronald Inglehart, *Silent Revolution: Changing Values and Political Styles among Western Publics* (Princeton, N.J.: Princeton University Press, 1977).

7. "Transcript," 33 and 35. Here and in the next paragraph, I build on the work of Samuel P. Hays, especially *Beauty, Health, and Permanence*, 1–39, and *Conservation and the Gospel of Efficiency: The Progressive Conservation Movement, 1890–1920* (Cambridge, Mass.: Harvard University Press, 1959). As a number of historians have argued, Hays's distinctions between conservation and environmentalism are overdrawn. But in the case of water pollution in Wisconsin, they offer an accurate model for understanding the two sides in the 1948 hearing. See David Stradling, *Smokestacks and Progressives: Environmentalists, Engineers, and Air Quality in America, 1881–1951* (Baltimore, Md.: Johns Hopkins University Press, 1999).

8. The best historical analysis of this phenomenon is William Cronon's *Nature's Metropolis: Chicago and the Great West* (New York: W. W. Norton, 1991). See also David Blanke, *Sowing the American Dream: How Consumer Culture Took Root in the Rural Midwest* (Athens: Ohio University Press, 2000); Hal S. Barron, *Mixed Harvest: The Second Great Transformation in the Rural North, 1870–1930* (Chapel Hill: University of North Carolina, 1997); and Ronald R. Kline, *Consumers in the Country: Technology and Social Change in Rural America* (Baltimore, Md.: Johns Hopkins University Press, 2002). On the history and environmental impact of consumption, see Lawrence B. Glickman, ed., *Consumer Society in American History: A Reader* (Ithaca, N.Y.: Cornell University Press, 1999), 399–414; Matthew W. Klingle, "Spaces of Consumption in Environmental History," *History and Theory* 42 (December 2003): 94–110; Thomas Princen, Michael Maniates, and Ken Conca, eds., *Confronting Consumption* (Cambridge, Mass.: MIT Press, 2002); Richard Wightman Fox and T. J. Jackson Lears, eds., *The Culture of Consumption: Critical Essays in American History, 1880–1980* (New York: Pantheon Books, 1983); and Lizabeth Cohen, *A Consumer's Republic: The Politics of Mass Consumption in Postwar America* (New York: Random House, 2003).

9. "Pollution of the Fox," 8.

10. The annual pollution surveys conducted at the valley's mills suggest that water quality improved slightly during the late 1920s before declining again through the 1930s and early 1940s. See CWP, Subject Files, Box 9. In 1944, the state Board of Health compiled a ten-year summary of these findings: "General Report on Pulp and Paper Mills Waste Surveys," CWP, Subject Files, Box 9. On pollution and human health, see Christopher Sellers, *Hazards of the Job: From Industrial Disease to Environmental Health Science* (Chapel Hill: University of North Carolina Press, 1997); Greg Mitman, Michelle Murphy, and Christopher Sellers, eds., *Landscapes of Exposure: Knowledge and Illness in Modern Environments* (Chicago: University of Chicago Press, 2004); and Adam Rome, "Coming to Terms with Pollution: The Language of Environmental Reform," *Environmental History* 1 (July 1996): 6–28. On the cultural roots of environmentalism,

see Thomas R. Dunlap, *Faith in Nature: Environmentalism as Religious Quest* (Seattle: University of Washington Press, 2004).

11. In some ways, this argument builds on the work of two recent essays, both in William Cronon, ed., *Uncommon Ground: Toward Reinventing Nature* (New York: W. W. Norton, 1995): Cronon, "The Trouble with Wilderness; or, Getting Back to the Wrong Nature," 69–90; and Richard White, "'Are You an Environmentalist or Do You Work for a Living?': Work and Nature," 171–185. On the complex history of wilderness in American culture, see Roderick Nash, *Wilderness and the American Mind,* 3rd ed. (New Haven, Conn.: Yale University Press, 1982); Peter Schmitt, *Back to Nature: The Arcadian Myth in Urban America* (New York: Oxford University Press, 1969); and Paul Sutter, *Driven Wild: How the Fight against Automobiles Launched the Modern Wilderness Movement* (Seattle: University of Washington Press, 2002).

CHAPTER 1: THE VOICE OF INDUSTRY

1. The best history of water pollution control in Wisconsin is Earl Finbar Murphy, *Water Purity: A Study in Legal Control of Natural Resources* (Madison: University of Wisconsin Press, 1961). On the evolution of the paper industry, see *The Progress of Paper: With Particular Emphasis on the Remarkable Industrial Development in the Past 75 Years and the Part that Paper Trade Journal Has Been Privileged to Share in that Development* (New York: Lockwood Trade Journal Company, 1947).

2. John D. Buenker, *The History of Wisconsin,* vol. 4, *The Progressive Era, 1893–1914* (Madison: SHSW, 1998), vii, emphasis in original. Biographical information on Kanneberg is derived from "Adolph Kanneberg Dies Here at 79," *Wisconsin State Journal,* August 5, 1949, 7; and the small collection of Adolph Kanneberg Papers, SHSW. See also Stanley Caine, "Railroad Regulation in Wisconsin, 1903–1910: An Assessment of a Progressive Reform" (Ph.D. thesis, University of Wisconsin–Madison, 1967).

3. "Fish Die Like Poisoned Rats in Polluted Waters of the Flambeau," Park Falls *Independent,* July 16, 1925, 1. See also "Fish Dying in Flambeau River," Park Falls *Herald,* July 17, 1925, 8; and Adolph Kanneberg, "The Past and Present of Water Pollution and Encroachment," in SHSW Archives, CWP, Subject Files, Box 5.

4. Kanneberg, "Past and Present of Water Pollution." For legislation concerning the Conservation Commission, the Board of Health, and the Railroad Commission, see the following, respectively: chap. 668, *Laws of Wisconsin, 1917,* 1197–1252; chap. 447, *Laws of Wisconsin, 1919,* 667–672; and chap. 380, *Laws of Wisconsin, 1915,* 409–422.

5. "Fish Dying in Flambeau River" and "Fish Die Like Poisoned Rats."

6. Adolph Kanneberg, "Conservation," 2, in Kanneberg Papers, SHSW. Information on the Park Falls hearing, including Kanneberg's stated aims for the investigation, can be found in CWP, Box 8, SHSW.

7. John D. Rue, "Pulp and Paper Mill Waste in Relation to the Pollution of Streams," in CWP, Box 8, SHSW. See also Vance Edwardes, "The Waste Water Problem in News Print Mills," in CWP, Box 8, SHSW; and "Hearing on Wisconsin Stream Conditions Now on in City Hall," Park Falls *Independent*, October 1, 1925, 1.

8. Rue, "Pulp and Paper Mill Waste," 7; and Edwardes, "Waste Water Problem in News Print Mills," 2.

9. Throughout this text, I use the historical spelling "sulphite" rather than the more recent "sulfite." I do this to avoid confusion for readers, because nearly every source I quote from the period uses the former spelling of the word.

10. Rue, "Pulp and Paper Mill Waste," 5, 11–14. See also Wisconsin State Board of Health, *Stream Pollution in Wisconsin* (Madison: Published by the Board, 1927), 74.

11. See the Railroad Commission's official ruling in *Opinions and Decisions of the Railroad Commission of Wisconsin*, vol. 29 (Madison: Published by the State, 1930), 284–345.

12. Kanneberg, "Conservation," 13; and Kanneberg, "Past and Present of Water Pollution," 18.

13. Kanneberg, "Past and Present of Water Pollution," 9, 10, and 12.

14. Adolph Kanneberg, "What of Wisconsin's Stream and Lake Pollution?," September 10, 1926, in CWP, Box 5, SHSW. Quotes from 10, 3, and 9, respectively.

15. Chapter 264, *Laws of Wisconsin, 1927,* 296–300. See also "Conflict of Power Blocks Conservation," Milwaukee *Journal*, September 6, 1925, part 4, 1; "Urges State Water Bill," Milwaukee *Journal*, September 26, 1926, 2; "Conservation Measure Will be Drawn Here," Madison *Capital Times*, October 21, 1926, 11; "Commends Bill on Pollution," Milwaukee *Journal*, March 6, 1927, 1; and "Two Sides to It," Milwaukee *Sentinel*, July 8, 1927, 6.

16. Kanneberg, "Past and Present of Water Pollution," 19; and "Two Sides to It." See also "Commends Bill on Pollution."

17. "Summary of Proceedings at the Conference Between Pulp and Paper Manufacturers and State Officials of Wisconsin," February 10, 1926, 1 in CWP, Subject Files, Box 7, SHSW.

18. *Stream Pollution in Wisconsin,* 127–129.

19. Ibid., 75–83; quote from 83.

20. C. E. Curran, "Pollution of Streams from Pulp and Paper Mills," 568, a report to the North American Wildlife Conference, February 3–7, 1936, in CWP, Box 5; and L. F. Warrick, "Industrial Wastes . . . Pulp and Paper Industry," *Industrial and Engineering Chemistry* 39 (May 1947): 675.

21. "Sewerage Systems in Wisconsin," undated report, CWP, Subject Files, Box 6.

22. Frank Sinclair, "How Wisconsin Cities and Industries Purified Lakes, Rivers," Milwaukee *Journal*, July 7, 1940, section 2, 4. See also the following items, all in CWP, Subject Files, Box 4: L. F. Warrick, "Fox River Valley CLEAN-UP the

Latest Step in Wisconsin's Sanitation Program," *Concrete Highways and Public Improvements*, March–April 1936, 8–10; "Sewage Treatment Plant Summary—1945, Lower Fox River"; "Progress Report, Fox River Clean-up Program," 1936; and Greeley & Hansen, Engineers, "City of Appleton, Wisconsin: Intercepting Sewers and Sewage Treatment Plant," undated publication.

23. L. F. Warrick to the Honorable Harold A. Lytie, Assemblyman, First District, May 12, 1938, in Kaftan Papers, Box 1; and "Green Bay's Rampaging River," GBPG, July 23, 1938, 6.

24. "Fish Die by Thousands in River; Chemical Content Seen as Cause," APC, September 20, 1937, 1, 10; quote from 1. See also "Botulism Killed Ducks; But What Caused Disease?" GBPG, October 17, 1936, 1–2; "Ducks Move South, Few Dying, Report," GBPG, October 20, 1936, 7; "Tracing Source of East River Smell," GBPG, June 13, 1936, 5; Ray Pagel, "Ducks Dying in Bay Again," GBPG, September 8, 1937, 15; and "Game Fish Die in Lower Fox," GBPG, September 21, 1937, 1.

25. "Chemist Spikes Acid Theory in River Fish Loss," APC, November 17, 1937, 12. See also "Acid Fish Test Not Conclusive, Doctor Asserts," APC, November 18, 1937, 2.

26. "Minutes of Meeting," January 21, 1938, 2, located in CWP, Box 1, SHSW.

27. Stanley Barnett, "Claim Pollution in Fox River Is Caused by Mills," GBPG, October 6, 1939, 1, 13; quote from 13. See also Wisconsin State Committee on Water Pollution and State Board of Health, *Investigation of the Pollution of the Fox and East Rivers and of Green Bay in the Vicinity of the City of Green Bay* (Madison: Published by the Committee, 1939).

28. "Mills Will Finance Study of River Pollution Elimination," GBPG, November 15, 1939, 1. See also "Board Seeks to Stop Pollution," 1; "Pollution Meeting Scheduled Tuesday," GBPG, November 13, 1939, 3; and "Mill Executives Meet in Appleton," GBPG, November 14, 1939, 2.

29. "Victory over Sulphite Pollution of State Rivers Now in Sight," GBPG, August 22, 1946, 1–2.

30. The second river referred to in the quote is the East River, which joined the Fox in Green Bay shortly before the Fox emptied into the bay. "Let Us Have a Swimming Pool," GBPG, September 11, 1946, 6.

31. "Transcript," 52.

32. Peter Kurowski, "Public Streams," GBPG, January 6, 1949, 8.

33. "Transcript," 52–53, 94, 145, and 150.

34. The bulk of the testimony from citizens is reported in "Transcript," 32–47. For quotes, see 33–36, 46, 176, and 178.

35. "Transcript," 33, 87, and 150. For testimony on fiber loss, see 23 and 131; for discussion of the credibility of industry science, see 63 and 129; for questions regarding possible treatment methods, see 61–87.

36. Tubbs, "Pollution: The Green Bay Story," 8.

CHAPTER 2: WORKING WITH NATURE

1. "Water Again," Appleton *Crescent*, May 11, 1895, 6; and "Shall We Drink It," Appleton *Crescent*, July 13, 1895, 1. See also "What Will the Water Be," Appleton *Crescent*, May 4, 1895, 3; and "No Water Power," Appleton *Crescent*, August 17, 1895, 6. On urban environments during the late nineteenth century, see Joel Tarr, *The Search for the Ultimate Sink: Urban Pollution in Historical Perspective* (Akron, Ohio: University of Akron Press, 1996); Martin V. Melosi, ed., *Pollution and Reform in American Cities, 1870–1930* (Austin: University of Texas Press, 1980); David Ward, *Cities and Immigrants: A Geography of Change in Nineteenth Century America* (New York: Oxford University Press, 1971); Lawrence H. Larsen, "Nineteenth Century Street Sanitation: A Study of Filth and Frustration," *Wisconsin Magazine of History* 52 (1968): 239–247; and Judith Walzer Leavitt, *The Healthiest City: Milwaukee and the Politics of Health Reform* (Madison: University of Wisconsin Press, 1982).

2. As will be discussed later in this chapter, such a diversion was possible only because the headwaters of the upper Fox River were separated from the Wisconsin by a distance of roughly a mile. A canal at the city of Portage in south-central Wisconsin connected the two rivers. See the following articles from the Appleton *Crescent*: "To Raise the Water," April 27, 1895, 1; "Water Power Question," May 11, 1895, 1; "Low Water Trouble," May 18, 1895, 1; "Many Mills Idle," May 18, 1895, 6; "Can Use Water," May 25, 1895, 1; "Saturday Closing Too," June 15, 1895, 1; "Cost of Engines," June 15, 1895, 1; "No Lights Tonight," July 20, 1895, 4; "Ask a Little Water," July 27, 1895, 1; "No Water Power," 1; "Let Us Not Talk About It, But Do It," August 24, 1895, 3; and "That Water Meeting," September 7, 1895, 4. See also these articles from the Green Bay *Gazette*: "It Will Help Green Bay," August 30, 1895, 1; "Will Receive the Visitors," August 31, 1895, 1; "Help for the Fox Valley," September 3, 1895, 5; and "The Fox River Conference," September 4, 1895, 4. The petition of valley residents to the Congress is recorded in U.S. Congress, 1896, *Memorial of the Citizens of Portage, Berlin, Oshkosh, Fond du Lac, Neenah, Menasha, Appleton, Kaukauna, De Pere, and Green Bay*, 54th Cong., 1st Sess., S. Doc. 52.

3. "Water Again," 6; and "Shall We Drink It," 1.

4. On the importance of the Fox in the valley's early settlement, see Smith, *Millstone and Saw*; Glaab and Larsen, *Factories in the Valley*; and Joseph Schafer, *The Winnebago-Horicon Basin: A Type Study in Western History* (Madison: SHSW, 1937), 77–89.

5. *Kaukauna, Wis.: "The Lion of the Fox"* (Kaukauna: Sun Publishing, 1891), 11.

6. "Fox River Improvement Completed," Green Bay *Advocate*, June 19, 1856, 1. See also "Opening of the Fox River Improvement," Appleton *Crescent*, June 21, 1856, 2; and Smith, *Millstone and Saw*, 28–29. The structures comprising the improvement are described in C. D. Westbrook Jr., *Fox and Wisconsin Improvement* (New York: Banks, Gould, 1854), 1–13.

7. "Opening of the Fox River Improvement," 2; and "Fox River Improvement Completed," 1.
8. "Fox River Improvement Completed," 1; and C. D. Westbrook Jr., *Fox and Wisconsin Improvement* (New York: S. S. Hommel, 1853), 5. Such attitudes remained central to the human relationship to nature in the United States well into the twentieth century, reaching their zenith perhaps during the great dam-building era of the 1930s through the 1950s. See Richard White, *The Organic Machine: The Remaking of the Columbia River* (New York: Hill and Wang, 1995), esp. 34–35; Leo Marx, *The Machine in the Garden: Technology and the Pastoral Ideal in America* (London: Oxford University Press, 1964); Lewis Mumford, *Technics and Civilization* (New York: Harcourt Brace, 1934); David E. Nye, *American Technological Sublime* (Cambridge, Mass.: MIT Press, 1994); John F. Kasson, *Civilizing the Machine: Technology and Republican Values in America, 1776–1900* (New York: Hill and Wang, 1999); and Thomas P. Hughes, *American Genesis: A Century of Invention and Technological Enthusiasm, 1870–1970* (New York: Penguin Books, 1989). For discussions specific to the improvement of rivers, see Theodore Steinberg, *Nature Incorporated: Industrialization and the Waters of New England* (New York: Cambridge University Press, 1991); Ari Kelman, *A River and Its City: The Nature of Landscape in New Orleans* (Berkeley: University of California Press, 2003); Jeffrey K. Stine, *Mixing the Waters: Environment, Politics, and the Building of the Tennessee-Tombigbee Waterway* (Akron, Ohio: University of Akron Press, 1993); and Harvey H. Jackson III, *Rivers of History: Life on the Coosa, Tallapoosa, Cahaba, and Alabama* (Tuscaloosa: University of Alabama Press, 1995).
9. "Fox River Improvement Completed," 1.
10. On the political and legal history of the Improvement, see Robert W. McCluggage, "The Fox-Wisconsin Waterway, 1836–1872: Land Speculation and Regional Rivalries, Politics and Private Enterprise" (Ph.D. thesis, University of Wisconsin–Madison, 1954); Samuel Mermin, *The Fox-Wisconsin Rivers Improvement: An Historical Study in Legal Institutions and Political Economy* (Madison: University of Wisconsin Extension, 1968); Smith, *Millstone and Saw*, 23–37; and Schafer, *Winnebago-Horicon Basin*, 79–131.
11. On the geography of the Fox and Wisconsin Rivers, see the report of Captain Thomas J. Cram, an engineer with the U.S. Army's Topographical Engineers: U.S. Congress, *Report from the Secretary of War*, 26th Cong., 1st Sess., 1840, S. Doc. 318, Serial 359. See also Whitbeck, *Geography of the Fox-Winnebago Valley*, 7–29.
12. On the history of the portage, see Frederica Hart Kleist, *Fox-Wisconsin "Portage": 1673–1987* (Portage, Wis.: Published by the Author, 1987); Schafer, *Winnebago-Horicon Basin*, 79–80; and Whitbeck, *Geography of the Fox-Winnebago Valley*, 24–29. On the route as a "natural" outlet for trade, see McCluggage, "Fox-Wisconsin Waterway," 43–45.
13. Reuben G. Thwaites, ed., "Narrative of Morgan L. Martin," in *Collections of the State Historical Society of Wisconsin* (Madison: Democrat Printing, 1888), 385–

415. See also Papers of Morgan Lewis Martin, 1645–1931, SHSW; Smith, *Millstone and Saw*, 23; and Schafer, *Winnebago-Horicon Basin*, 82–84.

14. Thwaites, "Narrative of Morgan L. Martin," 414–415, Schafer, *Winnebago-Horicon Basin*, 84; and McCluggage, "Fox-Wisconsin Waterway," 38–43.

15. U.S. Congress, *Report from the Secretary of War*, 1840, S. Doc. 318, esp. 4–11; quotes from 2. See also Fox and Wolf River Control Association, "A Brief History of the War Department Studies of the Fox and Wolf Rivers," in the Charles R. Seaborne Papers, Box 1, SHSW.

16. McCluggage, "Fox-Wisconsin Waterway," 86–147; Mermin, *Fox-Wisconsin Rivers Improvement*, 1–24.

17. Smith, *Millstone and Saw*, 24–28; McCluggage, "Fox-Wisconsin Waterway," 148–231; Mermin, *Fox-Wisconsin Rivers Improvement*, 25–86. A highly useful collection of documents related to the Fox-Wisconsin Improvement is housed in the SHSW Rare Book Collection (call number J87 W6 1834–1875). The collection is untitled and catalogued only by the title of individual documents, among which is a copy of Martin's 1851 proposal to the state, "Communication from Hon. Morgan L. Martin."

18. Westbrook, *Fox and Wisconsin Improvement* (1853), 5–7; and Westbrook, *Fox and Wisconsin Improvement* (1854), 67–79.

19. "Fox River Improvement Completed," 1.

20. Smith, *Millstone and Saw*, 33–35; McCluggage, "Fox-Wisconsin Waterway," 232–314; Mermin, *Fox-Wisconsin Rivers Improvement*, 61–101.

21. *Water Communication between the Mississippi and the Lakes* (Madison: Atwood & Rublee, 1869), 52 and 44; and *Letter of the River Improvement Committee* (Green Bay: Robinson & Brother, 1875), 3 (in SHSW Rare Book Collection).

22. McCluggage, "Fox-Wisconsin Waterway," 315–395; Mermin, *Fox-Wisconsin Rivers Improvement*, 103–165. See also U.S. Congress, *Wisconsin and Fox Rivers Improvement*, 42nd Cong., 2nd Sess., 1872, H. Exec. Doc. 185, Serial 1513.

23. U.S. Congress, *Report of the Chief of Engineers, U.S. Army*, 55th Cong., 3rd Sess., 1898–1899, H. Doc. 2, Serial 3748, 2366.

24. Westbrook, *Fox and Wisconsin Improvement* (1853), 13; and U.S. Congress, *Wisconsin and Fox Rivers Improvement*, 1872, H. Exec. Doc. 185, 5 and 13.

25. A. J. Reid, *The Resources and Manufacturing Capacity of the Lower Fox River Valley* (Appleton, Wis.: Reid & Miller, Steam Book and Job Printers, 1874); quotes from 6–8, 37. See also Charles N. Glaab in *Kansas City and the Railroads: Community Policy in the Growth of a Regional Metropolis* (Madison: SHSW, 1962), 18–20. According to Glaab, an emphasis on resources "was a necessary part of the ideological equipment of town boosters throughout the Midwest in the pre–Civil War era" (20).

26. Reid, *Resources*, 21, 37.

27. Ibid., 9. See also Whitbeck, *Geography of the Fox-Winnebago Valley*, 7–40; and Thwaites, *Historic Waterways: Six Hundred Miles of Canoeing Down the Rock, Fox, and Wisconsin Rivers* (Chicago: A. C. McClurg, 1888), 180–181.

28. Alice E. Smith, *Millstone and Saw,* 34; Publius V. Lawson, *The First Water Power of the Lower Fox River, Menasha, Wis.* (Menasha, Wis.: Press Printing House, 1885), 3–4; *Kaukauna, Wis.: "The Lion of the Fox,"* 12; and Neenah *Gazette,* January 2, 1875, 1.

29. Reid, *Resources,* 11. The valley's economy was more diversified than this list of activities suggests. See Glaab and Larsen, *Factories in the Valley,* 48–77; Schafer, *Winnebago-Horicon Basin,* 132–191.

30. Reid, *Resources,* 11 and 34.

31. John Giffin Thompson, *The Rise and Decline of the Wheat Growing Industry in Wisconsin* (Madison: University of Wisconsin, 1909).

32. Gustavus de Neveu, "Considerations on the Causes and Effects of the Diminution of American Crops," in *Report of the Commissioner of Patents for the Year 1858: Agriculture* (Washington, D.C.: James B. Steedman, Printer, 1859), 213–220, quotes from 214–216; H. Smith, "Agriculture of Outagamie County," in *Transactions of the Wisconsin State Agricultural Society,* vol. 1, 1851 (Madison: Beriah Brown, State Printer, 1852), 184–187, quote from 185; and William W. Daniells, "Agriculture," in *Historical Atlas of Wisconsin* (Milwaukee: Snyder, Van Vechten, 1878), 160 (emphasis in original).

33. Reid, *Resources,* 14. See also Thompson, *Rise and Decline,* 192–193, 196; Glaab and Larsen, *Factories in the Valley,* 48–77; Smith, *Millstone and Saw,* 63–65; and Frederick Merk, *Economic History of Wisconsin during the Civil War Decade,* 2nd ed. (Madison: SHSW, 1971), 15–58.

34. Reid, *Resources,* 12, 18. On lumbering in Wisconsin, see Robert F. Fries, *Empire in Pine: The Story of Lumbering in Wisconsin, 1830–1900* (Madison: SHSW, 1951); James Willard Hurst, *Law and Economic Growth: The Legal History of the Lumber Industry in Wisconsin, 1836–1915* (Madison: University of Wisconsin Press, 1984); and F. G. Wilson, *E. M. Griffith and the Early Story of Wisconsin Forestry, 1903–1915* (Madison: University of Wisconsin, Department of Natural Resources, 1982).

35. Glaab and Larsen, *Factories in the Valley,* 60–61; Smith, *Millstone and Saw,* 65–67; Fries, *Empire in Pine,* 239; and Merk, *Economic History of Wisconsin,* 59, 78–79, 142, 146–147.

36. For analyses of this dilemma, see Ray Hughes Whitbeck, *The Geography and Industries of Wisconsin,* Wisconsin Geological and Natural History Survey, Bulletin 26 (Madison: Published by the State, 1913), 45–47; Glaab and Larsen, *Factories in the Valley,* 64–74; and Thompson, *Rise and Decline,* 82–102, and 159–171.

37. Reid, *Resources,* 41. On early papermaking in Wisconsin, see Melvin R. Bartz, "Origin and Development of the Paper Industry in the Fox River Valley (Wisconsin)" (thesis, Iowa State University, 1940); *A History of the Wisconsin Paper Industry, 1848–1948* (Chicago: Howard Publishing, 1948); Bowman, *Paper in Wisconsin;* J. N. McGovern, "Development of the Paper Manufacturing Industry in Wisconsin," in *Proceedings of the Fourth Annual Meeting of the Forest History Association of Wisconsin* (Wausau: Published by the Association, 1979); Kimberly-Clark Cor-

poration, *Four Men and a Machine: Commemoration the Seventy-Fifth Anniversary of Kimberly-Clark Corporation* (Neenah, Wis.: Published by the Company, 1948); and Maurice Lloyd Branch, "The Paper Industry in the Lake States Region, 1834–1947" (Ph.D. thesis, University of Wisconsin–Madison, 1954).

38. Reid, *Resources,* 7, 39. See also Glaab and Larsen, *Factories in the Valley,* 79–84.

39. Reid, *Resources,* 41 (emphasis in original); and *Kaukauna, Wis.: "The Lion of the Fox,"* 57.

40. "Our Paper Industry," Milwaukee *Sentinel,* January 10, 1892, 9. See also Smith, *History of Papermaking,* 219–256; and Glaab and Larsen, *Factories in the Valley,* 109–126, 258–280.

41. "Our Paper Industry," 9.

42. Reid, *Resources,* 20–21, 37.

43. "Our Lumber Interests," Green Bay *Advocate,* November 23, 1893, 3; and "As to Water Power," Appleton *Crescent,* July 13, 1895, 1. See also Glaab and Larsen, *Factories in the Valley,* 276–280.

44. "An Awful Responsibility," Appleton *Weekly Post,* September 14, 1893, 4. See also David P. Thelen, *The New Citizenship: Origins of Progressivism in Wisconsin, 1885–1900* (Columbia: University of Missouri Press, 1972), 55–85.

45. Frederick Jackson Turner, "The Significance of the Frontier in American History," in Martin Ridge, ed. *Frederick Jackson Turner: Wisconsin's Historian of the Frontier* (Madison: SHSW, 1993), 26–47; quotes from 26 and 47.

46. Reid Badger, *The Great American Fair: The World's Columbian Exposition and American Culture* (Chicago: Nelson Hall, 1979), xiii; and Hubert Howe Bancroft, *The Book of the Fair: An Historical and Descriptive Presentation of the World's Science, Art, and Industry, as Viewed through the Columbian Exposition at Chicago in 1893* (New York: Bounty Books, 1894), 3.

47. On events in the *1890s,* see Hal R. Williams, *Years of Decision: American Politics in the 1890s* (New York: Wiley, 1978); Susan Harris Smith and Melanie Dawson, eds., *The American 1890s: A Cultural Reader* (Durham, N.C.: Duke University Press, 2000); H. W. Brands, *The Reckless Decade: America in the 1890s* (New York: St. Martin's Press, 1995); Carleton Beals, *The Great Revolt and Its Leaders: The History of Popular American Uprisings in the 1890s* (New York: Abelard-Schuman, 1968); Lawrence Goodwyn, *The Populist Moment: A Short History of the Agrarian Revolt in America* (New York: Oxford University Press, 1978); Paul Krause, *The Battle for Homestead, 1880–1892: Politics, Culture, and Steel* (Pittsburgh: University of Pittsburgh Press, 1992); Richard Schneirov, Shelton Stromquist, and Nick Salvatore, eds., *The Pullman Strike and the Crisis of the 1890s: Essays on Labor and Politics* (Urbana: University of Illinois Press, 1999); and Dee Brown, *Bury My Heart at Wounded Knee: An Indian History of the American West* (New York: Henry Holt, 1991).

48. For reports on urban water works, gas and electric service, local canneries, and other aspects of modern development, see the following newspaper articles: "A

Luxury of Modern Times," GBPG, July 7, 1895, 2; "The New Cannery," Green Bay *Advocate,* October 5, 1893, 3; "The Pickle Factory," Green Bay *Advocate,* October 12, 1893, 3; "The City Water Works," Green Bay *Advocate,* June 29, 1893, 3; "How Much Water We Use," Green Bay *Advocate,* October 26, 1893, 3; "Gas and Electric Light," Green Bay *Advocate,* November 9, 1893, 3; "A Modern Mill," Appleton *Crescent,* July 13, 1895, 1; and "The Old Reliable Meat Market," Appleton *Crescent,* June 19, 1895, 2. See also Mark H. Rose, *Cities of Light and Heat: Domesticating Gas and Electricity in Urban America* (University Park: Pennsylvania State University, 1995); and Siegfried Giedion, *Mechanization Takes Command: A Contribution to Anonymous History* (New York: Oxford University Press, 1948).

49. GBPG, July 7, 1895, 5; and "Lost Everything," Appleton *Crescent,* October 26, 1895, 1. See also Michael Lesy, *Wisconsin Death Trip* (New York: Random House, 1973).

50. "The Ice Harvest Is On," Appleton *Crescent,* January 19, 1895. See also the Green Bay *Advocate,* July 13, 1893, 3; and Lee E. Lawrence, "The Wisconsin Ice Trade," *Wisconsin Magazine of History* 48 (1965): 257–267.

51. B. C. Brett, *Report to the Board of Health of the City of Green Bay, for the Year Ending March 31, 1897* (Green Bay: Der Landsmann, 1897), 3. On public health in nineteenth-century Wisconsin, see Leavitt, *Healthiest City.* On the history of garbage collection, see Martin V. Melosi, *Garbage in the Cities: Refuse, Reform, and the Environment, 1880–1980* (College Station: Texas A&M University Press, 1981).

52. Appleton *Weekly Post,* September 6, 1894, 1. Reports of runaway horses appeared weekly in local newspapers. For examples, see Appleton *Weekly Post,* February 22, 1894, 1; Appleton *Crescent,* August 18, 1894, 1; and Green Bay *Advocate,* August 11, 1892, 3. The Green Bay *Gazette,* January 12, 1895, 4, notes two related incidents, one in which a "lost cow" was reported wandering through town and a second in which a butcher was attacked and severely injured by a steer on Main Street.

53. "Work in the Woods," Appleton *Crescent,* January 19, 1895, 6. See also Green Bay *Gazette,* January 4, 1895, 4, and January 11, 1895, 4. The first statewide survey of rural road conditions was conducted by mail carriers in the early twentieth century under the direction of the Wisconsin Geological and Natural History Survey. See the Survey's Records, 1899–1930, SHSW, Box 6.

54. "Let Us Not Talk About It, But Do It," 3 and "Many Mills Idle," 6. The federal regulation supporting navigation over manufacturing is explained in U.S. Congress, *Report of the Chief of Engineers, U.S. Army,* 55th Cong., 3rd Sess., 1898–1899, H. Doc. 2, Serial 3748, 2340–2344.

CHAPTER 3: THE RENEWAL OF PROGRESS

1. "Opening Address by the President," in *Proceedings of a Conference of Governors in the White House, Washington, D.C., May 13–15, 1908* (Washington, D.C.: Government Printing Office, 1909), 3–13; quotes from 4, 8, and 10. See also Hays, *Conservation and the Gospel of Efficiency;* Stephen Fox, *The American Conservation*

Movement: John Muir and His Legacy (Madison: University of Wisconsin Press, 1985); Gifford Pinchot, *Breaking New Ground* (New York: Harcourt, Brace, 1947); and Charles R. Van Hise, *The Conservation of Natural Resources in the United States* (New York: Macmillan, 1910).

2. "Meetings of the Wisconsin Legislative Committee on Water Powers, Forestry and Drainage, Volume I," in Paul O. Husting Papers, 1909–1918, SHSW, Box 21; quote from 28. On conservation in Wisconsin, see Huffman, *Protectors of the Land and Water*, 1–31; Dennis East, "Water Power and Forestry in Wisconsin: Issues of Conservation, 1890–1915" (Ph.D. thesis, University of Wisconsin–Madison, 1971); Donald Edward Boles, "Administrative Rule Making in Wisconsin Conservation" (Ph.D. thesis, University of Wisconsin–Madison, 1956); Alfred Allan Schmid, "Water Allocation and Development in Wisconsin" (Ph.D. thesis, University of Wisconsin–Madison, 1959). In addition to the Green Bay and Mississippi Canal Company, there was a second, smaller enterprise that owned significant rights to the power of the Fox River: the Neenah and Menasha Water Power Company. See the company's "Records, 1896–1946," in SHSW. See also "Uncle Sam's Dams Prove Pot of Gold," Milwaukee *Journal*, October 11, 1936, 6; and Glaab and Larsen, *Factories in the Valley*, 262–264.

3. "Committee on Water Powers, Forestry and Drainage, Volume I," 17.

4. "Opening Address by the President," 10. See also, Hays, *Conservation and the Gospel of Efficiency*, 1–4.

5. "Opening Address by the President," 10. See also Kendrick A. Clements, *Hoover, Conservation, and Consumerism: Engineering the Good Life* (Lawrence: University Press of Kansas, 2000), 3–4; and Daniel O. Buehler, "Permanence and Change in Theodore Roosevelt's Conservation Jeremiad," *Western Journal of Communication* 62 (Fall 1998): 439–458.

6. The growing array of conservation activities during the period is best followed in Wisconsin State Conservation Commission, *Biennial Report* (Madison: Published by the State, 1909–1930), in SHSW. See also Walter E. Scott, "Conservation's First Century in Wisconsin: Landmark Dates and People," in *Conservation Centennial Symposium: The Quest for Quality in Wisconsin*, ed. Norma Cournow Camp (Madison: University of Wisconsin, 1967), 14–39.

7. "Opening Address by the President," 3 and 6.

8. "Kurz Recalls First Days in Light Plant," APC, September 29, 1932, 30; and from "Electric Light," Appleton *Crescent*, October 7, 1882, 3. See also "Light Transaction," Appleton *Post*, July 27, 1882, 1; "Glory Hallelujah!," Appleton *Post*, August 3, 1882, 5; "The Electric Light," Appleton *Crescent*, September 9, 1882, 3; "The Electric Light," Appleton *Post*, October 5, 1882; "Creation of Electric Forces," Appleton *Post*, November 30, 1882, 2; and "The Incandescent Electric Light," Appleton *Crescent*, December 2, 1882, 3. For historical accounts, see Louise P. Kellogg, "The Electric Light System at Appleton," *Wisconsin Magazine of History* 6 (December 1922): 189–194; Wisconsin Michigan Power Company, *Souvenir Booklet Commemorating the*

50th Anniversary of the Opening of the World's First Hydro-Electric Central Station at Appleton, Wisconsin (Appleton: Published by the Company, 1932); Wisconsin Michigan Power Company, . . . *They Turned on the Lights* (Appleton: Published by the Company, 1957); A. C. Langstadt, "Early Experiences in Electrical Work at Appleton, Wisconsin," March 24, 1922, in Outagamie County Historical Society, Wisconsin Electric Power Company (WEPCO) Collection, Box 9; and Forrest Mc-Donald, *Let There Be Light: The Electric Utility Industry in Wisconsin, 1881–1955* (Madison: American History Research Center, 1957), 16, 34–35.

9. "Electric Light," Appleton *Crescent*, 3; and "Creation of Electric Forces," 2. See also Harold C. Passer, *The Electrical Manufacturers, 1875–1900: A Study in Competition, Entrepreneurship, Technical Change, and Economic Growth* (Cambridge, Mass.: Harvard University Press, 1953), 90–91, 119–121.

10. "Creation of Electric Forces," 2. On electrification in the United States, see Passer, *Electrical Manufacturers;* Thomas P. Hughes, *Networks of Power: Electrification in Western Society, 1880–1930* (Baltimore, Md.: Johns Hopkins University Press, 1983); Rose, *Cities of Light and Heat;* David E. Nye, *Consuming Power: A Social History of American Energies* (Cambridge, Mass.: MIT Press, 1998); David E. Nye, *Electrifying America: Social Meanings of a New Technology* (Cambridge, Mass.: MIT Press, 1990); Nye, *American Technological Sublime*, 143–198; and Lois C. Hunter and Lynwood Bryant, *A History of Industrial Power in the United States, 1780–1930*, vol. 3, *The Transmission of Power* (Cambridge, Mass.: MIT Press, 1991).

11. On earlier efforts to transmit energy, see Hunter and Bryant, *Transmission of Power*, 115–184.

12. See Kellogg, "Electric Light System," 189–193; McDonald, *Let There Be Light*, 15–16 and 34–37; Wisconsin Michigan Power Company, *Souvenir Booklet;* Lagstadt, "Early Experiences"; and "Electric Light," Appleton *Crescent*, 3.

13. "Electric Light," Appleton *Post*.

14. Langstadt, "Early Experiences," 1–3.

15. On the economics of load factor, see Hughes, *Networks of Power*, 216–221; Passer, *Electrical Manufactures*, 105–207; McDonald, *Let There Be Light*, 34–45, 109–110; and Langstadt, "Early Experiences."

16. Langstadt, "Early Experiences," 1–3; and McDonald, *Let There Be Light*, 25–26. On alternating current, see Hughes, *Networks of Power*, 93–95, 129–135; and Passer, *Electrical Manufactures*, 276–320.

17. Transformers were comprised of two separate coils of wire wound on a magnetic core. When electricity was passed through the first, or primary, coil, it induced a corresponding flow of electricity in the secondary coil, whose voltage and current depended on the relative number of turns in each. If the secondary had more turns than the primary, then the voltage in the original circuit was increased or "stepped up," and the current "stepped down" accordingly.

18. McDonald, *Let There Be Light*, 98; and Hunter and Bryant, *Transmission of Power*, 361–364.

19. Hunter and Bryant, *Transmission of Power*, 243, 254–272; and Passer, *Electrical Manufactures*, 310–337.

20. McDonald, *Let There Be Light*, 131–133, 229–230.

21. Nye, *Electrifying America;* Nye, *Consuming Power.* See also McDonald, *Let There Be Light*, 270–275.

22. Violet Christensen, "Replica of First Hydro-Electric Plant Dedicated," APC, October 1, 1932, 1, 4.

23. "Electricity Celebrates," APC, September 29, 1932, 6.

24. "Big Territory Served from Modern Plant," APC, September 29, 1932, 36, 38.

25. Solomon Fabricant, *Labor Savings in American Industry, 1899–1939* (New York: National Bureau of Economic Research, 1945), 20.

26. "Pioneer Work Still Going on in Electricity," APC, September 29, 1932, 31.

27. "Cities Ready for Highway 15 Tour," Milwaukee *Sentinel*, evening edition, August 21, 1922, 3. See also "Highway 15 Opening Tour Number," a special section of the Milwaukee *Evening Sentinel*, September 14, 1922, 17; "Progressive Twins Welcome Highway 15 Tour Party," Neenah and Menasha *Daily News and the Times*, September 14, 1922, 1, 8; "Expect 1,000 Visitors Here for Opening of Highways 15," GBPG, September 13, 1922, 1; "Hundreds of Cars Aid in Road Opening," GBPG, September 14, 1922, 1; "Hirst Issues Plea for Tax to Aid Roads," GBPG, September 15, 1922, 1, 4; "Appleton Ready for Motorcade's Visit Thursday," APC, September 13, 1922, 12; "Kaukauna Turns Out for Parade," APC, September 15, 1922, 6; "Praise County and Conway for Boost Given Good Roads," APC, September 15, 1922, 16; and "Highway 15 Opened with Enthusiastic Acclaim," *Wisconsin Motorist* 13 (September 1922): 54.

28. "Hirst Issues Plea for Tax to Aid Roads," 4. See also William Otis Hotchkiss, *Rural Highways of Wisconsin*, Bulletin 18, Wisconsin Geological and Natural History Survey (Madison: Published by the State, 1906), 77–80, 89–96; and Arthur R. Hirst, *Earth Roads*, Road Pamphlet 1, Wisconsin Geological and Natural History Survey (Madison: Published by the State, 1907), 1.

29. "Hirst Issues Plea for Tax to Aid Roads," 4. See also "Facts about Wisconsin's New $4,000,000 Highway," Milwaukee *Sentinel*, special section on Highway 15, September 14, 1922, 3. For the 1921–1922 fiscal year, the total budget for the state of Wisconsin was a mere $34.4 million, nearly a third of which, or roughly $11.3 million, was allocated to the State Highway Commission. See *Wisconsin State Budget* (Madison: State Board of Public Affairs, 1923), 7–12.

30. Arthur Brisbane, "Buy an Automobile! It Means Freedom; Saves Time and Money," *Wisconsin Motorist* 14, no. 3 (January 1923): 135; and F. A. Cannon, "Turn Back the Pages of History and Take Glimpse at Highway 15 in 1826," GBPG, September 14, 1922, 1, 3; quote from 3. My description of highways as industrialized spaces is based on similar analyses of railroads in the nineteenth century: Alfred Runte, *Trains of Discovery: Western Railroads and the National Parks* (Flagstaff, Ariz.: Northland Press, 1984); Wolfgang Schivelbusch, *The Railway Journey: The*

Industrialization of Time and Space in the 19th Century (Berkeley: University of California Press, 1977); and John R. Stilgoe, *Metropolitan Corridor: Railroads and the American Scene* (New Haven, Conn.: Yale University Press, 1983). See also Carol Sheriff, *The Artificial River: The Erie Canal and the Paradox of Progress, 1817–1862* (New York: Hill and Wang, 1996).

31. Robert Fargo, *Our Country Roads,* Wisconsin Farmers' Institutes, 1887, Bulletin 1 (Madison: Democrat Printing, 1887), 209–215, quote from 209; and John M. Olin, "Better Roads — A Plan for Improving County Highways in Wisconsin," in *Transactions of the Wisconsin State Agricultural Society* 31 (1893): 283–323, quote from 288–289. See also M. G. Davis et al., eds., *A History of Wisconsin Highway Development, 1835–1945* (Madison: Department of Transportation, 1947), 14–16; Ballard Campbell, "The Good Roads Movement in Wisconsin, 1890–1911," *Wisconsin Magazine of History* 49 (Summer 1966): 273–293; Merk, *Economic History of Wisconsin,* 238–239; and Hurst, *Law and Economic Growth,* 21–22, 169.

32. *Laws of Wisconsin,* 1911 (Madison: Published by the State, 1911), chap. 337, 353–368; and State Highway Commission, *The New State Aid Highway Law,* Bulletin 1 (Madison: Published by the State, 1911). The creation of the State Highway Commission did not guarantee acceptance of the agency or its authority, but the new commission's achievements quickly overcame most opposition. See also Barron, *Mixed Harvest,* 7–42; Campbell, "Good Roads Movement"; Bruce R. Seely, *Building the American Highway System: Engineers as Policy Makers* (Philadelphia: Temple University Press, 1987), 11–23; Hays, *Conservation and the Gospel of Efficiency;* Stephen Skowronek, *Building a New American State: The Expansion of National Administrative Capacities, 1877–1920* (New York: Cambridge University Press, 1982); Thomas K. McCraw, *Prophets of Regulation: Charles Francis Adams, Louis D. Brandeis, James M. Landis, Alfred E. Kahn* (Cambridge, Mass.: Harvard University Press, 1984); and Charles McCarthy, *The Wisconsin Idea* (New York: Macmillan, 1912).

33. Arthur R. Hirst, "Story of the Wisconsin Highway System," in Victor F. Pettric, *Motoring in Wisconsin: 1922 Official Yearbook of the Wisconsin Motorists Association* (Milwaukee: Burdick-Allen, 1922), 41–48, quote from 41; and "Who Is Hirst?," in *Good Roads for Wisconsin* (May–June, 1924): 19–20, quote from 19. The latter is included in Arthur R. Hirst, Papers, SHSW Archives, Madison, Wisconsin. Additional biographical information on Hirst from "Arthur Roscoe Hirst," in *Ninth Biennial Report of State Highway Activities* (Madison: Published the State, 1932), 9–11.

34. Wisconsin Highway Commission, *Fifth Biennial Report of State Highway Activities* (Madison: Published by the State, 1924), 29; and Arthur R. Hirst, *Wisconsin's Highway Problem* (Madison: Good Roads Association of Wisconsin, 1921), 15.

35. Numerous plans for Highway 15 — which later became U.S. Highway 41 — are located in the offices of the Wisconsin Department of Transportation in Green Bay. See, for example, Wisconsin Highway Commission, "Plan and Profile of Proposed Appleton–Green Bay Road: Appleton–Little Chute, Outagamie County,

Federal Aid Project 582 B," 1935, File No. Outagamie 27. The commission's manuals on road construction spanning the period between the 1920s and 1950s can be found in the SHSW library. The oldest is Wisconsin Highway Commission, *Federal Aid Construction: Contract and Specifications* (Madison: Published by the State, 1926). See also "How Wisconsin's Great Highway Became a Concrete Reality," Milwaukee *Sentinel,* evening edition, September 14, 1922, 3, in special edition on Highway 15; and Seely, *Building the American Highway System,* 118–135.

36. The commission's growing power over nature is reflected in the increasing size and specificity of its regulations. Compare, for example, Wisconsin Highway Commission, *Federal Aid Construction: Contract and Specifications* (1926), a small pamphlet of merely 78 pages, with the commission's *Standard Specifications for Road and Bridge Construction* (Madison: Published by the State, 1935), a densely printed book of 640 pages.

37. Arthur R. Hirst, "Underlying Principles Controlling the Laying Out, Marking and Maintaining of a State Trunk Highway System," in the *Fourth Biennial Report Showing State Aid Highway Operations under the Supervision of the Wisconsin Highway Commission from January 1, 1916, to January 1, 1918* (Madison: Published by the State, 1918), 45–60; quotes from 45 and 47. See also Harry D. Blake, *Highway Location and Surveying,* Wisconsin Highway Commission, Bulletin 13 (Madison: Published by the State, 1922), 24.

38. Blake, *Highway Location and Surveying,* 18. See also A. R. Whitson and C. W. Stoddart, "Studies of Wisconsin Soils," in *Twenty-second Annual Report of the Agricultural Experiment Station of the University of Wisconsin* (Madison: Democrat Printing, 1905), 262–281; Whitbeck, *Geography of the Fox-Winnebago Valley,* 7–12; and W. O. Hotchkiss and Edward Steidtmann, *Limestone Road Materials of Wisconsin* (Madison: Published by the State, 1914).

39. Wisconsin Highway Commission, *Federal Aid Construction: Contract and Specifications* (1926), 8. Although published several years after the period I am here discussing, this set of standards likely resembles fairly closely the specifications in place from 1918 through 1922, when the paving of Highway 15 was first completed. Similar precautions are suggested in George R. Chatburn, *Highway Engineering: Rural Roads and Pavements* (New York: Wiley, 1921), 140.

40. Arthur R. Hirst, *The Earth Road Drag,* Road Pamphlet 2, Wisconsin Geological and Natural History Survey (Madison: Published by the State, 1907), 6. The changing technology of highway construction during the 1910s and 1920s can be followed through *Good Roads,* a monthly publication sponsored by the American Road Builders Association, an organization of private contractors.

41. Portland cement was produced by heating a mixture of limestone and clay and then grinding the resulting substance into a fine powder. It was so named for its resemblance to limestone quarried in Portland, England. See Wisconsin Highway Commission, *Federal Aid Construction: Contract and Specifications* (1926), 24–29; and Chatburn, *Highway Engineering,* 233–288.

42. Quote from Arthur R. Hirst, *Earth Roads,* Road Pamphlet 1, 2nd ed., Wisconsin Geological and Natural History Survey (Madison: Published by the State, 1909), 10. See also Wisconsin Highway Commission, *Federal Aid Construction: Contract and Specifications* (1926), 57–60; and Chatburn, *Highway Engineering,* 87–122.

43. "Unused Roads Are a Poor Investment from Standpoint of the Taxpayer," *Wisconsin Motorist* 11, no. 6 (April 1920): 60–62; quote from 60. See also *Laws of Wisconsin,* 1931, chap. 22, 20–39; and the following articles from the *Wisconsin Motorist:* "Can We Drive Cars in Winter," 11, no. 4 (February 1920), 42–43; "Campaign to Keep Roads Open in Winter Meets with Favor," 11, no. 5 (March 1920), 33–35; F. A. Cannon, "Open Highways Next Winter Means You Must Act Now," 11, no. 12 (October 1920), 48–49; and "Members Asked to Aid in Fight for Open Roads," 12, no. 1 (November 1920), 45.

44. "A Milestone of Progress," Milwaukee *Evening Sentinel,* September 14, 1922, special section on Highway 15, 3; and "Opening Highway 15," APC, September 16, 1922, 20.

45. Hirst, *Wisconsin's Highway Problem,* 5 and 14.

46. Wisconsin Highway Commission, *Sixth Biennial Report of State Highway Activities* (Madison: Published by the State, 1926), 15; and *Eighth Biennial Report of State Highway Activities* (Madison: Published by the State, 1930), 144. Statistics compiled from "Motor Vehicle Registrations for the Year 1922," *Wisconsin Motorist* 14, no. 3 (January 1923): 105; United States Department of Commerce, Bureau of the Census, *Fourteenth Census of the United States Taken in the Year 1920,* vol. 1, *Population, 1920, Number and Distribution of Inhabitants* (Washington, D.C.: Government Printing Office, 1921), 137–138; and United States Department of Commerce, Bureau of the Census, *Fifteenth Census of the United States: 1930, Population,* vol. 1, *Number and Distribution of Inhabitants* (Washington, D.C.: Government Printing Office, 1931), 1182–1183. See also John B. Rae, *The Road and the Car in American Life* (Cambridge, Mass.: MIT Press, 1971); James J. Flink, *The Automobile Age* (Cambridge, Mass.: MIT Press, 1988); Flink, *America Adopts the Automobile, 1895–1910* (Cambridge, Mass.: MIT Press, 1970); Virginia Scharff, *Taking the Wheel: Women and the Coming of the Motor Age* (New York: The Free Press, 1991); Kenneth T. Jackson, *Crabgrass Frontier: The Suburbanization of the United States* (New York: Oxford University Press, 1985), 157–171; Clay McShane, *Down the Asphalt Path: The Automobile and the American City* (New York: Columbia University Press, 1994), 125–148; and Robert and Helen Lynd, *Middletown: A Study in American Culture* (New York: Harcourt Brace, 1929).

47. "Visit County to Gain Ideas for Farming," APC, July 9, 1924, 1; and "Western Visitors Liked Valley Best of All Tour Area," APC, July 10, 1924, 7. For the visiting delegation's report, see *Dairying in Wisconsin and Its Possibilities in Kansas, Missouri and Oklahoma* (Kansas City, Mo.: Good Roads Association of Greater Kansas City, 1924). See also Eric E. Lampard, *The Rise of the Dairy Industry in Wisconsin: A Study in Agricultural Change, 1820–1920* (Madison: SHSW, 1963).

48. *Dairying in Wisconsin,* 22 and 4, respectively.
49. Ibid., 27–28. Members of the delegation had every reason to argue that Wisconsin's natural advantages were no greater than those of their own states because they hoped to promote dairying. Nevertheless, their comments accurately reflect the industrialized use of nature in Wisconsin farming. See also Lampard, *Rise of the Dairy Industry,* 145–242.
50. Ray W. Ingham, *Grass Silage and Dairying* (New Brunswick, N.J.: Rutgers University Press, 1949), 11. See also E. Jane Homan and Michael A. Wattiaux, *Technical Dairy Guide: Lactation and Milking* (Madison: Babcock Institute for International Dairy Research and Development, 1995), 3–39; Colin T. Whittemore, *Lactation of the Dairy Cow* (London: Longman Group, 1980), 5–28; and W. A. Henry and F. B. Morrison, *Feeds and Feeding: A Handbook for the Student and Stockman,* 15th ed. (Madison: Henry-Morrison Company, 1915), 338–340.
51. Again, the discussion that follows is based on Lampard, *Rise of the Dairy Industry,* esp. 91–242.
52. P. H. Smith, "Agriculture of Outagamie County," and L. B. Brainard, "Agriculture of Brown County," in *Transactions of the Wisconsin State Agricultural Society,* vol. 1, 1851 (Madison: Beriah Brown, State Printer, 1852), 184–187 and 128–132, respectively. During the early decades of the twentieth century, the Wisconsin Geological and Natural History Survey, in cooperation with the United States Department of Agriculture, produced soil surveys of each county in the state. The surveys of Brown, Outagamie, Calumet, Winnebago, and Fond du Lac counties can be found in the survey's bulletins (Madison: Published by the State), numbers 62A (1929), 54D (1921), 61B (1927), 61A (1925), and 37 (1914), respectively.
53. Fred H. Scribner and Roy T. Harris, *The Winter Feeding of Dairy Cows,* Wisconsin Bankers' Farm Bulletin 17 (Milwaukee: Wisconsin Bankers' Association, 1914), 1. Statistics drawn from Wisconsin Department of Agriculture, *Agricultural Statistics for Wisconsin,* 1915, Bulletin 4 (Madison: Published by the State, 1916), 13–14; and *Wisconsin Agricultural Statistics for 1920,* Bulletin 34 (Madison: Wisconsin Cooperative Crop Reporting Service, 1920), 52–53. See also N. S. Fish, "The History of the Silo in Wisconsin," *Wisconsin Magazine of History* 8 (December 1924): 158–170; Lampard, *Rise of the Dairy Industry,* 155–162; W. H. Peterson, et al., "A Study of the Principal Changes which Take Place in the Making of Silage," *Bulletin No. 61 of the Agricultural Experiment Station of the University of Wisconsin* (Madison: University of Wisconsin, 1925); and Peter McDonald, *The Biochemistry of Silage* (Chichester, U.K.: Wiley, 1981).
54. Lampard, *Rise of the Dairy Industry,* 152–169; quote from 152. See also Steven Stoll, *Larding the Lean Earth: Soil and Society in Nineteenth-Century America* (New York: Hill and Wang, 2002); G. C. Humphrey and F. B. Morrison, *Feeding Dairy Cows* (Madison: University of Wisconsin Extension Service, 1923); and P. E. McNall and D. R. Mitchell, *Getting the Most from the Dairy Herd by Right Feeding* (Madison: University of Wisconsin Agricultural Experiment Station, 1928).

55. Humphrey and Morrison, *Feeding Dairy Cows,* 1. During the same period, re-searchers also perfected a variety of tests to detect disease in cattle, particularly bovine tuberculosis. See H. L. Russell and E. G. Hastings, *Bovine Tuberculosis in Wisconsin,* Bulletin 84 (Madison: University of Wisconsin Agricultural Experi-ment Station, 1901). On the evolution of cow testing, selective breeding, and the Babcock test, see Lampard, *Rise of the Dairy Industry,* 178–190 and 197–204.

56. S. M. Babcock and H. L. Russell, *The Cheese Industry: Its Development and Possi-bilities in Wisconsin,* Bulletin 60 (Madison: University of Wisconsin Agricultural Experiment Station, 1897). See also Lampard, *Rise of the Dairy Industry,* 91–144. A second technology known as the hand cream separator also proved useful to farmers, providing them an efficient and dependable means of separating cream from skim milk and permitting them to make fewer trips to local factories to deliver milk.

57. Emory C. Wilcox, Orville E. Krause, and Lawrence Brereton, *Utilization of Wis-consin Milk* (Madison: Wisconsin State Department of Agriculture, 1950); Wis-consin Crop Reporting Service, *Wisconsin Dairying at Mid-Century* (Madison: Wisconsin State Department of Agriculture, 1955); and Emory C. Wilcox, *Trans-portation of Wisconsin Milk: Farm to Market* (Madison: Wisconsin State Depart-ment of Agriculture, 1951). On milk as a danger to public health, see Leavitt, *Healthiest City,* 156–189. See also Lampard, *Rise of the Dairy Industry,* 227–242, and 453.

58. "Opening Address by the President," 8–9.

59. *Dairying in Wisconsin,* 25.

60. Ibid., 33; and APC, April 28, 1923, 39. See also Blanke, *Sowing the American Dream;* and Kline, *Consumers in the Country.*

61. APC, April 28, 1923, 54. See also Cronon, *Nature's Metropolis,* 364–369.

CHAPTER 4: THE CONSUMER'S METROPOLIS

1. "We Are Going to Organize," APC, March 27, 1920, 4; and "Chamber of Com--merce Organized," APC, March 30, 1920, 1. In addition, see the following reports in the APC: "Interest Growing in Chamber of Commerce Meeting Monday," March 27, 1920, 1; "City's Welfare Live Issue with Appleton's Men," March 27, 1920, 1, 6; "All Set for Mass Meeting at Elk Hall This Evening," March 29, 1920, 1, 8; "Urges Cooperation," March 30, 1920, 1, 8; "663 Members in New Commerce Chamber; Still Going Strong," March 31, 1920, 1; and "Directors for New Com-merce Chamber Elected Last Night," April 13, 1920, 1, 3. See also the minutes of an earlier, smallerorganizational meeting in the Yearbook, Appleton Chamber of Commerce Records (hereafter Yearbook, ACC), 1920, 1–3, SHSW Archives. For a listing of the chamber's early members, see "Membership List Classified," in *Community Betterment,* the publication of the ACC, vol. 1, no. 1 (August 1920): 2–4. The initial priorities of the chamber were derived from a survey of its mem-bers. See "Plenty To Do for Appleton," in *Community Betterment* 1, no. 1 (August

1920): 6–7 in Yearbook, ACC, 1920. See also the minutes of the Board of Directors, September 10, 1920, in Yearbook, ACC, 1920, 32–33.

2. "Nineteen Twenty-One," *Community Betterment* 1, no. 6 (January 1921): 1. See also T. J. Jackson Lears, *No Place of Grace: Antimodernism and the Transformation of American Culture, 1880–1920* (Chicago: University of Chicago Press, 1981), 7–11; Lynn Dumenil, *The Modern Temper: American Culture and Society in the 1920s* (New York: Hill and Wang, 1995), 3–13, 56–97; William Leach, *Land of Desire: Merchants, Power, and the Rise of a New American Culture* (New York: Vintage Books, 1993); Cohen, *Consumer's Republic;* and Sarah Elvins, *Sales and Celebrations: Retailing and Regional Identity in Western New York State, 1920–1940* (Athens: Ohio University Press, 2004).

3. "Nineteen Twenty-One," 1; and "City's Welfare Live Issue with Appleton Men," 1.

4. Calvin Coolidge, "The Press under a Free Government," in *Foundations of the Republic: Speeches and Addresses* (New York: Books for Libraries Press, 1968), 183–190; quotes from 187–188. See also "Interest Growing in Chamber," 1; and "City's Welfare Live Issue with Appleton Men," 6; Arthur M. Schlesinger Jr., *The Crisis of the Old Order, 1919–1933* (Boston: Houghton Mifflin, 1956), 54–76; and Thomas B. Silver, *Coolidge and the Historians* (Durham, N.C.: Carolina Academic Press, 1982).

5. Yearbook, ACC, September 17, 1926, 81–82 and October 1, 1926, 21. See also "Here's Where Appleton Gets Its Business," APC, October 9, 1926, 25.

6. "32 Great Bargains to Open 'Motor to Appleton Week'!," APC, October 9, 1926, 28–29; "Low Everyday Prices Point to Economy . . ."; and "Motor to Appleton Week, Geo. Walsh Co.," APC, October 9, 1926, 7 and 15.

7. "Rural Affairs," *Community Betterment* 1, no. 8 (March 1921): 6, in Yearbook, ACC, 1921, attached following 63; and "Community Not Bounded by City Lines, C. C. Told," in Yearbook, ACC, 1922.

8. "The Caravan on College Avenue," APC, January 14, 1928, 5. See also "Merchandise Sales in Appleton Stores to Reach Total of Over $12,000,000 a Year," APC, April 28, 1923, 49 and 52; and "College Avenue Historic District Nomination Report," located in the Historic Preservation Office, SHSW. Appleton's trading area is described in *Report of Committee: Town and Country Relations,* Chamber of Commerce Collection, Outagamie County Historical Society. On the history of American main streets, see Elvins, *Sales and Celebrations,* 21–46.

9. "Report of the Road Committee," August 31, 1923, Board of Directors, September 12, 1923, Yearbook, ACC, following 20; and Board of Directors, March 19, 1924, Yearbook, ACC, 44. See also William R. Childs, *Trucking and the Public Interest: The Emergence of Federal Regulation, 1914–1940* (Knoxville: University of Tennessee Press, 1985), 7–24; and Rae, *The Road and the Car,* 87–132.

10. "The Tenth Year's Work," 9, Yearbook, ACC, 1929. For discussions of the sign campaign, see the minutes of the chamber's Community Welfare Committee, Yearbook, ACC, May 14, 1929, and May 21, 1929, 138–141; and June 26, 1930, and July 10, 1930, 93–98.

11. Leonard S. Smith, "Appleton Today and Tomorrow," *Community Betterment* 2, no. 2 (June–August 1921): 3 in Yearbook, ACC, 1921.

12. Wisconsin Highway Commission, *Eighth Biennial Report*, 57–59.

13. Yearbook, ACC, Board of Directors, September 21, 1934, 28–30, SHSW. See also Wisconsin Highway Commission, *Sixth Biennial Report*, 39–45, 80–81; and W. O. Hotchkiss, "U.S. Routes in Wisconsin," *Badger Highways* (August 1925): 12.

14. As with the initial construction of Highway 15, the rerouting of Highway 41 was an evolutionary process that never fully came to an end. See "U. S. H. 41 So. Co. Line Winnebago to CTH 'JJ' (McCarty's Crossing), Winnebago and Outagamie County," an unpublished, handwritten chronology of the development of Highway 41, located in the files of the Wisconsin Department of Transportation's office in Green Bay. That office also possesses plans for several sections of the highway, listed under the following file numbers: Outagamie 26, 27, 31, 36, 45, 127, 141, 148; and Brown 46. In addition, several newspaper articles tracked the progress of the belt line effort. See these reports in the APC: "Road Officials Conduct Hearing on New 41 Route," June 15, 1935, 2; "Asylum Route for New 41 Will Meet Firm Opposition," July 29, 1937, 4; and "City and Chamber Oppose Proposed Highway 41 Route," July 30, 1937, 4. For discussion of the U.S. 41 business route, see the following entries in Yearbook, ACC: Highway Committee, July 6, 1936; Board of Directors, August 14, 1936; Board of Directors, November 20, 1936; Board of Directors, July 23, 1937; Board of Directors, August 27, 1937; Road Committee, September 26, 1939; Board of Directors, November 29, 1940; Board of Directors, January 10, 1941; Board of Directors, June 20, 1941; Highway Committee, July 10, 1941; Highway Committee, July 22, 1941; Highway Committee, August 18, 1941; Highway Committee, November 7, 1941; Board of Directors, September 28, 1944; "Extension of West College Avenue," May 31, 1946; Board of Directors, August 19, 1948; Highway Committee, May 12, 1949; Retail Division, October 5, 1949; and Retail Board of Governors, October 13, 1949.

15. The editorial is included in Yearbook, ACC, 1931, attached following 23. See also "Special Report," in Yearbook, ACC, 1931, 41.

16. See these entries from Yearbook, ACC: Board of Directors, January 6, 1928; Retail Division, June 9, 1930; Retail Division, July 7, 1930; and Retail Division, May 13, 1936.

17. Parking Committee, Yearbook, ACC, May 12, 1949, 111. For discussion of the parking meter issue, see the following in Yearbook, ACC: Retail Division, July 15, 1936; Retail Division, September 2, 1936; Special Retail Committee on Parking, September 15, 1936; Board of Directors, June 14, 1940; Retail Division, May 12, 1948; Board of Directors, August 19, 1948; Board of Directors, October 21, 1948; Board of Directors, January 20, 1949; and "Minutes of Parking Committee," 1948, 115–127. See also "What Parking Meters Have Done," GBPG, April 26, 1948, 6; "Start Erection of New Parking Signs," APC, July 30, 1937, 2; and "Parking Meter Law Sent Back to Committees," APC, December 16, 1948, 25.

18. *Report of Committee: Town and Country Relations,* Chamber of Commerce Collection, Outagamie County Historical Society. See also Don S. Kirschner, *City and Country: Rural Responses to Urbanization in the 1920s* (Westport, Conn.: Greenwood Press, 1970); Blanke, *Sowing the American Dream;* Kline, *Consumers in the Country;* and Barron, *Mixed Harvest.*

19. On the social functions organized by the chamber, see the following entries from Yearbook, ACC: "Outline of Letter and Questionnaire to Be Sent to 100 Leading Appleton Farmers," November 2, 1920; "Farm Picnic," June 18, 1924; and "Farm and City Tied Together at Big Meeting," November 3, 1924. On the question of public restrooms, see Rural Affairs Committee, June 18, 1924 in Yearbook, ACC. For discussions of highway snow removal, see Yearbook, ACC: "Brusewitz Tells Why Roads Are Not Opened in Winter," March 26, 1924; Rural Affairs Committee, June 18, 1924; and Road Committee, January 27, 1927. For dairy promotions, see Yearbook, ACC: Board of Directors, July 10, 1936; Dairy Day Committee, August 12, 1936; Retail Meeting, September 18, 1940; and "Annual Report," March 31, 1941, 3, 6. On the stock fairs, see "Report of Committee: Town and Country Relations," c1924, Chamber of Commerce Collection, Outagamie County Historical Society, 142–143.

20. "Wiegle's Illness Prevented Speech at C. of C. Dinner," in Yearbook, ACC, 1922; and Retail Division, Yearbook, ACC, 1929, 165.

21. APC, November 7, 1934, special Appleton Day section, 1; APC, June 20, 1932, 11; Kaukauna *Times,* June 21, 1931, 3; and "Trade Expansion Days at Gloudemans,'" Kaukauna *Times,* June 16, 1931, 3. See also "If you can't get it at home . . . ," Hilbert *Favorite,* June 23, 1932, 8. On the chamber's rural advertising, see Retail Division, Yearbook, ACC: August 1, 1934; October 31, 1934; January 23, 1935; July 31, 1935; August 28, 1935; October 30, 1935; April 24, 1940; and May 3, 1940.

22. APC, June 17, 1931, 5; and "The Fashion Shop," APC, June 17, 1931, 19.

23. Retail Division, Yearbook, ACC, August 1, 1929, 200. On timing sales with large gatherings in Appleton, see the following entries from Yearbook, ACC: Retail Division, March 12, 1928; Retail Division, August 1, 1929; Board of Directors, September 20, 1929; Retail Division, February 26, 1940; and "Annual Report," 1942, 8. On the annual Christmas sales, see Yearbook, ACC, 1939: Christmas Program Committee, October 11; Retail Division, October 26; Special Retail Committee, November 1; Special Retail Committee, November 4; "Prospectus for 1939 Christmas Season," attached to Retail Division, 56; and "Annual Report," 1940, 7. See also "Children Will Compete for Three Prizes in Christmas Procession, Friday, Dec. 1," APC, November 22, 1939, 1; "City Stores Hold Christmas Opening Today; Santa Claus Will Head Procession Dec. 1," APC, November 23, 1939, 1; and "Children Give Santa Claus Tremendous Greeting Today," APC, December 2, 1939, 1, 7. In 1948, Santa Claus made his first arrival in the city in a helicopter. See "4,000 Greet Santa on Arrival from North Pole Saturday," APC, November 15, 1948, 10.

24. According to Lizabeth Cohen, *Consumer's Republic,* 18–61, the 1930s were an important period in the evolution of mass consumption as a political and cultural

force in the United States. "A paradox arose in the midst of the Great Depression of the 1930s," she writes. "Hard times forced many Americans to struggle to find and keep work, to feed their families, and to hold on to their homes or pay their rent. Yet increasingly they were being viewed by policymakers—and were thinking of themselves—as consumers, as purchasers of goods in the marketplace" (18).

25. Alice G. Marquis, *Hopes and Ashes: The Birth of Modern Times, 1929–1939* (New York: The Free Press, 1986); and Nye, *American Technological Sublime*, 199–224.

26. *Markets by Incomes: A Study of the Relation of Income to Retail Purchases in Appleton, Wisconsin* (New York: Time Incorporated, 1932), 1:7–9.

27. See the following sections in *Markets by Incomes:* "Groceries," 1:41–66; "Public Utilities," 2:43–44; "Automobiles," 1:13–20; and "Public Utilities," 2:43–44.

28. APC, October 20, 1928, 13, and June 2, 1928, 18.

29. This estimate remains very rough because it fails to account for the declining value of the dollar caused by inflation. Nevertheless, as the next paragraph argues, the point I am making here is of secondary importance. Statistics drawn from the following sources: "Merchandise Sales in Appleton Stores to Reach Total of Over $12,000,000 a Year," 49; U.S. Department of Commerce, *United States Census of Business,* 1948, vol. 3, *Retail Trade-Area Statistics* (Washington, D.C.: Government Printing Office, 1951), 48.09; U.S. Department of Commerce, *Fourteenth Census of the United States Taken in the Year* 1920, vol. 1, *Population,* 1920, *Number and Distribution of Inhabitants* (Washington, D.C.: Government Printing Office, 1921), 137–138; U.S. Department of Commerce, *Report of the Seventeenth Decennial Census of the United States: Census of Population: 1950,* vol. 1, *Number of Inhabitants* (Washington, D.C.: Government Printing Office, 1952); 49.11–49.19; and Convention Committee, "You'll Be Glad You Came to Appleton," in Yearbook, ACC, 1947.

30. "Chamber of Commerce Organized," 1.

31. "City Cut Off from Outside World," APC, February 22, 1922, 1; and "Heavy Loss in City's Worst Storm," APC, February 23, 1922, 1, 12 (quote from 1). See also "City's Isolation May End Saturday," APC, February 24, 1922, 1, 16; "Storm Plight Ends as Trains Move," APC, February 25, 1922, 1; "Wire Circuits Again Unite Valley," APC, February 27, 1922, 1, 10; and "Hundreds of Men Work Untiringly to Restore Pre-Storm Conditions," APC, February 28, 1922, 1.

32. "Says Storm Is Worst in More than 50 Years," APC, February 24, 1922, 1. See also "Storm Recalls Hard Times of Yester-Year," APC, February 24, 1922, 2. On natural disasters, see Theodore Steinberg, *Acts of God: The Unnatural History of Natural Disaster in America* (New York: Oxford University Press, 2000); and Donald Worster, *Dust Bowl: The Southern Plains in the 1930s* (New York: Oxford University Press, 1979).

33. "Huge Force Is Building Up Power Lines," APC, February 27, 1922, 1; "City Cut Off from Outside World," 1; and "Heavy Loss in City's Worst Storm," 1, 12.

34. "Draws History of Industry in Valley Region," APC, October 1, 1932, 3. Sensen-brenner was unable to attend the dedication of the replica plant, so a colleague read his address.

35. W. W. Spratt, "Electricity in the Paper Industry," *Paper Trade Journal* 78 (June 19, 1924): 46–50. See also Hunter and Bryant, *Transmission of Power*, 209–217, 283–289. The *Paper Trade Journal* provides by far the best means of following the gradual adoption of electricity by manufacturers of paper. See, for example, the following selected articles: C. C. Batchelder, "Electrical Equipment of Pulp and Paper Mills," 60 (February 18, 1915): 213–223; W. F. Schaphorst, "The Steam Turbine in the Paper Mill," 61 (August 19, 1915): 44–50; and W. W. Cronkhite, "Electric Motor Application to Paper Machinery," 64 (February 8, 1917): 97–107.

36. Ronald C. Tobey, *Technology as Freedom: The New Deal and the Electrical Modernization of the American Home* (Berkeley: University of California Press, 1996), 5–13. In Appleton, the relative importance of industrial as compared to residential power consumption was apparent from an early date. In 1916, the local utility had 3,221 total consumers, only 306 of whom purchased electricity for manufacturing power. Nonetheless, the company's industrial customers still accounted for over half the energy purchased from the utility. *Tenth Annual Report of the Railroad Commission of Wisconsin* (Madison: Democrat Printing, 1917), 450–481, 566–579, and 616–659.

37. Kaukauna *Times*, June 12, 1931, 2; GBPG, June 2, 1948, 8; GBPG, March 31, 1948, 15; and APC, May 11, 1940, 5. New appliances failed to liberate women from the responsibilities of hearth and home, but it did nonetheless alter the character of their labor, reducing the physical demands of housework and eliminating many of its former discomforts. See Ruth Schwartz Cowan, *More Work for Mother: The Ironies of Household Technology from the Open Hearth to the Microwave* (New York: Basic Books, 1983); and Suellen Hoy, *Chasing Dirt: The American Pursuit of Cleanliness* (New York: Oxford University Press, 1995). On the marketing of electric appliances, see Rose, *Cities of Light and Heat*.

38. APC, March 16, 1920, 12. See also Wolfgang Schivelbusch, *Disenchanted Night: The Industrialization of Light in the Nineteenth Century* (Berkeley: University of California Press, 1995).

39. Kaukauna *Times*, June 12, 1931, 2. See also Gail Cooper, *Air-conditioning America: Engineers and the Controlled Environment, 1900–1960* (Baltimore, Md.: Johns Hopkins University Press, 1998).

40. McDonald, *Let There Be Light*, 225, 328–330, and 382–383. See also Lemant Richardson, *Wisconsin REA: The Struggle to Extend Electricity to Rural Wisconsin, 1935–1955* (Madison: University of Wisconsin Experiment Station, 1961), 31.

41. GBPG, March 22, 1948, 17; and "The Farmer Turns on the Juice," GBPG, May 12, 1948, 12. See also Maureen Ogle, *All the Modern Conveniences: American Household Plumbing, 1840–1890* (Baltimore, Md.: Johns Hopkins University

Press, 1996); Paul W. Glad, "Innovations and Adaptations of a New Era: Science, Technology, and Agriculture in Wisconsin, 1920–1930," *Wisconsin Magazine of History* 74 (1990): 9–16; Susan Burdick Davis, *And There Was Light* (Madison: Published by the Author, 1948); and Richardson, *Wisconsin REA,* 146–149.

42. State Highway Commission, Division 3, *Sixteenth Annual Report* (Green Bay: Published by the Division, 1949), 3; and State Highway Commission, *Wisconsin Highway Traffic,* 1948 (Madison: Highway Planning Survey, 1948). See also George B. Sowers, *The Wisconsin Highway Picture in 1952* (Madison: Public Expenditure Survey of Wisconsin, 1952); and *Highway Transportation Links Wisconsin's Economy* (Madison: Wisconsin Highway Users Conference, 1947), 6–15.

43. State Highway Commission, Division 3, *Sixteenth Annual Report,* 27–28, 47–57, and 62.

44. Kaukauna *Times,* June 2, 1931, 2; GBPG, March 22, 1948, 10; GBPG, June 2, 1948, 8; and GBPG, April 10, 1948, 8.

45. "Unparalleled Savings!," APC, June 17, 1931, 31.

46. "Cars Skid, Bus Schedules Hit as Freezing Rain Makes Roads Slick," APC, December 15, 1948, 1. See also "Ice Coated Highways Paralyze Traffic," GBPG, December 15, 1948, 1.

47. APC, July 29, 1937, 17.

48. Howard I. Wood, "Marinette to Take Part in Opening," Milwaukee *Evening Sentinel,* September 14, 1922, 4 of the "Highway 15 Opening Tour Number."

49. Edmund Charles Kratsch, "Motoring over the Great Trails," *Wisconsin Motorist* 11, no. 8 (June 1920): 60–65. See also Robert Gough, *Farming the Cutover: A Social History of Northern Wisconsin, 1900–1940* (Lawrence: University Press of Kansas, 1997); and Timothy Bawdin, "The Northwoods: Back to Nature?," in Robert C. Ostergren and Thomas R. Vale, *Wisconsin Land and Life* (Madison: University of Wisconsin Press, 1997), 450–469.

50. Nye, *American Technological Sublime,* 52–64; quote from 53.

51. Brisbane, "Buy an Automobile!," 135; "Cloverland, the Upper Peninsula of Michigan," *Wisconsin Motorist* 11, no. 8 (June 1920): 45; Asa K. Owen, "A Bit of Old Wisconsin," *Wisconsin Motorist* 14, no. 8 (June 1923): 22–24; and Walter H. Reed, "Joys of Motoring and Living in Northern Wisconsin," *Wisconsin Motorist* 11, no. 8 (June 1920): 68–69.

52. Henry David Thoreau, "Walking," in *The Writings of Henry David Thoreau* (Boston: Houghton Mifflin, 1906), 5:205–248; quotes from 5:224, 5:226, and 5:213, respectively. See also Reed, "Joys of Motoring," 68.

53. William K. Gibbs, "Nature's Rendezvous and the Motorists' Paradise," *Wisconsin Motorist* 11, no. 8 (June 1920): 53–57; quote from 53. Gibbs was referring to a specific location, namely the Upper Peninsula of Michigan. But even so, what made that location so attractive in his mind were the highways that cut through the landscape.

54. Brisbane, "Buy an Automobile!," 135; and Reed, "Joys of Motoring," 69.

55. "Closed Cars and the Summer Touring Season," *Wisconsin Motorist* 11, no. 9 (July 1920): 62. See also Scharff, *Taking the Wheel*, 122–126; and "Why the Popularity of the Closed Car?" *Wisconsin Motorist* 12, no. 2 (December 1920): 65.

56. Conway's ad is located in *Automobile Blue Book of Wisconsin* (1910), 248. See also Reed, "Joys of Motoring," 69. On accommodations for tourists in valley communities, see the *Wisconsin Motorist:* "Oshkosh Opens Fishing Park to Tourists," 14, no. 5 (March 1923): 67; "Many Cities Provide Accommodations for Tourists," 12, no. 3 (January 1921): 91; "Camp Sites in Wisconsin," 13, no. 8 (June 1922): 46; "Badger Cities to Give Tourists Free Camp Sites," 13, no. 9 (July 1921): 48. See also Warren J. Belasco, *Americans on the Road: From Autocamp to Motel, 1910–1945* (Cambridge, Mass.: MIT Press, 1979); and John A. Jakle, Keith A. Sculle, and Jefferson S. Rogers, *The Motel in America* (Baltimore, Md.: Johns Hopkins University Press, 1996).

57. Kaukauna *Times,* June 10, 1932, 5, and June 24, 1932, 3.

58. Owen, "A Bit of Old Wisconsin," 22; and "Cloverland," 45. See also *Ninth Biennial Report,* 78.

59. Wisconsin Highway Commission, *Eighth Biennial Report,* 59, and *Ninth Biennial Report,* 61. The state legislature authorized the commission to begin its program of highway beautification in 1931. See *Laws of Wisconsin,* 1931, chap. 295, 484–485. On the related development of scenic parkways, see Marilyn E. Weigold, *Pioneering in Parks and Parkways: Westchester County, New York, 1895–1945* (Chicago: Public Works Historical Society, 1988); John Nolen and Henry V. Hubbard, *Parkways and Land Values* (Cambridge, Mass.: Harvard University Press, 1957); and State Highway Commission, *Wisconsin Scenic Roads and Parkway Study* (Madison: Published by the Commission, 1965).

60. State Highway Commission, *Eleventh Biennial Report of Highway Activities* (Madison: Published by the State, 1936), 21; and State Highway Commission, "Beautifying the Highway," *Ninth Biennial Report,* 78–81; quote from 79. See also Karl Raitz, ed., *The National Road* (Baltimore, Md.: Johns Hopkins University Press, 1996); and John Brinckerhoff Jackson, *A Sense of Place, a Sense of Time* (New Haven, Conn.: Yale University Press, 1994), 187–205.

CHAPTER 5: ENJOYING THE GREAT OUTDOORS

1. David Prerau, *Seize the Daylight: The Curious and Contentious Story of Daylight Saving Time* (New York: Thunder's Mouth Press, 2005); and Michael Downing, *Spring Forward: The Annual Madness of Daylight Saving* (Washington, D.C.: Shoemaker & Hoard, 2005).

2. John A. Campbell, "Brother Farmer," GBPG, March 14, 1947, 4.

3. "From a Daughter," GBPG, March 18, 1947, 6; "City Speaks for Farm," GBPG, March 15, 1947, 4; "And the Farmer," GBPG, March 18, 1947, 6; "Health and Daylite [*sic*] Saving," GBPG, March 29, 1947, 4; and E. Wacek, "City and Country," GBPG, March 18, 1947, 6.

4. "County Joins Rest of State in Voting Down Daylight Saving Plan," APC, April 2, 1947, 1. See also GBPG, April 2, 1947, 1.

5. "From a Daughter," 6; "City Speaks for Farm," 4; "Doesn't Want Daylight Saving," APC, March 20, 1947, 10; and "Settle Own Problem," APC, March 31, 1947, 6.

6. *Laws of Wisconsin, 1957,* chap. 6 (Madison: Published by the State, 1957), 13; and *Wisconsin Statutes,* 1957 (Madison: Published by the State, 1957), 2377.

7. *First Report of the Conservation Commission of the State of Wisconsin* (Madison: Published by the State, 1909), quotes from 3–4, 28.

8. Leopold's many comments on outdoor recreation are collected in Curt Meine and Richard L. Knight, eds., *The Essential Aldo Leopold: Quotations and Commentaries* (Madison: University of Wisconsin Press, 1999), 32–44; quotes from 37–38, and 43. See also Sutter, *Driven Wild,* 54–99.

9. *Biennial Report* (1916), 7; and (1918), 15.

10. *Biennial Report* (1916), 43–67; quotes from 64. See also Louis S. Warren, *The Hunter's Game: Poachers and Conservationists in Twentieth-Century America* (New Haven, Conn.: Yale University Press, 1997); and John F. Reiger, *American Sportsmen and the Origins of Conservation* (Norman: University of Oklahoma Press, 1986).

11. *Biennial Report* (1916), 15–24, 139–140, 145–146, 151–156; and *Biennial Report* (1926), 17–18.

12. *Biennial Report* (1932), 30. Information on hatcheries and stream improvement taken from *Biennial Report* (1937), 53–59, 67–69. The Conservation Commission was represented by the Commissioner of Fisheries on the Committee on Water Pollution. Yet as noted, the CWP remained reluctant to impose restrictions on certain kinds of industrial waste despite the obvious harm to fish life.

13. *Biennial Report* (1937), 73. Carp had been planted intentionally throughout Wisconsin, including in Lake Winnebago, during the 1880s. See John D. Black, *Nature's Own Weed Killer: The German Carp* (Madison: State Conservation Department, 1946).

14. *Biennial Report* (1916), 25; and *Biennial Report* (1937), 110. See also *Biennial Report* (1937), 73–82. On the removal of rough fish, see also the William J. P. Aberg Papers, SHSW Archives, especially Box 11.

15. *Biennial Report* (1916), 47, 53. See also the following editions of *Biennial Report:* (1916), 46–67; (1930), 83–96; (1934), 58–66; (1937), 177–184.

16. *Biennial Report* (1916), 95–97; and *Biennial Report* (1924), 15–16. For evidence of the kinds of pressures faced by the Conservation Commission to improve the amenities at state parks, see Ernest Swift to E. J. Vanderwall, June 6, 1947, in Aberg Papers, SHSW, Box 7.

17. *First Report,* 28–29. See also Wilson, *E. M. Griffith and the Early Story of Wisconsin Forestry;* East, "Water Power and Forestry in Wisconsin," 1–98, 260–342; and *The Wisconsin Forest Crop Law* (Madison: State Conservation Department, 1952).

18. *Biennial Report* (1928), 5–6. On recreational forests, see *Biennial Report* (1939), 2–3.

19. *Fifteenth Biennial Report of the State Conservation Commission of Wisconsin* (Madison: Published by the State, 1937), 107–108. See also chap. 365, *Laws of Wisconsin*, 1935.

20. *Biennial Report* (1937), 107–113.

21. Meine and Knight, *Essential Aldo Leopold*, 36; and *Biennial Report* (1934), 5. Tabulations of hunting, fishing, deer, and trapping licenses can be found in Aberg Papers, SHSW, Box 10. Between 1932 and 1948, the number of hunting licenses sold in the four-county region comprising the Fox River Valley more than doubled, climbing from 14,799 to 30,957. This pattern was even more pronounced in the number of fishing licenses sold during the same period, which rose from 10,025 to 48,215, a nearly fivefold increase.

22. *Biennial Report* (1937), 7–8; Gifford Pinchot, *The Fight for Conservation* (Garden City, N.Y.: Harcourt, Brace, 1910), 42.

23. Wisconsin Regional Planning Committee, *A Study of Wisconsin: Its Resources, Its Physical, Social and Economic Background* (Madison: Published by the State, 1934); quote from the foreword.

24. Ibid., 157–185; quotes from 157.

25. Wisconsin State Planning Board and State Conservation Commission, *A Park, Parkway, and Recreational Area Plan*, Bulletin 8 (Madison: Published by the State, 1939), 1. Three years earlier, the planning board had produced a less comprehensive recreational study of the region surrounding Milwaukee, but most of its conclusions were incorporated into the larger statewide report in 1939. See Wisconsin State Planning Board, *A Conservation and Recreation Plan for Southeastern Wisconsin*, Bulletin 3 (Madison: Published by the State, 1936).

26. Wisconsin State Planning Board, *Park, Parkway*, 5–8.

27. Ibid., 5–8.

28. Ibid., 5–44; quotes from 5, 42.

29. Ibid., 45–66; quote from 56.

30. Ibid., 45–87; quote from 68.

31. Wisconsin State Planning Board, *A Recreational Plan for Vilas County*, Bulletin 12 (Madison: Published by the State, 1941), 1–4.

32. Ibid., 4–11; quotes from 10–11.

33. Ibid., 14–41; quote from 36.

34. Ibid., 22. See also Walter Rowlands, Fred Trenk, and Raymond Penn, *Rural Zoning in Wisconsin*, Bulletin 479 (Madison: University of Wisconsin, 1948); and Wisconsin State Planning Division, *Rural Planning and Zoning*, Bulletin 19 (Madison: Published by the State, 1954).

35. The kind of planning described in this section extended to the local level and was typically carried out by city parks commissions. For an example in the Fox River

Valley, see *Annual Report of the Board of Parks Commissioners of the City of Green Bay* (Green Bay: Green Bay Printing Company, 1931).

36. *Vacation in Door County, Wisconsin's Outdoor Living Room* (Sturgeon Bay: Door County Chamber of Commerce, 1945). Information and quotes in this and the following two paragraphs are compiled from two similar versions of the brochure, both of which appear to date from 1945. They are located in the SHSW library's pamphlet collection.

37. *Kaukauna, Wis.: "The Lion of the Fox,"* 11, 43.

38. "Press-Gazette Sports Show," GBPG, March 19, 1948, 3. See also John Torinus, "First Post-War Press-Gazette Sports Show Opens Tuesday," GBPG, March 29, 1948, 25.

39. Torinus, "First Post-War Press-Gazette Sports Show," 25. See also John Sears, *Sacred Places: American Tourist Attractions in the Nineteenth Century* (New York: Oxford University Press, 1989); Anne Farrar Hyde, *An American Vision: Far Western Landscape and National Culture, 1820–1920* (New York: New York University Press, 1990); Earl Pomeroy, *In Search of the Golden West: The Tourist in Western America* (New York: Alfred A. Knopf, 1957); Sutter, *Driven Wild,* 19–53; Clements, *Hoover, Conservation, and Consumerism;* and Roy Rosenzweig, *Eight Hours for What We Will: Workers and Leisure in the Industrial City, 1870–1920* (New York: Cambridge University Press, 1983).

40. See the following ads from merchants who exhibited at the Sports Show: GBPG, March 29, 1948, 14, 16, 17, 19, 24, 28–29. Quotes from 16 and 24, respectively.

41. GBPG, March 29, 1948, 28 and 19, respectively.

42. GBPG, March 29, 1948, 14–19. See also Jenny Price, *Flight Maps: Adventures with Nature in Modern America* (New York: Basic Books, 1999); and Miles Orvell, *The Real Thing: Imitation and Authenticity in American Culture, 1880–1940* (Chapel Hill: University of North Carolina Press, 1989).

43. Meine and Knight, *Essential Aldo Leopold,* 43.

44. Torinus, "First Post-War Press-Gazette Sports Show," 25.

CHAPTER 6: "POLLUTION CONCERNS YOU!"

1. Joseph R. McCarthy, "The Wisconsin Citizen," November 1946, 2, in SHSW pamphlet collection.

2. Michael O'Brien, *McCarthy and McCarthyism in Wisconsin* (Columbia: University of Missouri Press, 1980), 55–80.

3. Donald Soquet, interview by Paul Wozniak, April 20, 1995, in SHSW Archives, Green Bay Area Research Center. Hereafter referred to as "Soquet Interview."

4. Tubbs, "Pollution: The Green Bay Story," 1. According to Soquet, he was so angered at the degraded condition of the Fox after his 1946 canoe trip that he wrote a letter to the editor of the GBPG expressing his disappointment. A paper worker named Orrin Wilson read the letter. Wilson contacted Soquet and suggested forming a chapter of the Izaak Walton League in order to make his lone voice

more significant. Unfortunately, I have been unable to locate Soquet's letter to confirm its existence. Nonetheless, his story seems consistent with other facts.

5. Wozniak, Soquet interview. See also Bowman, *Paper in Wisconsin,* 21.

6. "Victory over Sulphite Pollution of State Rivers Now in Sight," GBPG, August 22, 1946, 1–2. Quotes from the following, respectively: Lloyd Geniesse, "Pollution in the Bay," GBPG, March 18, 1948; L. H. Kingston and Ira G. Smith, "Pollution of the Fox River," GBPG, April 10, 1948, 4; and "Be Practical about Pools," GBPG, March 30, 1948, 4.

7. On consumption in American politics, see Thelen, *New Citizenship,* 1–4, 55–85; Cohen, *Consumer's Republic,* 18–61; Robert H. Wiebe, *The Search for Order, 1877–1920* (New York: Hill and Wang, 1967); and Oliver Zunz, *Making America Corporate, 1870–1920* (Chicago: University of Chicago Press, 1990).

8. Joseph Moore, "The Swimming Problem," GBPG, March 2, 1948, 6; "Be Practical about Pools"; and "Why We Need Pools," GBPG, April 2, 1948, 6.

9. Moore, "The Swimming Problem"; "Be Practical about Pools"; L. H. Kingston and Ira G. Smith, "Pollution of the Fox River," GBPG, April 10, 1948, 4; and "Why We Need Pools," 6.

10. Joseph Moore, "Making a Choice," GBPG, April 19, 1948, 10; and Kingston and Smith, "Pollution of the Fox River." See also Rome, *Bulldozer in the Countryside,* 189–219.

11. Clayton Ewing, "The Paper Mill's Side," GBPG, April 10, 1948, 4; and "The Swimming Pools," GBPG, April 2, 1948, 6.

12. "Be Practical about Pools"; and Jantz, "The Swimming Pool in Menasha."

13. "Kaftan Victor in Senate Contest," GBPG, September 22, 1948, 1; "Lytie Defeated for Senate Post," GBPG, November 3, 1948, 1; and Wozniak, "They Thought We Were Dreamers," 168.

14. "Plan Probe of Pollution Here," GBPG, October 22, 1948, 4. See also "Rennebohm Talk Slated Tonight," GBPG, October 21, 1948, 7; and Wozniak, Soquet interview.

15. The advertisements appeared in the GBPG on the following dates: December 11, 1948, 3; December 15, 1948, 24; and December 31, 1948, 3.

16. Vandereer, "What Price Pollution?"; *Stream Pollution in Wisconsin,* 99 and 7, respectively; and "Pollution of the Fox," 8.

17. Paul G. Steckart, "Pollution," GBPG, December 21, 1948, in Kaftan Papers, Green Bay Micro 36.

18. Minutes, January 21, 1949, in CWP, Committee Meetings, 1928–1950, Box 1, 4–7, quotes from 5–6; and Minutes, June 21, 1949 in CWP, Committee Meetings, 1928–1950, Box 1, 4–5, quote from 5. For Kanneberg's letter, see Kanneberg and Harold M. Wilkie to Committee on Water Pollution, June 20, 1949, in Kaftan Papers, Box 1.

19. Kaftan cosponsored his legislation with two other state senators. The bills were numbered 206, S through 210, S. Copies are located in Kaftan Papers, Box 1. See also "Kaftan Outlines Pollution Curbs," GBPG, February 9, 1949, in Kaftan Papers, Green Bay Micro 36.

20. Virgil Muench, Arthur Kaftan, and Donald Soquet to the Committee on Water Pollution, May 11, 1949, in CWP, Basin Studies, 1940–, E–K, Box 2, File 2-49J; and "Compromise on Anti-Pollution Bills Sought," GBPG, April 8, 1949, in Kaftan Papers, Green Bay Micro 36.

21. Wisconsin Manufacturers's Association to All Members, March 16, 1949, in Kaftan Papers, Box 1.

22. Green Bay Association of Commerce to Fellow Members, March 18, 1949, in Kaftan Papers, Box 1. The advertisements sponsored by the paper industry were produced by two Green Bay companies, Northern Paper Mills and Hoberg Paper Mills. See "What Is Pollution?" GBPG, January 8, 1949, 3; "A Practical Problem," GBPG, January 12, 1949, 20; and "The Logical Approach," GBPG, January 15, 1949, 3. See also "New Tack in Fight on Stream Pollution," *Business Week,* February 5, 1949, 38, 40.

23. "Heated Arguments Feature Pollution Hearing," GBPG, March 25, 1949, in Kaftan Papers, Green Bay Micro 36. See also Lewis C. French, "Five Hour Battle Rages Over Antipollution Bills," Milwaukee *Journal,* March 25, 1949, in Kaftan Papers, Green Bay Micro 36.

24. "Heated Arguments Feature Pollution Hearing."

25. "Watered Down Anti-Pollution Bill Passes State Senate," GBPG, June 3, 1949, in Kaftan Papers Green Bay Micro 36; Lewis C. French, "Pollution Making Lower Fox 'Dead Water,'" Milwaukee *Journal,* March 6, 1949, 24; and John Wyngaard, "Government and Politics," GBPG, March 29, 1949, in Kaftan Papers, Green Bay Micro 36. See also "Compromise on Anti-Pollution Bills Sought." On the position of organized labor during the debate, see Brown County CIO to State Committee on Water Pollution, January 11, 1949, in Kaftan Papers, Box 1; "A Resolution on River, Bay & Lake Pollution," Brown County CIO Council, undated, in Kaftan Papers, Box 1; "Sulphite Men Ask Boex About Jobs," GBPG, January 10, 1949, in Kaftan Papers, Green Bay Micro 36; "CIO Supports Pollution Ban," Milwaukee *Sentinel,* January 13, 1949, in Kaftan Papers, Green Bay Micro 36; and Izaak Walton League's response to Northern Paper Mill union, undated and untitled statement in Kaftan Papers, Box 1.

26. "Sen. Kaftan Is Satisfied With Fund for Pollution Control," GBPG, July 5, 1949, 6. See also *Laws of Wisconsin,* 1949, chap. 603, 546–548.

27. "Pollution Concerns You!," fifth in the series, in Kaftan Papers, Green Bay Micro 36. See also Murphy, *Water Purity,* 92–93.

28. Lewis C. French, "Mills Granted Pollution Stay," Milwaukee *Journal,* December 23, 1949, in Kaftan Papers, Green Bay Micro 36; "Fox Pollution Hearing Opens," GBPG, December 22, 1949, 1, 10; and "Green Bay Mills Lead Way in Clean Up," GBPG, December 23, 1949, 1. See also "Open Pollution Case Thursday," GBPG, December 19, 1949, in Kaftan Papers, Green Bay Micro 36; and "Paper Mills Get More Time for Cleanup," GBPG, undated, in Kaftan Papers, Green Bay Micro 36.

29. "Transcript of Re-Hearing," December 22, 1949, 156–159, in CWP, Box 27.

CONCLUSION: THE MEANING OF NATURE

1. As noted in the introduction, this argument builds on the ideas of William Cronon and Richard White: Cronon, "Trouble with Wilderness," 69–90; and White, "Are You an Environmentalist?," 171–185; both in Cronon, ed., *Uncommon Ground.*

SELECTED BIBLIOGRAPHY

I. MANUSCRIPT COLLECTIONS

Aberg, William J. P. Papers, 1925–1964. State Historical Society of Wisconsin.

Appleton Chamber of Commerce Collection. Outagamie County Historical Society, Appleton, Wisconsin.

Appleton Chamber of Commerce. Records, 1920–1967. State Historical Society of Wisconsin, Green Bay Area Research Center.

Committee on Water Pollution. Records, 1921–1966. State Historical Society of Wisconsin.

Hirst, Arthur R. Papers, 1924. State Historical Society of Wisconsin.

Husting, Paul O. Papers, 1909–1918. State Historical Society of Wisconsin.

Kaftan, Arthur. Papers, 1929–1972. State Historical Society of Wisconsin, Green Bay Area Research Center.

Kanneberg, Adolph. Papers, 1920–1944. State Historical Society of Wisconsin.

Kimberly-Clark. Records, 1880–1952. State Historical Society of Wisconsin.

Neenah and Menasha Water Power Company. Records, 1896–1946. State Historical Society of Wisconsin.

Seaborne, Charles R. Papers, 1936–1950. State Historical Society of Wisconsin, Green Bay Area Research Center.

Wisconsin Electric Power Company Collection. Outagamie County Historical Society, Appleton, Wisconsin.

Wisconsin Geological and Natural History Survey. Records, 1899–1930. State Historical Society of Wisconsin.

II. PERIODICALS

Appleton *Crescent*, 1856–1895
Appleton *Post*, 1882
Appleton *Post-Crescent*, 1920–1950
Appleton *Weekly Post*, 1894
Green Bay *Advocate*, 1856–1893
Green Bay *Gazette*, 1895
Green Bay *Press-Gazette*, 1915–1950
Hilbert *Favorite*, 1932
Kaukauna *Times*, 1931
Madison *Capital Times*, 1926
Milwaukee *Journal*, 1925–1949
Milwaukee *Sentinel*, 1892–1949
Neenah *Gazette*, 1875
Neenah and Menasha *Daily News and the Times*, 1922

Paper Trade Journal (New York: Vance Publishing, 1895–1950)
Park Falls *Independent*, 1925
Park Falls *Herald*, 1925
Wisconsin Motorist (Milwaukee: M. C. Moore, 1910–1928)

III. BOOKS

Ainsworth, John H. *The Lower Fox . . . A River of Paper: A Discussion of Pollution, Plankton and Paper*. Kaukauna, Wis.: Thimany Pulp & Paper Company, 1957.

Badger, Reid. *The Great American Fair: The World's Columbian Exposition and American Culture*. Chicago: Nelson Hall, 1979.

Bancroft, Hubert Howe. *The Book of the Fair: An Historical and Descriptive Presentation of the World's Science, Art, and Industry, as Viewed through the Columbian Exposition at Chicago in 1893*. New York: Bounty Books, 1894.

Barron, Hal S. *Mixed Harvest: The Second Great Transformation in the Rural North, 1870–1930*. Chapel Hill: University of North Carolina Press, 1997.

Beals, Carleton. *The Great Revolt and Its Leaders: The History of Popular American Uprisings in the 1890s*. New York: Abelard-Schuman, 1968.

Belasco, Warren J. *Americans on the Road: From Autocamp to Motel, 1910–1945*. Cambridge, Mass.: MIT Press, 1979.

Bess, Michael. *The Light-Green Society: Ecology and Technological Modernity in France, 1960–2000*. Chicago: University of Chicago Press, 2003.

Blanke, David. *Sowing the American Dream: How Consumer Culture Took Root in the Rural Midwest*. Athens: Ohio University Press, 2000.

Bowman, Francis F., Jr. *Paper in Wisconsin: Ninety-Two Years Industrial Progress*. N.p.: N.p., 1940.

Brands, H. W. *The Reckless Decade: America in the 1890s*. New York: St. Martin's Press, 1995.

Brown, Dee. *Bury My Heart at Wounded Knee: An Indian History of the American West*. New York: Henry Holt, 1991.

Buenker, John D. *The History of Wisconsin*, vol. 4, *The Progressive Era, 1893–1914*. Madison: State Historical Society of Wisconsin, 1998.

Camp, Norma Cournow, ed. *Conservation Centennial Symposium: The Quest for Quality in Wisconsin*. Madison: University of Wisconsin, 1967.

Carson, Rachel. *Silent Spring*. Boston: Houghton Mifflin, 1962.

Chatburn, George R. *Highway Engineering: Rural Roads and Pavements*. New York: John Wiley & Sons, 1921.

Childs, William R. *Trucking and the Public Interest: The Emergence of Federal Regulation, 1914–1940*. Knoxville: University of Tennessee Press, 1985.

Clements, Kendrick A. *Hoover, Conservation, and Consumerism: Engineering the Good Life*. Lawrence: University Press of Kansas, 2000.

Cohen, Lizabeth. *A Consumer's Republic: The Politics of Mass Consumption in Postwar America*. New York: Random House, 2003.

Cooper, Gail. *Air-conditioning America: Engineers and the Controlled Environment, 1900–1960.* Baltimore, Md.: Johns Hopkins University Press, 1998.

Cowan, Ruth Schwartz. *More Work for Mother: The Ironies of Household Technology from the Open Hearth to the Microwave.* New York: Basic Books, 1983.

Cronon, William, *Nature's Metropolis: Chicago and the Great West.* New York: W. W. Norton, 1991.

———, ed. *Uncommon Ground: Toward Reinventing Nature.* New York: W. W. Norton, 1995.

Dairying in Wisconsin and Its Possibilities in Kansas, Missouri and Oklahoma. Kansas City, Mo.: Good Roads Association of Greater Kansas City, 1924.

Davis, Susan Burdick. *And There Was Light.* Madison: Published by the Author, 1948.

Dewey, Scott Hamilton. *Don't Breathe the Air: Air Pollution and U.S. Environmental Politics, 1945–1970.* College Station: Texas A&M University, 2000.

Downing, Michael. *Spring Forward: The Annual Madness of Daylight Saving.* Washington, D.C.: Shoemaker & Hoard, 2005.

Dumenil, Lynn. *The Modern Temper: American Culture and Society in the 1920s.* New York: Hill and Wang, 1995.

Dunlap, Thomas R. *Faith in Nature: Environmentalism as Religious Quest.* Seattle: University of Washington Press, 2004.

Easton, Robert. *Black Tide: The Santa Barbara Oil Spill and Its Consequences.* New York: Delacorte Press, 1972.

Elvins, Sarah. *Sales and Celebrations: Retailing and Regional Identity in Western New York State, 1920–1940.* Athens: Ohio University Press, 2004.

Fabricant, Solomon. *Labor Savings in American Industry, 1899–1939.* New York: National Bureau of Economic Research, 1945.

Flink, James J. *America Adopts the Automobile, 1895–1910.* Cambridge, Mass.: MIT Press, 1970.

———. *The Automobile Age.* Cambridge, Mass.: MIT Press, 1988.

Fox, Richard Wightman, and T. J. Jackson Lears, eds. *The Culture of Consumption: Critical Essays in American History, 1880–1980.* New York: Pantheon Books, 1983.

Fox, Stephen. *The American Conservation Movement: John Muir and His Legacy.* Madison: University of Wisconsin Press, 1985.

Fries, Robert F. *Empire in Pine: The Story of Lumbering in Wisconsin, 1830–1900.* Madison: State Historical Society of Wisconsin, 1951.

Giedion, Siegfried. *Mechanization Takes Command: A Contribution to Anonymous History.* New York: Oxford University Press, 1948.

Glaab, Charles N. *Kansas City and the Railroads: Community Policy in the Growth of a Regional Metropolis.* Madison: State Historical Society of Wisconsin, 1962.

Glaab, Charles N., and Lawrence H. Larsen. *Factories in the Valley: Neenah-Menasha, 1870–1915.* Madison: State Historical Society of Wisconsin, 1969.

Glickman, Lawrence B., ed. *Consumer Society in American History: A Reader.* Ithaca, N.Y.: Cornell University Press, 1999.

Goodwyn, Lawrence. *The Populist Moment: A Short History of the Agrarian Revolt in America*. New York: Oxford University Press, 1978.

Gottlieb, Robert. *Forcing the Spring: The Transformation of the American Environmental Movement*. Washington, D.C.: Island Press, 1993.

Gough, Robert. *Farming the Cutover: A Social History of Northern Wisconsin, 1900–1940*. Lawrence: University Press of Kansas, 1997.

Harvey, Mark. *A Symbol of Wilderness: Echo Park and the American Conservation Movement*. Seattle: University of Washington Press, 2000.

Hays, Samuel P. *Beauty, Health, and Permanence: Environmental Politics in the United States, 1955–1985*. New York: Cambridge University Press, 1987.

———. *Conservation and the Gospel of Efficiency: The Progressive Conservation Movement, 1890–1920*. Cambridge, Mass.: Harvard University Press, 1959.

Henry, W. A., and F. B. Morrison. *Feeds and Feeding: A Handbook for the Student and Stockman*. 15th ed. Madison: Henry-Morrison Company, 1915.

A History of the Wisconsin Paper Industry, 1848–1948. Chicago: Howard Publishing, 1948.

Homan, E. Jane, and Michael A. Wattiaux. *Technical Dairy Guide: Lactation and Milking*. Madison: Babcock Institute for International Dairy Research and Development, 1995.

Hoy, Suellen. *Chasing Dirt: The American Pursuit of Cleanliness*. New York: Oxford University Press, 1995.

Huffman, Thomas R. *Protectors of the Land and Water: Environmentalism in Wisconsin, 1961–1968*. Chapel Hill: University of North Carolina Press, 1994.

Hughes, Thomas P. *American Genesis: A Century of Invention and Technological Enthusiasm, 1870–1970*. New York: Penguin Books, 1989.

———. *Networks of Power: Electrification in Western Society, 1880–1930*. Baltimore, Md.: Johns Hopkins University Press, 1983.

Hunter, Louis C., and Lynwood Bryant. *A History of Industrial Power in the United States, 1780–1930*, vol. 3, *The Transmission of Power*. Cambridge, Mass.: MIT Press, 1991.

Hurley, Andrew. *Environmental Inequalities: Class, Race, and Industrial Pollution in Gary, Indiana, 1945–1980*. Chapel Hill: University of North Carolina Press, 1995.

Hurst, James Willard. *Law and Economic Growth: The Legal History of the Lumber Industry in Wisconsin, 1836–1915*. Madison: University of Wisconsin Press, 1984.

Hyde, Anne Farrar. *An American Vision: Far Western Landscape and National Culture, 1820–1920*. New York: New York University Press, 1990.

Ingham, Ray W. *Grass Silage and Dairying*. New Brunswick, N.J.: Rutgers University Press, 1949.

Inglehart, Ronald. *Silent Revolution: Changing Values and Political Styles among Western Publics*. Princeton, N.J.: Princeton University Press, 1977.

Jackson, Harvey H., III. *Rivers of History: Life on the Coosa, Tallapoosa, Cahaba, and Alabama*. Tuscaloosa: University of Alabama Press, 1995.

Jackson, John Brinckerhoff. *A Sense of Place, a Sense of Time.* New Haven, Conn.: Yale University Press, 1994.

Jackson, Kenneth T. *Crabgrass Frontier: The Suburbanization of the United States.* New York: Oxford University Press, 1985.

Jakle, John A., Keith A. Sculle, and Jefferson S. Rogers. *The Motel in America.* Baltimore, Md.: Johns Hopkins University Press, 1996.

Kasson, John F. *Civilizing the Machine: Technology and Republican Values in America, 1776–1900.* New York: Hill and Wang, 1999.

Kaukauna, Wis.: "The Lion of the Fox." Kaukauna, Wis.: Sun Publishing, 1891.

Kelman, Ari. *A River and Its City: The Nature of Landscape in New Orleans.* Berkeley: University of California Press, 2003.

Kimberly-Clark Corporation. *Four Men and a Machine: Commemoration the Seventy-Fifth Anniversary of Kimberly-Clark Corporation.* Neenah, Wis.: Published by the Company, 1948.

Kleist, Frederica Hart. *Fox-Wisconsin "Portage": 1673–1987.* Portage, Wis.: Published by the Author, 1987.

Kline, Ronald R. *Consumers in the Country: Technology and Social Change in Rural America.* Baltimore, Md.: Johns Hopkins University Press, 2002.

Krause, Paul. *The Battle for Homestead, 1880–1892: Politics, Culture, and Steel.* Pittsburgh: University of Pittsburgh Press, 1992.

Lampard, Eric E. *The Rise of the Dairy Industry in Wisconsin: A Study in Agricultural Change, 1820–1920.* Madison: State Historical Society of Wisconsin, 1963.

Lawson, Publius V. *The First Water Power of the Lower Fox River, Menasha, Wis.* Menasha, Wis.: Press Printing House, 1885.

Leach, William. *Land of Desire: Merchants, Power, and the Rise of a New American Culture.* New York: Vintage Books, 1993.

Lears, T. J. Jackson. *No Place of Grace: Antimodernism and the Transformation of American Culture, 1880–1920.* Chicago: University of Chicago Press, 1981.

Leavitt, Judith Walzer. *The Healthiest City: Milwaukee and the Politics of Health Reform.* Madison: University of Wisconsin Press, 1982.

Lesy, Michael. *Wisconsin Death Trip.* New York: Random House, 1973.

Lynd, Robert and Helen. *Middletown: A Study in American Culture.* New York: Harcourt Brace, 1929.

Markets by Incomes: A Study of the Relation of Income to Retail Purchases in Appleton, Wisconsin. 2 vols. New York: Time Incorporated, 1932.

Marquis, Alice G. *Hopes and Ashes: The Birth of Modern Times, 1929–1939.* New York: The Free Press, 1986.

Marx, Leo. *The Machine in the Garden: Technology and the Pastoral Ideal in America.* London: Oxford University Press, 1964.

McCarthy, Charles. *The Wisconsin Idea.* New York: Macmillan, 1912.

McCraw, Thomas K. *Prophets of Regulation: Charles Francis Adams, Louis D. Brandeis, James M. Landis, Alfred E. Kahn.* Cambridge, Mass.: Harvard University Press, 1984.

McDonald, Forrest. *Let There Be Light: The Electric Utility Industry in Wisconsin, 1881–1955*. Madison: American History Research Center, 1957.

McShane, Clay. *Down the Asphalt Path: The Automobile and the American City*. New York: Columbia University Press, 1994.

Meine, Curt, and Richard L. Knight, eds. *The Essential Aldo Leopold: Quotations and Commentaries*. Madison: University of Wisconsin Press, 1999.

Melosi, Martin V., ed. *Garbage in the Cities: Refuse, Reform, and the Environment, 1880–1980*. College Station: Texas A&M University Press, 1981.

———. *Pollution and Reform in American Cities, 1870–1930*. Austin: University of Texas Press, 1980.

Merk, Frederick. *Economic History of Wisconsin during the Civil War Decade*. Madison: State Historical Society of Wisconsin, 1916.

Mermin, Samuel. *The Fox-Wisconsin Rivers Improvement: An Historical Study in Legal Institutions and Political Economy*. Madison: University of Wisconsin Extension, 1968.

Mitman, Greg, Michelle Murphy, and Christopher Sellers, eds. *Landscapes of Exposure: Knowledge and Illness in Modern Environments*. Chicago: University of Chicago Press, 2004.

Mumford, Lewis. *Technics and Civilization*. New York: Harcourt Brace, 1934.

Murphy, Earl Finbar. *Water Purity: A Study in Legal Control of Natural Resources*. Madison: University of Wisconsin Press, 1961.

Nash, Roderick. *Wilderness and the American Mind*. 3rd ed. New Haven, Conn.: Yale University Press, 1982.

Nolen, John, and Henry V. Hubbard. *Parkways and Land Values*. Cambridge, Mass.: Harvard University Press, 1957.

Nye, David E. *American Technological Sublime*. Cambridge, Mass.: MIT Press, 1994.

———. *Consuming Power: A Social History of American Energies*. Cambridge, Mass.: MIT Press, 1998.

———. *Electrifying America: Social Meanings of a New Technology*. Cambridge, Mass.: MIT Press, 1990.

O'Brien, Michael. *McCarthy and McCarthyism in Wisconsin*. Columbia: University of Missouri Press, 1980.

Ogle, Maureen. *All the Modern Conveniences: American Household Plumbing, 1840–1890*. Baltimore, Md.: Johns Hopkins University Press, 1996.

Orvell, Miles. *The Real Thing: Imitation and Authenticity in American Culture, 1880–1940*. Chapel Hill: University of North Carolina Press, 1989.

Ostergren, Robert C., and Thomas R. Vale. *Wisconsin Land and Life*. Madison: University of Wisconsin Press, 1997.

Passer, Harold C. *The Electrical Manufacturers, 1875–1900: A Study in Competition, Entrepreneurship, Technical Change, and Economic Growth*. Cambridge, Mass.: Harvard University Press, 1953.

Pinchot, Gifford. *Breaking New Ground*. New York: Harcourt, Brace, 1947.

————. *The Fight for Conservation*. Garden City, N.Y.: Harcourt, Brace, 1910.

Pomeroy, Earl. *In Search of the Golden West: The Tourist in Western America*. New York: Alfred A. Knopf, 1957.

Prerau, David. *Seize the Daylight: The Curious and Contentious Story of Daylight Saving Time*. New York: Thunder's Mouth Press, 2005.

Price, Jenny. *Flight Maps: Adventures with Nature in Modern America*. New York: Basic Books, 1999.

Princen, Thomas, Michael Maniates, and Ken Conca, eds. *Confronting Consumption*. Cambridge, Mass.: MIT Press, 2002.

The Progress of Paper: With Particular Emphasis on the Remarkable Industrial Development in the Past 75 Years and the Part that Paper Trade Journal Has Been Privileged to Share in that Development. New York: Lockwood Trade Journal Company, 1947.

Rae, John B. *The Road and the Car in American Life*. Cambridge, Mass.: MIT Press, 1971.

Raitz, Karl, ed. *The National Road*. Baltimore, Md.: Johns Hopkins University Press, 1996.

Reid, A. J. *The Resources and Manufacturing Capacity of the Lower Fox River Valley*. Appleton, Wis.: Reid & Miller, Steam Book and Job Printers, 1874.

Reiger, John F. *American Sportsmen and the Origins of Conservation*. Norman: University of Oklahoma Press, 1986.

Ridge, Martin, ed. *Frederick Jackson Turner: Wisconsin's Historian of the Frontier*. Madison: State Historical Society of Wisconsin, 1993.

Rome, Adam. *The Bulldozer in the Countryside: Suburban Sprawl and the Rise of American Environmentalism*. New York: Cambridge University Press, 2001.

Rose, Mark H. *Cities of Light and Heat: Domesticating Gas and Electricity in Urban America*. University Park: Pennsylvania State University Press, 1995.

Rosenzweig, Roy. *Eight Hours for What We Will: Workers and Leisure in the Industrial City, 1870–1920*. New York: Cambridge University Press, 1983.

Rothman, Hal. *The Greening of a Nation? Environmentalism in the United States since 1945*. Fort Worth, Tex.: Harcourt Brace, 1998.

Runte, Alfred. *Trains of Discovery: Western Railroads and the National Parks*. Flagstaff, Ariz.: Northland Press, 1984.

Scarpino, Philip V. *Great River: An Environmental History of the Upper Mississippi, 1890–1950*. Columbia: University of Missouri Press, 1985.

Schafer, Joseph. *The Winnebago-Horicon Basin: A Type Study in Western History*. Madison: State Historical Society of Wisconsin, 1937.

Scharff, Virginia. *Taking the Wheel: Women and the Coming of the Motor Age*. New York: The Free Press, 1991.

Schivelbusch, Wolfgang. *Disenchanted Night: The Industrialization of Light in the Nineteenth Century*. Berkeley: University of California Press, 1995.

————. *The Railway Journey: The Industrialization of Time and Space in the 19th Century*. Berkeley: University of California Press, 1977.

Schlesinger, Arthur M., Jr. *The Crisis of the Old Order, 1919–1933.* Boston: Houghton Mifflin, 1956.

Schmitt, Peter. *Back to Nature: The Arcadian Myth in Urban America.* New York: Oxford University Press, 1969.

Schneirov, Richard, Shelton Stromquist, and Nick Salvatore, eds. *The Pullman Strike and the Crisis of the 1890s: Essays on Labor and Politics.* Urbana: University of Illinois Press, 1999.

Schrepfer, Susan R. *The Fight to Save the Redwoods: A History of Environmental Reform, 1917–1978.* Madison: University of Wisconsin Press, 1983.

Sears, John. *Sacred Places: American Tourist Attractions in the Nineteenth Century.* New York: Oxford University Press, 1989.

Seely, Bruce R. *Building the American Highway System: Engineers as Policy Makers.* Philadelphia: Temple University Press, 1987.

Sellers, Christopher. *Hazards of the Job: From Industrial Disease to Environmental Health Science.* Chapel Hill: University of North Carolina Press, 1997.

Sheriff, Carol. *The Artificial River: The Erie Canal and the Paradox of Progress, 1817–1862.* New York: Hill and Wang, 1996.

Silver, Thomas B. *Coolidge and the Historians.* Durham, N.C.: Carolina Academic Press, 1982.

Skowronek, Stephen. *Building a New American State: The Expansion of National Administrative Capacities, 1877–1920.* New York: Cambridge University Press, 1982.

Smith, Alice E. *Millstone and Saw: The Origins of Neenah-Menasha.* Madison: State Historical Society of Wisconsin, 1966.

Smith, David C. *History of Papermaking in the United States, 1691–1969.* New York: Lockwood Publishing, 1970.

Smith, Susan Harris, and Melanie Dawson, eds. *The American 1890s: A Cultural Reader.* Durham, N.C.: Duke University Press, 2000.

Steinberg, Theodore. *Acts of God: The Unnatural History of Natural Disaster in America.* New York: Oxford University Press, 2000.

———. *Nature Incorporated: Industrialization and the Waters of New England.* New York: Cambridge University Press, 1991.

Stilgoe, John R. *Metropolitan Corridor: Railroads and the American Scene.* New Haven, Conn.: Yale University Press, 1983.

Stine, Jeffrey K. *Mixing the Waters: Environment, Politics, and the Building of the Tennessee-Tombigbee Waterway.* Akron, Ohio: University of Akron Press, 1993.

Stoll, Steven. *Larding the Lean Earth: Soil and Society in Nineteenth-Century America.* New York: Hill and Wang, 2002.

Stradling, David. *Smokestacks and Progressives: Environmentalists, Engineers, and Air Quality in America, 1881–1951.* Baltimore, Md.: Johns Hopkins, 1999.

Sutter, Paul. *Driven Wild: How the Fight against Automobiles Launched the Modern Wilderness Movement.* Seattle: University of Washington Press, 2002.

Tarr, Joel. *The Search for the Ultimate Sink: Urban Pollution in Historical Perspective.* Akron, Ohio: University of Akron Press, 1996.

Thelen, David P. *The New Citizenship: Origins of Progressivism in Wisconsin, 1885–1900.* Columbia: University of Missouri Press, 1972.

Thompson, John Giffin. *The Rise and Decline of the Wheat Growing Industry in Wisconsin.* Madison: University of Wisconsin, 1909.

Thoreau, Henry David. *The Writings of Henry David Thoreau.* Boston: Houghton Mifflin, 1906.

Thwaites, Reuben Gold. *Historic Waterways: Six Hundred Miles of Canoeing Down the Rock, Fox, and Wisconsin Rivers.* Chicago: A. C. McClurg, 1888.

Titus, William A., ed. *History of the Fox River Valley: Lake Winnebago and the Green Bay Region.* Vols. 1–3. Chicago: S. J. Clarke Publishing, 1930.

Tobey, Ronald C. *Technology as Freedom: The New Deal and the Electrical Modernization of the American Home.* Berkeley: University of California Press, 1996.

Van Hise, Charles R. *The Conservation of Natural Resources in the United States.* New York: Macmillan, 1910.

Ward, David. *Cities and Immigrants: A Geography of Change in Nineteenth Century America.* New York: Oxford University Press, 1971.

Warren, Louis S. *The Hunter's Game: Poachers and Conservationists in Twentieth-Century America.* New Haven, Conn.: Yale University Press, 1997.

Weigold, Marilyn E. *Pioneering in Parks and Parkways: Westchester County, New York, 1895–1945.* Chicago: Public Works Historical Society, 1988.

Wellock, Thomas Raymond. *Critical Masses: Opposition to Nuclear Power in California, 1958–1978.* Madison: University of Wisconsin Press, 1998.

Westbrook, C. D., Jr. *Fox and Wisconsin Improvement.* New York: S. S. Hommel, 1853.

———. *Fox and Wisconsin Improvement.* New York: Banks, Gould, 1854.

White, Richard. *The Organic Machine: The Remaking of the Columbia River.* New York: Hill and Wang, 1995.

Whittemore, Colin T. *Lactation of the Dairy Cow.* London: Longman Group, 1980.

Wiebe, Robert H. *The Search for Order, 1877–1920.* New York: Hill and Wang, 1967.

Williams, Hal R. *Years of Decision: American Politics in the 1890s.* New York: Wiley, 1978.

Wilson, F. G. *E. M. Griffith and the Early Story of Wisconsin Forestry, 1903–1915.* Madison: University of Wisconsin, Department of Natural Resources, 1982.

Wisconsin Michigan Power Company. *Souvenir Booklet Commemorating the 50th Anniversary of the Opening of the World's First Hydro-Electric Central Station at Appleton, Wisconsin.* Appleton: Published by the Company, 1932.

———. *... They Turned on the Lights.* Appleton: Published by the Company, 1957.

Worster, Donald. *Dust Bowl: The Southern Plains in the 1930s.* New York: Oxford University Press, 1979.

Zunz, Oliver. *Making America Corporate, 1870–1920.* Chicago: University of Chicago Press, 1990.

IV. ARTICLES

Buehler, Daniel O. "Permanence and Change in Theodore Roosevelt's Conservation Jeremiad." *Western Journal of Communication* 62 (Fall 1998): 439–458.

Campbell, Ballard. "The Good Roads Movement in Wisconsin, 1890–1911." *Wisconsin Magazine of History* 49 (Summer 1966): 273–293.

Fish, N. S. "The History of the Silo in Wisconsin." *Wisconsin Magazine of History* 8 (December 1924): 158–170.

Fleming, Donald. "Roots of the New Conservation Movement." *Perspectives in American History* 6 (1972): 7–91.

Glad, Paul W. "Innovations and Adaptations of a New Era: Science, Technology, and Agriculture in Wisconsin, 1920–1930." *Wisconsin Magazine of History* 74 (1990): 9–16.

Kellogg, Louise P. "The Electric Light System at Appleton." *Wisconsin Magazine of History* 6 (December 1922): 189–194.

Klingle, Matthew W. "Spaces of Consumption in Environmental History." *History and Theory* 42 (December 2003): 94–110.

Larsen, Lawrence H. "Nineteenth Century Street Sanitation: A Study of Filth and Frustration." *Wisconsin Magazine of History* 52 (1968): 239–247.

Lawrence, Lee E. "The Wisconsin Ice Trade." *Wisconsin Magazine of History* 48 (1965): 257–267.

Rome, Adam. "Coming to Terms with Pollution: The Language of Environmental Reform." *Environmental History* 1 (July 1996): 6–28.

Wozniak, Paul. "Cleaning Up the Dirty Brown Fox." *Voyageur: Northeast Wisconsin's Historical Review* 6 (Summer/Fall 1990): 18–28.

———. "They Thought We Were Dreamers: Early Anti-Pollution Efforts on the Lower Fox and East Rivers of Northeast Wisconsin, 1927–1949." *Transactions of the Wisconsin Academy of Sciences, Arts and Letters* 84 (1996): 161–175.

V. THESES

Bartz, Melvin R. "Origin and Development of the Paper Industry in the Fox River Valley (Wisconsin)." Thesis, Iowa State University, 1940.

Boles, Donald Edward. "Administrative Rule Making in Wisconsin Conservation." Ph.D. thesis, University of Wisconsin–Madison, 1956.

Branch, Maurice Lloyd. "The Paper Industry in the Lake States Region, 1834–1947." Ph.D. thesis, University of Wisconsin–Madison, 1954.

Caine, Stanley. "Railroad Regulation in Wisconsin, 1903–1910: An Assessment of a Progressive Reform." Ph.D. thesis, University of Wisconsin–Madison, 1967.

East, Dennis. "Water Power and Forestry in Wisconsin: Issues of Conservation, 1890–1915." Ph.D. thesis, University of Wisconsin–Madison, 1971.

McCluggage, Robert W. "The Fox-Wisconsin Waterway, 1836–1872: Land Speculation and Regional Rivalries, Politics and Private Enterprise." Ph.D. thesis, University of Wisconsin–Madison, 1954.

Schmid, Alfred Allan. "Water Allocation and Development in Wisconsin." Ph.D. thesis, University of Wisconsin–Madison, 1959.

VI. GOVERNMENT DOCUMENTS

Proceedings of a Conference of Governors in the White House, Washington, D.C., May 13–15, 1908. Washington, D.C.: Government Printing Office, 1909.

United States Congress, 1840. *Report from the Secretary of War.* 26th Cong., 1st Session, Senate Document 318, Serial 359.

United States Congress, 1872. *Wisconsin and Fox Rivers Improvement.* 42nd Cong., 2nd Session, House Executive Document 185, Serial 1513.

United States Congress, 1896. *Memorial of the Citizens of Portage, Berlin, Oshkosh, Fond du Lac, Neenah, Menasha, Appleton, Kaukauna, De Pere, and Green Bay.* 54th Cong., 1st Session, Senate Document No. 52.

United States Congress, 1898–1899. *Report of the Chief of Engineers, U.S. Army.* 55th Cong., 3rd Session, House Document 2, Serial 3748.

Whitbeck, Ray Hughes. *The Geography and Industries of Wisconsin.* Wisconsin Geological and Natural History Survey, Bulletin 26. Madison: Published by the State, 1913.

———. *The Geography of the Fox-Winnebago Valley.* Wisconsin Geological and Natural History Survey, Bulletin 42. Madison: Published by the State, 1915.

Wisconsin Regional Planning Committee. *A Study of Wisconsin: Its Resources, Its Physical, Social and Economic Background.* Madison: Published by the State, 1934.

Wisconsin State Board of Health. *Stream Pollution in Wisconsin.* Madison: Wisconsin State Board of Health, 1927.

Wisconsin State Committee on Water Pollution and State Board of Health. *Investigation of the Pollution of the Fox and East Rivers and of Green Bay in the Vicinity of the City of Green Bay.* Madison: Published by the Committee, 1939.

Wisconsin State Conservation Commission. *Biennial Report.* Madison: Published by the State, 1909–.

Wisconsin State Highway Commission. *Biennial Report.* Madison: Published by the State, 1911–.

Wisconsin State Planning Board. *A Conservation and Recreation Plan for Southeastern Wisconsin.* Bulletin 3. Madison: Published by the State, 1936.

———. *A Recreational Plan for Vilas County.* Bulletin 12. Madison: Published by the State, 1941.

Wisconsin State Planning Board and State Conservation Commission. *A Park, Parkway, and Recreational Area Plan.* Bulletin 8. Madison: Published by the State, 1939.